WOMEN OF THE MIDAN

PUBLIC CULTURES OF THE MIDDLE EAST
AND NORTH AFRICA

Paul A. Silverstein, Susan Slyomovics, and Ted Swedenburg, editors

WOMEN OF THE MIDAN

*The Untold Stories of
Egypt's Revolutionaries*

Sherine Hafez

Indiana University Press

This book is a publication of

Indiana University Press
Office of Scholarly Publishing
Herman B Wells Library 350
1320 East 10th Street
Bloomington, Indiana 47405 USA

iupress.indiana.edu

Manufactured in the United States of America

Cataloging information is available from the Library of Congress.

ISBN 978-0-253-04060-2 (hardback)
ISBN 978-0-253-04061-9 (paperback)
ISBN 978-0-253-04064-0 (ebook)

1 2 3 4 5   24 23 22 21 20 19

To all revolutionary people

"The intellectual who claims ownership of the Truth is the other leg of the dictator. When an intellectual claims to own the Truth, he becomes the dictator's servant."

nasr hamid abu zayd

Contents

Acknowledgments

This book would not have been possible without the generosity of heart and spirit that the women of the *midan* invested in this project. They have shared their most poignant rememories with me, even when it was too difficult for them to continue to do so, because of emotional as well as safety issues. They grace this book with their narratives. To them goes my deepest gratitude. I humbly dedicate this book to them and to all revolutionaries, wherever they may be.

I am deeply indebted to Professor Hoda Elsadda for reading this manuscript and commenting on it. You continue to inspire me with your grace, your ideals, your dedication, and your boundless activism.

I gratefully acknowledge the support of my anthropologist friend and colleague, Selim Shahine, for encouraging me to write this book and for being the first one to read it in draft form. I am thankful for his insights and for generously sharing his photographs and memories of the revolution with me. My sincere thanks to Wael Abed, an accomplished former news photographer and reporter, for giving me permission to publish many of the pictures in the book as well as the cover photograph. Wael's gift for capturing images will always be an immense contribution to the visual documentation of the revolution. My immense gratitude as well goes to my old friend Minou Hammam, an international artist and award-winning photographer, for generously sharing her evocative and poignant photographs with me and consequently with everyone who picks up this book.

My sincere thanks to the series editors of Popular Cultures in the Middle East at Indiana University Press, Susan Slyomovics, Paul Silverstein and Ted Swedenburg. I would also like to extend my gratitude to the editors of IUP for their insights and support throughout the publishing process, Dee Mortensen and Paige Rasmussen, and to my anonymous reviewers for their suggestions and advice that helped strengthen the message of this book. Thank you to Suad Joseph, my friend and mentor of many years; your insights were instrumental to the writing of this book.

My thanks to Angie Abdelmonem, Marta Agosti and Susana Galan with whom I have the pleasure of collaborating in a research collective on Theorizing MENA Bodies, which we began in 2017. Our discussions and energetic panels have invigorated my own research on corporeal dissent. I hope this book will contribute to our work on the topic.

I would like to extend my thanks to those who offered me collegial guidance and support over the years. To the members of my department at the University of California, Riverside for reading my work and for their never-ending support. I am so lucky to be able to share my journey toward completing this book with you all. Sondra Hale, Azza Basarudin, Khanum Shaikh, Catherine Sameh for your incredible support as well and for all the colleagues whose comments on my work helped shape it for what it is today.

My thanks to the University of California, Riverside for providing the fellowships and grants that enabled me to take these multiple research trips to Egypt.

To my family and friends in Egypt, I thank you with all my heart. My children and my mother, my most cherished in the world, you are my inspiration as well as my backbone; thank you for understanding and for always being there for me.

Finally I would like to mention that this book includes excerpts from previously published journal and book articles which I wrote since the revolution. I therefore wish to acknowledge the following journals: *American Ethnologist* for permission to publish excerpts from my article, "No Longer a Bargain," in chapter one. Chapter five contains excerpts from my article published in *The Journal of North African Studies*, "The Revolution Shall Not Pass Through Women's Bodies," and excerpts from my article, "The Virgin Trials: Piety, Femininity and Authenticity in Muslim Brotherhood Discourse," were originally published in *Gender and Sexuality in Muslim Cultures*, Gul Ozyegin, editor and appear in the same chapter. Chapter seven is a version of an article published in *The Middle East Report*.

Timeline

Recentering Gender in Revolution

January 25, 2011
On National Police Day and in response to nationwide protests from the April 6th Movement, thousands of Egyptians take to the streets and principal squares of various Egyptian metropolises. The "Day of Rage" demonstrations are countered by tear gas, batons, and water cannons. In Suez, two protestors are killed as well as one policeman.

January 27, 2011
Clashes between protestors and security forces take place as demonstrations continue. Facebook and Twitter are blocked by the government. Mohamed El Baradei arrives in Cairo in response to calls for his participation.

January 28, 2011
Protests increase to massive proportions after Friday prayers. Women are a prominent presence in the demonstrations. Cell phones and internet are temporarily shut down by the regime. Mobs burn the National Democratic Party headquarters down and wreak havoc on the streets as police withdraw. Military troops are deployed to Tahrir and take a neutral stance toward the protests.

January 29, 2011
A state of insecurity prevails as neighborhood vigilantes organize and take up arms to protect their streets. Mubarak names a vice president for the first time, Omar Soliman, chief of the secret police.

January 30, 2011
Chaos is on the rise as prisoners break out of jails, weapons and ammunition are looted. For the first time since the beginning of the protests, the Muslim Brotherhood demands that the regime step down.

February 2, 2011
Pro-Mubarak supporters ride into Tahrir Square on donkeys, horses, and camels, attacking peaceful protestors. Hundreds are dead or injured as a result. This incident was named "The Battle of the Camel."

The Coalition of Egyptian Feminist Organizations is established, comprising sixteen women's groups.

February 11, 2011

Mubarak steps down and turns power over to the military. The military dissolves parliament and suspends the constitution in response to protestors' demands. A council of "wise men" made up largely of prominent male tycoons in Egypt meets with SCAF to discuss the transition. No women are invited to attend.

CBS reporter Lara Logan is sexually assaulted in Tahrir Square by a mob of forty men.

February 14, 2011

The military announces it will take charge for six months, after which elections will be held. While liberals and secularists recognize the importance of building political coalitions and agendas, preferring to postpone elections, Islamists call for speeding things up. The latter manage to accelerate the timetable.

February 25, 2011

The military forces unleash violence on protestors who are still demanding a quicker transition and the removal of PM Ahmed Shafik. While protestors are savagely beaten and their tents torn down in Tahrir, there is no response from the Muslim Brotherhood.

March 8, 2011

Thugs claiming to be pro-Mubarak and Islamist attack the International Women's Day march in Tahrir. The few hundred women who showed up were groped and heckled. The square was later dispersed.

March 9, 2011

The military clear out Tahrir, burning tents, arresting hundreds of men and women who are then beaten and tortured. Women are questioned about their marital status; they are assaulted and threatened to be charged with prostitution.

March 10, 2011

The military conducts virginity tests on Samira Ibrahim and six other female detainees in a military prison in Hikestep. Samira Ibrahim takes the military to court. The court finds the military physician who conducted these tests innocent. However, an administrative court in Cairo finds these practices illegal and orders the military to ban them in female prisons a year later.[2]

March 19, 2011

Committee to amend the constitution does not include women; 77 percent vote yes on the military proposed amendments.

April 30, 2011

The Freedom and Justice Party is established. The MB states that they have no objection toward women or Copts assuming cabinet positions. Neither, however, is considered by them to be suitable for the office of president.[3]

July 2011
The SCAF cancels 12 percent quota for women for anticipated parliamentary elections.

July 2, 2011
FJP sponsors conference called "Women from the Revolution to the Renaissance." Camellia Helmy FJP executive, calls for prioritizing homemaking over political action.[4]

September 27, 2011
The Egyptian Coalition for Civic Education and Women's Participation is established, linking more than 454 NGOs from twenty-seven governorates.[5]

October 9, 2011
A Coptic Christian protest demands retribution for attacks on Churches in Maspero. Twenty-five protestors are massacred by army bullets. Army vehicles run over bystanders. Mina Daniel, a young activist, is remembered as a martyr.

November 19, 2011
The clashes, which rage on Mohamed Mahmoud Street in downtown Cairo, continue for five straight days from November 19 to November 25.[6] Police fire tear gas at unarmed protesters under the pretext that they are preventing them from attacking the Ministry of Interior (four streets away).[7]

Between forty and ninety protestors are reported to have been killed and hundreds injured.

Women are clearly observed playing a part in the violent clashes, as noted in the documentaries by Amr Nazeer. An eyewitness account by a woman on CBC directly attests to officers killing protestors. This woman, who belongs to no particular political party, states, "As God is my witness, if I see another officer attack a young man in Tahrir again, I will cut him to pieces."[8]

November 28, 2011 to February 15, 2012
Parliamentary elections begin. Islamists, the Muslim Brotherhood, and the Salafis win most of the seats.

Each party list is required by SCAF to include one woman, which each party includes at the end of the list, which severely limits women's participation.

As a result, women win only 1.97 percent of the seats.

December 16, 2011
Cabinet clashes leave seventeen people dead when protestors call for a peaceful sit-in, in front of the Cabinet building on Qasr al Aini Street, which branches off Tahrir Square.

Protestors agitate outside of the Cabinet building. Rocks and heavy furniture are thrown down from atop the building, injuring many of them. As they retreat, state security forces attack the field hospital with tear gas while patients are inside. The protests continue for several days.

Ghada Kamal, a 6th of April activist from Mansoura is arrested and dragged by her hair while stopping to help another woman, Sanaa, a doctor who was thrown on the floor and viciously beaten. Kamal recounts how soldiers and military personnel not only used force against the protestors but were inciting anger by using sexually explicit gestures.

December 17, 2011
Human rights activist Hend Nafea is also brutally attacked by a gang of soldiers. She is tortured and assaulted by army forces with nine other women in the Shura Council building.

A young woman is dragged by her cloak, beaten, and stomped on by army personnel. The incident is known as the blue bra incident. Azza Hilal Suleiman, who tries to free her, is beaten almost to death.

Blogger and doctor Farida El Hessy is beaten by army batons on the ground and dragged by her hair to the People's Assembly building.

Also, on the same day, the Scientific Building that contains rare books dating to the eighteenth century is torched. The army accuses minors of receiving money to incite violence, broadcasting a tape showing their confession. This tape is considered a violation of children's rights by human rights organizations.

December 20, 2011 (Tuesday)[9]
A "Million Woman March," which later is called "Egyptian Women Are a Red Line," is a march to object to state violence against women. The march, which is comprised of approximately two thousand people, begins from Tahrir Square and spreads to nearby locations. Marchers, mostly women, are accompanied by groups of men, arms interlaced to protect the march, more as a gesture than actual protection. They carry large posters of the blue bra girl and iconic feminist and powerful women from Egyptian history.[10]

2012

January 21, 2012
Sixty-seven percent of parliament seats go to Islamists. Women win less than 2 percent (eight seats of 508).[11]

May 23–24, 2012
The top two finalists in the presidential elections are Ahmed Shafiq (considered part of the old regime) and Mohamed Morsi, the MB candidate.

June 17–18, 2012
SCAF seizes substantial authority over government at the expense of the office of president.

June 30, 2012
Mohamed Morsi is sworn in as president of Egypt.

August 6, 2012
Morsi appoints Pakinam Al Sharkawi as his "assistant for political affairs." Al Sharkawi, a political science professor at Cairo University, claims no ties to any Muslim party.

November 21–22, 2012
Morsi grants himself immunity and protects his parliament from constitutional court. This sparks more protests.

November 29, 2012
Controversy arises over Morsi rushing new constitutional changes that limit citizen rights. No provisions are made for women's rights in the constitution.
    Military power receives a boost in these changes.

December 4–5, 2012
Demanding an equitable constitution, one hundred thousand protestors march on the presidential palace, where they are attacked by armed pro-Morsi supporters. At least ten people are killed.

December 15–22, 2012
In a low turnout, a majority supports the referendum.

2013

January 25, 2013
Hundreds of thousands of protestors demonstrate in the second anniversary of the revolution, demanding that Mohamed Morsi step down as president. Many are injured.

February to March 2013
As fuel and electricity shortages increase, more people join the protests.

March 4–5, 2013
Pakinam al Sharkawi is appointed head of the Egyptian delegation to the United Nations 57th Commission on the Status of Women in 2013. Al Sharkawi is heavily criticized for her support of the MB constitution in her speech and her claims that the organization assured equality between men and women. The MB also hastens to post a condemnation of the CSW on their website, declaring it to be against the principles of Islam.

April 7, 2013
Following the attack on a Coptic Orthodox church in El Khosus during a funeral for four dead in similar violence, Morsi fails to conduct an investigation.
    The group "Tamarod" starts a signature campaign to depose Morsi.

May 7, 2013
Negotiations with the International Monetary Fund resume.

June 21, 2013
While Tamarod gathers twenty-two million signatures, Al Sisi warns Morsi of a growing split in society.

June 30, 2013
Millions of people demonstrate, demanding that Morsi step down; eight people are killed.

July 1, 2013
Widespread demonstrations continue while the forty-eight hours ultimatum is coming to a close.

July 3, 2013
With no agreement reached, Mohamed Morsi is placed under house arrest. Three hundred Muslim Brotherhood prominent figures are arrested.

July 4, 2013
Interim president Adly Mansour is sworn in.

July 7, 2013
Pro- and anti-Morsi protests create havoc.

July 8, 2013
Morsi supporters are shot as military police claim self-defense. Fifty-one people are killed at the Republican Guard headquarters.

July 26, 2013
General Al Sisi asks the people for a mandate to fight terrorism amid claims that Morsi conspired with Hamas.

July 27, 2013
At least seventy-four Morsi supporters are killed in clashes with police outside Rab'a sit-in.

August 11–12, 2013
Siege of MB sit-in begins, and an ultimatum is given. Thousands of protestors reinforce the sit-in as the army backs off.

August 14, 2013
Rab'a sit-in is dispersed by force, and more than six hundred people are killed and 3,700 wounded. Martial law and curfews return. Vice President el Baradei resigns in protest.[12]

August 16, 2013
Violent reactions to the Rab'a massacre ensue, as gunfire is exchanged between MB supporters and armed vigilantes. Civilian and army casualties climb to 173. Violence continues.

More than twenty women are reportedly assaulted by officers in Al Tawheed Mosque.[13]

August 19, 2013
Islamist militants execute twenty-five soldiers in the Sinai.

August 22, 2013
Mubarak is released from prison after military court ruling.

August 25, 2013
Badie, MB supreme guide, is tried for murder of civilians.

September 5, 2013
A bomb targets a convoy of the interior minister.

September 10, 2013
Campaign calling for Al Sisi to run for president begins.

September 23, 2013
The Muslim Brotherhood is declared a banned organization by the court.

October 6, 2013
Clashes between Islamist protestors and army end in the death of fifty-one protestors.

November 26, 2013
Women were beaten and sexually assaulted by security forces as they protest outside Shura Council in Cairo. Women activists report the incident to the police the next day.[14]

December 7, 2013
For their violation of the protest laws, fourteen young women members of the Muslim Brotherhood receive one year's suspended sentence, and seven others are released under probation by an Alexandrian court.[15]

December 19, 2013
Mona Mina is elected secretary general of the Doctor's syndicate. Dr. Mina, a Coptic woman activist, is the first non-MB member to head the syndicate in decades.[16]

2014

January 14, 2014
Women constitute only 12 percent of committee members (twelve out of ninety-nine total) tasked with new draft of the constitution, which was passed by 98 percent approval.

January 24, 2014
As violent incidents continue, fifteen MB members die in clashes with police. Six more protestors are killed in Cairo.

January 25, 2014
Third anniversary of the revolution ends in violent clashes leaving sixty-six people dead.
    Television airs live mob attack on woman in Tahrir Square.

January 26, 2014
Ansar Beit Al-Maqdis shoots at a military helicopter with a land-to-air missile that raises questions about the source of this advanced weaponry.

February 16, 2014
Ansar Beit Al-Maqdis claims responsibility for shooting at a civilian bus, killing four in the Sinai.

February 21, 2014
Hala Shukrallah elected as president of al Dostour Party, becoming Egypt's first female elected party leader.[17]

March 19, 2014
Student protests against the regime result in two student deaths due to violent treatment of protests by the state.

March 22, 2014
Court sentences 529 people to death in absentia till retrial of the escaped accused.

March 24 and April 28, 2014
Court in Minya hands out death sentences to 529 Muslim Brotherhood and then to 683 others in April.

April 28, 2014
The Cairo Court for Urgent Matters outlaws the April 6th Youth Movement on charges of espionage.

May 4, 2014
Al Azhar University expels seventy-six students for rioting.

June 3, 2014
Abdel Fattah Al-Sisi wins the presidential elections by 96.9 percent of the vote.

June 5, 2014
Interim president Adly Mansour decrees amendment of anti-sexual harassment law.

He also reinstates 12 percent quota for women in parliamentary elections.[18]

June 9, 2014
Twenty-five Egyptian rights groups call for law to combat violence against women.[19]

June 11, 2014
Abdel Fatah Al Sisi visits victim of mob assault in hospital, publicly apologizing for the incident. He forms a committee to get at the causes of rampant sexual harassment of women.[20]

By means of a reinstated antiprotest law, the court sentences activist Alaa Abdel Fattah and twenty-four others to fifteen years in prison.

June 23, 2014
Court sentences three Al Jazeera journalists and twenty others to prison for up to ten years. The decision causes an international uproar.

August 5, 2014
President Al-Sisi collects sixty billion EGP from the public in the form of investments in a new Suez Canal, which will take a year to build.

August 25, 2014
Providing no justification or rationale, minister of local development announces new government reshuffle will not include women. A coalition of sixteen women's groups condemns the announcement.[21]

September 13, 2014
Arrests of eight men accused of taking part in a same-sex marital union ceremony.

October 11, 2014
Hundreds of students are arrested as clashes erupt between private security firm hired by Egyptian campuses and large numbers of protestors.

October 24, 2014
Ansar Beit Al-Maqdis (later declaring themselves State of Sinai) kills thirty-one Egyptian soldiers and injures many others in the Sinai.

November 28, 2014
Protests on the "Islamic Youth Uprising" respond to a call by the Salafi Front. As three senior army officers are shot in different locations, four protesters are killed (mostly in Delta) when they come under open fire by security forces.[22]

November 29, 2014
Charges are dismissed against Hosni Mubarak and other business associates.

December 8, 2014
Twenty-six men are arrested for allegedly engaging in "gay bathhouse orgy."

2015

January 12, 2015
They are found innocent of alleged homosexual prostitution by a Cairo judge in a case called *"bab al bahr"* that had sparked much controversy.

January 24, 2015
Shaimaa al Sabbagh shot dead while peacefully commemorating the first uprising of January 25, 2011.

January 26, 2015
A court declares FGM an illegal practice, sending both a doctor and a father of young victim to jail over her death.

February 4, 2015
Hend Nafea is sentenced to life in prison with 230 others for demonstrating in November-December 2011.

February 27, 2015
Seven alleged transsexual youths are arrested by a morality police unit on charges of prostitution at a club in touristic Haram District.

February 18, 2015
Twenty-six Egyptian women are appointed to the judiciary.

September 19, 2015
While women's groups decry the limited number of women in government, only three (out of a total of thirty-three) are appointed to cabinet positions by current president Abdel Fattah El Sisi.

Women are still excluded from the state council.

December 15, 2015
Twelve female candidates win individual parliamentary seats out of 462, which is 4.22 percent of the Egyptian parliament.[23] With the year's-end application of the quota system, women won seventy-three seats in all.[24]

Notes

1. For a general timeline of 2011, see "Timeline: What's Happened Since Egypt's Revolution?" Sarah Childress, *Frontline*, September 17, 2013, http://www.pbs.org/wgbh/frontline/article/timeline-whats-happened-since-egypts-revolution/.

2. Human Rights Watch, "Egypt: Military 'Virginity Test' Investigation a Sham: Impunity Highlights Lack of Independence of Justice System," November 9, 2011, https://www.hrw.org/news/2011/11/09/egypt-military-virginity-test-investigation-sham.

3. http://www.ikhwanweb.com/article.php?id=28077.

4. Amany A. Khodair and Bassant Hassib. "Women's Political Participation in Egypt: The Role of the National Council for Women," *International Journal of Political Science and Development* 3, no. 7 (2015): 326–337. https://www.psa.ac.uk/sites/default/files/conference/papers/2015/Women's%20political%20participation%20in%20Egypt.pdf.

5. Nemat Guenena, "Women in Democratic Transition: Political Participation Watchdog UNIT," 2013, http://www.un.org/democracyfund/sites/www.un.org.democracyfund/files/UDF-EGY-08-241_Final%20UNDEF%20evaluation%20report.pdf.

6. Three shifts in security strategy toward demonstrations occurred at this time:
- Riot police respond with more violence against protesters.
- Tear gas use accelerated and charges of chemical ingredients that were never proven, as people coughed up blood and collapsed.
- The "eye sniper" and release of video showing an officer aiming his rifle at a protester as his colleagues cheered him on for "getting the boy's eye" led to calls for his arrest and investigations into what is now known as the eye sniper. Ahmed had lost an eye on January 28 and was known around Tahrir Square for wearing an eye patch that carried that date. On November 19, Ahmed was shot in his other eye. http://www.bbc.com/news/world-middle-east-20395260.

7. November 20 A 1000 chant with the downfall of Tantawi, (الألف في التحرير يهتفوا بإسقاط طنطاوي 20 نوفمب), https://www.youtube.com/watch?v=SdSLmh6P61s.

8. An Egyptian lady worth a million men attacks an officer after he assaulted a protestor (سيدة مصرية بمليون راجل تهاجم ظابط بعد تعديه علي شاب في التحرير), https://www.youtube.com/watch?v=Z4i59_EAmjM.

9. Salma Shukralla, "10,000 Egyptian Women March Against Military Violence and Rule," Jadaliyya, December 20, 2011, http://www.jadaliyya.com/pages/index/3671/10000-egyptian-women-march-against-military-violen.

10. Mohamed Fadel Fahmy and Mohammed Jamjoom, "Women March in Cairo to Protest Violence; Military Promises to Listen," CNN, December 21, 2011, http://www.cnn.com/2011/12/20/world/africa/egypt-unrest/.

11. Lulu Garcia-Navarro, "In Egypt's New Parliament, Women Will Be Scarce," NPR, January 19, 2012, http://www.npr.org/2012/01/19/145468365/in-egypts-new-parliament-women-will-be-scarce.

12. MEE Staff, "Egypt: Timeline of Key Human Rights Violations Since the 2011 Revolution," November 4, 2014, http://www.middleeasteye.net/news/egypt-timeline-key-human-rights-violations-2011-revolution-872433931.

13. FIDH, Nazra for Feminist Studies, New Women Foundation and Uprising of Women in the Arab World. "Egypt: Keeping Women Out: Sexual Violence Against Women in the Public Sphere," https://www.fidh.org/IMG/pdf/egypt_sexual_violence_uk-webfinal.pdf.

14. Ibid.

15. Human Rights Watch, "Egypt: Dangerous Message for Protesters: Harsh Sentences for Pro-Morsy Women, Girls Violate Rights," 2013, https://www.hrw.org/news/2013/12/07/egypt-dangerous-message-protesters.

16. Alahram Online, "PROFILE: Mona Mina, New Sec-Gen of the Doctors Syndicate: The First Non-Brotherhood Syndicate Head in Decades Is a Campaigner for Doctors' Rights

and Improved Healthcare," December 20, 2013, http://english.ahram.org.eg/NewsContent /1/64/89596/Egypt/Politics-/PROFILE-Mona-Mina,-new-secgen-of-the-Doctors-Syndi.aspx.

17. AbdelHalim H. AbdAllah, "Al-Dostour Elects Egypt's First Female Party Leader. Hala Shukrallah Will Succeed Mohamed ElBaradei," *Daily News Egypt*, February 22, 2014, http://www.dailynewsegypt.com/2014/02/22/al-dostour-elects-egypts-first-female-party-leader/.

18. Shounaz Meky, "Egypt Criminalizes Sexual Harassment," Al Arabiya English, June 6, 2014, http://english.alarabiya.net/en/News/middle-east/2014/06/06/Egypt-criminalizes -sexual-harassment.html.

19. Human Rights Watch, "Egypt: Take Concrete Action to Stop Sexual Harassment, Assault Committee Assessment Should Lead to Reforms," June 13, 2014, https://www.hrw .org/news/2014/06/13/egypt-take-concrete-action-stop-sexual-harassment-assault.

20. David Kirkpatrick, "Egyptian Leader Apologizes to Victim of Sexual Assault in Tahrir Square," June 11, 2014, http://www.nytimes.com/2014/06/12/world/middleeast/president-sisi -of-egypt-apologizes-to-victim-of-mass-sexual-assaults.html?_r=0.

21. Hend Kortam, "NGOs Condemn Minister's Intention to Exclude Women from Governor Reshuffle: Head of the Media Division in the Ministry Says Minister's Statements 'Were Taken out of Context,'" Daily News Egypt, August 25, 2014, http://www .dailynewsegypt.com/2014/08/25/ngos-condemn-ministers-intention-exclude-women -governor-reshuffle/.

22. "Deaths in Egypt Anti-Government Protest: Three Army Officers Killed in Separate Attacks Along with Four Demonstrators on a Day of Rallies Called by Salafi Front," Al Jazeera, November 28, 2014, http://www.aljazeera.com/news/middleeast/2014/11/egypt -tightens-security-salafist-protests-2014112861348838826.html.

23. Egyptian Center for Women's Rights, "12 Successful Female Candidates on Individual Seats out of 18," ecwronline.org, December 6, 2015, http://ecwronline.org/?p=6693.

24. Omneya Talal, "Egypt: Women's Achievements in 2015—Presiding Judges and Elected Parliamentarians," All Africa, December 28, 2015, http://allafrica.com/stories /201512282073.html.

Introduction

"*ANA MISH NASHITA, ana thawragiyya.*" I am not an activist; I am a revolutionary. Like many Egyptians who took to the streets to protest the erosion of their rights, the woman who sat across from me proudly carried the mantle of revolution in all its glory. Revolution marks her life like nothing else has or ever will. To this woman, revolution is not just activism, social work, or reform; it is, as she puts it, "The only way forward." Yet, before 2011, she had never acted to further a political or social cause. At thirty years old, Noha had never once been to a protest or ever carried a sign in a demonstration. On January 25 of that year, however, the day that was to mark the beginning of the Egyptian Revolution, she describes how she pushed with her body through the throngs of people attempting to cross Qasr El Nil Bridge into Tahrir Square. Noha, who drives her car everywhere, even a few blocks down the street, marched for hours that day. She recalled how she raised her voice with the crowd, pushing her vocal cords beyond their limit to call for the regime to fall, until her voice got so hoarse she could not speak for days. How she held her clenched fist high above her head, her face flushed and suffused with revolutionary fervor. And then, only a few weeks later, how deftly her hands wrapped themselves around the neck of a Molotov cocktail bottle as she willed her arm to cast a wide circle in the air before it jettisoned the burning liquid as far as it could go in the direction of armed security forces.

While she retold her story, Noha's forehead creased as if pushing against the pressure to forget. Still, her words spilled out, describing the popping sounds of bullets as they rained on the protestors and the muffled thud of bodies as they fell screaming in agony and the loss of life and limb that invariably followed. She continued speaking against a self-preserving impulse to attenuate the intensity of her emotions by forgetting the fear and violence of the days and months of protest. Despite the lure of forgetting, Noha—emboldened by her memories—relived those days of revolution with me one morning in her Cairo home. As she carefully walked me through her memories of the first eighteen days of revolution, then the next months, then the next and the next, her vivid recollections soon assumed a palpability of their own as the sights and sounds of Tahrir Square during the protests loomed in front of our eyes and pounded in our ears as she and I were both transported into the drama of revolution.

*　　*　　*

Rememory as a Corporeal Act

Since the uprisings that began with January 25, 2011, women like Noha have radically transformed the political landscape of Egypt. They are at the center of this book, which attempts to redress an androcentric bias in the accounts of revolution. The book, however, is not about setting the record straight—rather, the pages that follow aim to bring a gender-inclusive lens to the task of examining how politics and gender are fluidly intertwined and shape one another. At the core of this mutually creative process is the dissenting body. The protesting body is embodied in women's narratives of the uprisings, in the social and political discourses that circulated during and after the protests, and in the often brutal encounters with those invested in maintaining the status quo. In Egypt, the processes that delimit women's political participation are continuously being reconstituted through vociferous corporeal processes in the wake of a revolution; after an Islamic-styled state—under a current militaristic regime. As women's bodies protest on the streets of Arab nations, demanding democracy and social justice, they negotiate a variety of sociopolitical factors that both repress and discipline their bodies on one hand and become sites of resistance on the other. State control, Islamism, neoliberal market changes, the military establishment, and sociocultural patriarchal systems act as intersectional forces that demarcate the boundaries of corporeal dissent, while women's resistance to them simultaneously forges new paths of sociopolitical transformation.

Central to the process of (re)membering the uprisings that began in the Arab world since 2011 to this day is the gendered revolutionary body. It pivots at the heart of the multilayered, rapidly changing patriarchal power of a neoliberalizing system and of an increasingly necropolitical state.

In this book dealing with women's role in the Egyptian revolution, I am interested in fleshing out—so to speak—the conditions within which the gendered body comes to be a signifying agent of collective action and of transformation; how it can be (re)constituted in revolutionary narrative and in the (re)articulation of revolutionary desire and civil disobedience. Women's bodies are central to the processes of citizenship-making after the so-called "Arab Spring." This study aims at theorizing gendered corporeality in the Middle Eastern and North African contexts by examining the relationship between bodies and memory, governmentality and neoliberal transformations in Egypt and the emerging forms of violence, dissent, and gendered identities in the region. Specifically, this book asks the following questions: What are the practices and processes through which the gendered body in the Middle East and North Africa is constituted, experienced, regulated, and represented? How do bodies intervene within these spaces of regulation? And how can we begin to articulate an analysis of the contours of corporeality in the region?

Because bodies are media of transmitted knowledge, they archive information, convey meaning, and perform memory, thereby becoming catalysts of social transformation. To refer to the heightened forms of remembering as repeated experience, I borrow the term "rememory" from Toni Morrison's *Beloved* (1987) because it is helpful in representing the deliberate potency of memory. In her epic saga about the history of American slavery, Morrison uses the term "rememory" to illustrate how women experiencing the scars of trauma and slavery come to engage with their repressed memories. Her characters exhume their painful memories against an impulse to move on and forget, against a spiral of refusal and acceptance. Rememories become a powerful mechanism for them to restore their identities, histories, and sense of community. To be quite clear, I am in no means equating the prolonged and horrific suffering of African women under slavery with the incidents of trauma revolutionary women experienced in Tahrir Square. The process Morrison describes in *Beloved* resonates with what takes place in ethnographic retellings of revolution in women's narratives. The term does not merely refer to oral recollection, nor does it simply recount memories of experience, but is a combination of both.

In my use of rememory, I am particularly interested in capturing the intellectual and the emotional *as well as* the corporeal. In some ways, the revolutionary women interviewed here continue through rememory to engage with their struggle to reconcile their revolutionary experiences with a difficult present and an unknown future. Acts of remembering can be visceral, since the body is the locus of memory. The use of rememory here alludes more to a process than to a sporadic act of recollection. The process of rememory emphasizes the inseparability of the corporeal and material with the narrative and discursive. Rememory and the body are inseparable in reconceiving the transformative potential of revolutionary historiography. This is because, as I began to understand it, the process of writing on the body—of intextuating it with rebellion often takes place in the narratives of revolutionary women.

The rememories of protest narrated in this volume are where bodies and narratives both take shape and where, I believe, lie their potential to reactivate revolutionary bodies. By linking corporeal practices to recollected knowledge, anthropologist Paul Connerton (1989) describes this process as one that shapes subjectivities and identities through shared social memory. Societies remember through the memory of action and how it reconstitutes the body, Connerton asserts in his work

"*Ana mish nashita, ana thawragiyya.*" I am not an activist, I am a revolutionary, evokes just how a rememory of resistance can be transformative. Words, uttered with emphasis, as Noha looked me straight in the eye. They were not only for my benefit. She drew on them for her own self-sustenance. Both consciously as a revolutionary who espouses that identity, yet also physically as she embodies the memories that, in the retelling, emboldens a revolutionary identity that is now inextricably bound with the corporeal.

An Ethnography of Rememory

Anthropologists have invested considerable attention into studying the phenomenology of memory since the postmodern turn in the social sciences. Much of this interest perhaps has to do with the reflexive turn in anthropology and with the surge in studies that take on a discursive critique of metanarratives (Berliner 2005). Studies widely range from a focus on collective memory (Climo and Cattell 2002; Connerton 1989; Slyomovics 1998), to nostalgia and colonial memory (Nora 1989; Smith 2006; Fabian 2003), to gender and feminism and more specifically the ethnography of memory (Boyarin 1991; De Nardi 2014; Hale 2013). While studies in anthropology have paid less attention to women's roles, feminism, or gender issues (exceptions include Haug 1987; Al-Ali 2007; Hale 2013) the burgeoning field of memory work and gender has received extensive feminist examination in other fields, however (Henderson 2016; Hirsch & Smith 2002; DuPlessis & Snitow 2007; Aikau, Erickon, and Pierce 2007).

Memory-making and memories are treated in these works as negotiated, fluid, and always evolving. Memory and remembering are always contested acts. Memory is contested because the act of recollection is posited against a status quo, against forgetting, or against others' narratives. In short, memory is not a straightforward linear mental exercise in recollection; rather, it can be best described as a Möbius strip of multiple surfaces that fluidly interfuse and seamlessly evolve over time. The power of memory and its potential to debunk metanarratives lies in its fluidity and ability to reanimate the body. The diversity of experience and multiplicity of memories and how people remember enhance the countering potential of these narratives in the face of hegemonic discourses appropriating revolutionary history in Egypt and elsewhere in the Arab world. In developing this ethnography of rememory, these were all parameters that framed open-ended interviews, observations, and connections with the memory-makers of revolution.

Enjoining the study of memory and microhistory with embodiment and bodily experiences, on the other hand, requires that we problematize how the body acts as a corporeal archive, as a conveyor of meaning, and ultimately as an active agent in the production of narrative. Recreating the world of revolution through women's rememories relies first and foremost on an ethnography of their embodied narratives—one that emphasizes the phenomenology of embodied recollection. "Rememory," as it is used here, emphasizes memory as lived experience. It situates the body as "the field of remembering," where repetitions, gesturing, and lamenting communicate bodily experiences (Rakowski 2006). Through an ethnographic lens that draws on memory and oral history methods, the data collected for this book is both attentive to context and its relationship to meaning, as well as to the intersubjectivity of the in-depth interview experience (Di Leonardo 1987). In the open-ended interviews, discussions, and conversations I had with revolutionary women, it was therefore an important task to refer back to the body, to bridge their memories with their expressions and bodily comportment, so as to situate the women within their physical and historical context as closely as possible.

What this entails is a close reading of women's accounts, while paying equal attention to their bodily comportments, their physical surroundings, and their facial and vocal expressions as they engage in dialogue and rememorying. Integral to reading the body as text is ensuring that women's social and embodied rememories are read within their material and discursive settings. Each account in this book is the product of a detailed layering of meaning, impressions, reflections, intonation, as well as time, place, and personal history. Building on layer upon layer of conversation with my interlocutors, I include my own reactions to these accounts as well, so that readers can ascertain for themselves the vantage point from which these dialogues are written. Writing about rememory is a labor of detail that takes into account both the material and the discursive as closely interwoven and fluid but always partial. An ethnography of rememory goes beyond oral history to consider bodily experience as a form of memorial transmission. It is an approach that is cognizant of the fact that when these revolutionary women recount their stories, they document a history of civil disobedience in which their own bodies were instrumental in struggling for, as well as archiving social justice.

The study draws on accounts by close to a hundred Egyptian women from a cross-section of society who witnessed and shaped the realities of the revolutionary period that began on January 25, 2011. I focused on a heterogeneous sample of women who were involved in a variety of ways with the uprising. During a five-year period and over the course of several visits to Egypt, I interviewed women from various backgrounds, ages, classes, and religious faiths. From semirural to suburban and urban and industrial areas, my conversations with revolutionary women took me all around Cairo in ways I had never expected. I followed the stories as they were told, and they led me to others, who connected me to many more, and so on. The intricate web of relationships I followed and the distances I traveled (and the Cairo traffic I weathered) helped me envision the magnitude of what Tahrir Square had achieved—acting as the space where all these people once congregated, ate, slept, protested, celebrated, and mourned together.

Whether from Zamalek or Saft al Laban, Christian or Muslim, rich or poor, young or old, they came together en masse—a collective block of people whose paths would never have otherwise crossed. In their solidarity, they posed the biggest threat to government. The diverse backgrounds of the women who are the backbone of this work cannot be overemphasized as an important historical and ethnographic factor. This is because it demonstrates how the revolution in Egypt rose above deep-seated differences between people. Acknowledging this phenomenon is aside from subscribing to the romance of revolution, which assumes the utopian erasure of all differences between people—but to note that despite these various markers of difference, protestors learned to rise above them and unite around common goals. More specifically, this diversity among my women interlocutors testifies to the awe-inspiring momentum that galvanized this diverse collective—defying class, gender, religion, generational difference, even traffic and distance—into the sheer human magnitude of the Egyptian uprising against the regime.

Another caveat that must be acknowledged at the outset of this book is that it focuses on groups that opposed the regime and worked relentlessly to bring change to Egypt. This focus, however, does not intend to silence alternative points of view or those groups who supported the regime or engaged in protest and activism to defend their political beliefs. The book deals with gendered revolutionary activism and is specifically concerned with those invested in change and transformation and not the maintenance of the status quo or its modification. This choice does not reflect a preoccupation with change for change's sake or a view of change as a synonym for progress. Emphasis on change as progress is the product of a particular liberal disposition as Talal Asad has often pointed out. This perspective often influences research topics produced through a particular western liberal lens. Nor is progress necessarily an end in itself. The choice of focusing on revolutionaries is not arbitrary. There are implicit assumptions that inform this positioning which are informed by my own commitment to individual and political freedom, the right for self-determination, and the right to access resources unhampered by markings such as gender, race, ethnicity, religious affiliation, and/or political points of view. My vested interest in a gendered lens as a means of understanding the historical events of revolution derives from the assumption that as an organizing principle of any human society, gender is key to understanding social inequality. Consequently, political transformation cannot be accurately assessed without accounting for gender systems.

I intentionally avoided interviews with those who became celebrities of the media or those whose work was already publicly highlighted, choosing instead to feature those whose activism went unrecognized. While everyone's contributions are important and I have made every effort to reference them here, it was my research priority to bring the stories of ordinary women into the discussion of women's role in the revolution, the stories of those who are seldom heard. For it is only when all of the perspectives are brought together that we can begin to see the rich tapestry of embodied revolutionary action.

When I began recording my fieldwork observations in the tail end of 2011, it was with the intent to write about the revolutionary women I grew to know, using their real names. Without exception was their belief (and consequently mine) that their real names had to be included, not out of a particular need to glorify their work but out of a commitment to historical documentation. Although this ran counter to the conventional wisdom of ethnographic practice, where pseudonyms are used in lieu of real names to protect the privacy of research interlocutors, their assurances that this anonymity was not needed convinced me otherwise. Information was shared so freely and with such openness and excitement about their revolutionary activism, it was infectious. There was a sparkle, a vitality born out of a sense of hope and longing for a future that only then seemed possible. In the years following 2011, this enthusiasm for the historical revolutionary moment and their place in it began to wane.

When Mohamed Morsi was elected to the presidency in 2012, I began noticing how a few of the women would say that they were starting to "forget" and that it was an effort to remember. I sensed that there were unresolved issues and dissatisfaction with the approach of the new Islamist ruling government who frequently implied their loyalty was to the Islamic "*umma*"[1] and not to the state. A few of my interviewees seemed to hesitate about recalling their activism in Tahrir, reasoning that the present situation of rebuilding compelled them to look forward toward the future now. Consequently, a small number of the women did not wish to have their names mentioned in a book about events that have "passed." By the time General Abdel Fattah Al Sisi assumed office, the few women who preferred not to be named became the majority, until a year into his presidency in early 2015, practically no revolutionary woman would even speak to me unless I assured her that her name was not going to be mentioned. As the ethnographic narrative will detail, these forebodings were not unfounded, since the new regime not only clamped down heavily on civil liberties but also conducted wide campaigns imprisoning unprecedented numbers of protestors by means of a new antiprotest law, making unpermitted protests illegal. With the exception of those names that are known to the public, all the other names in this book are pseudonyms, and many of the identifying markers of each have been changed to preserve the anonymity and safety of my informants.

Despite the bravery and generosity of spirit of the revolutionary women I spoke with who insisted that they were not afraid of the government, there were, according to my observations, some underlying feelings of emotional stress and fear as the daily headlines announced more arrests of protestors. In the last year of my research, in 2015, only a few women would actually agree to discuss the revolution with me. A few would agree to meet, only to later keep rescheduling our appointments, forgetting we ever arranged one, or they would suddenly disappear—not replying to calls or texts. In the instances when I was able to ask why this had happened, it became apparent that a notable number of the revolutionary women who were "frontliners"—a term used by the women to describe those who were in the front lines fighting Internal Security soldiers with rocks and

Molotov bombs—were suffering from what was believed to be post-traumatic stress disorder (PTSD). In the cases that went undiagnosed, doctors were unable to explain sudden illnesses, chronic fatigue or pain, and even sudden collapse.

Although the demonstrations and the sit-ins and the violence they were subjected to shattered both mind and body, these were not the only reasons behind the trauma many of the women were feeling. For them, the sacrifices they made and the death and violence they witnessed could be tolerated, but as long as the revolution brought about the results they were hoping for. The losses they suffered could only then not be in vain. Yet, the advent of the current military regime saw the reversal of the demands of the revolution and the redeployment of repressive forces in society that limited the civil freedoms and collapsed the space of public politics that these revolutionaries had worked so hard to build. Trying to navigate health, emotional, and security issues made the research project difficult at times, especially because of the time constraints involved. Being mindful about the state of mind of my informants and the trials and tribulations they had experienced dictated how the ethnographic process proceeded.

Telling the stories of revolutionary women through a feminist ethnography of rememory is an endeavor that must navigate ethical and representational hurdles as well. While retelling any story is already a complicated process fraught with issues of power and ethics, these issues seemed to me even more so when dealing with emotional and often traumatic recollections. Memories can be elusive and slippery things to begin with. Retelling these memories is a process that often has to submit to the limitations of language and comprehension. How does one truly capture one's own memory, let alone someone else's? How can the intricate web of memory be translated into legible language (Mehrez 2012)? As a listener, how can I capture another's moment, thought, or feeling and in turn express it as faithfully, as gently as one can so as not to disturb its fragility. Retelling has to be consciously sensitive to this vulnerability of memory in the transaction that occurs between speaker and listener.

Tracing women's revolutionary activism over a period of five years has had both its challenges as well as its insights. Witnessing how the women who braved overwhelming social and physical harm while engaging in revolution evolve over time was both humbling as well as a privilege that I cannot overemphasize. From this privileged position of knowing them, it became clear that their stories— aside from reflecting their own experiences—also mirrored the impact of wider sociopolitical changes in Egypt. The storytellers were still immersed in their context, still affected by their memories, besieged by campaigns of social repression and of forgetting January 25, 2011, while I—I had the privilege of moving between borders and of occupying a position of entitlement by asking them to remember what many of them were being pressured to forget. These ethical issues were a heavy burden to carry. They made me aware of the incredible responsibility one assumes in retelling people's stories. All the more so when both the teller and the listener recognize that their exchange could effectively be the closest narrative to the events that made history in 2011 and the years that followed.

The process of rewriting history had already begun through official channels even then, as my interlocutors were retelling their version of it. Despite all the distortive complications inherent in the ethnographic process, this moment of retelling could very well be their only chance of documenting what happened. Finally, this book represents one version, my own interpretations of what they entrusted to me—retold with awareness of ethnographic privilege and my own positionality as a transnational Egyptian feminist living and teaching in the United States. Despite the risks of reproducing hegemonic structures of power/ knowledge and my own disclaimers that I do not speak for the subjects of this ethnography, I present these stories in their always-partial, nonlinear narrative, as incomplete, often contradictory, and occasionally discontinuous form.

As a feminist anthropologist who is keenly aware of hierarchizing forms of power that inhere in the text and in the ethnographic process, I am also aware of the need to acknowledge these relations of power, rather than assume that critical engagement can eliminate them completely. In Dipesh Chakravarty's often-quoted statement, he calls for a narrative that "deliberately makes visible, within the very structure of its narrative forms, its own repressive strategies and practices" (1992, 344). My account of these women's lives yields to these parameters of research and the ethnographic method.

During the five years of work on this project, I was often in and out of Egypt. Social media helped maintain ties and relationships with women between my absences. We continued to text, email, Facebook, and often Skyped, bridging the months of my absence with virtual face time. These various forms of communication often made me think about multisited ethnography in this millennium and the extent to which it is affected by social media. While it would not be at all accurate to describe this research as a "cyber ethnography," a term often used for studies of online communities, my fieldwork did rely in some part on forms of social media. Facebook Messenger was high on the list of social media forms of communication for almost all of the women who were involved in the uprising. Even if they themselves were unable to use the Net or Facebook, others at home were invariably available to help them connect. Although most of their posts and messages were in Arabic text, many of them also used English for texting and messaging. Facebook postings were in both languages discussing a wide array of topics, from poetry to art to memorials dedicated to the fallen martyrs of Tahrir, in addition to the news of arrests and occasional cartoons or jokes about the new regime.

In the Arab uprisings and in Egypt specifically, social media played a very important role in mobilizing people for demonstrations and disseminating information. In fact, the term "Facebook revolution" has often been erroneously used to describe the events of January 25. Wael Ghoneim, the Google executive who started the Facebook page "We Are All Khaled Said," comments on this in his memoirs, *Revolution 2.0. The Power of the People Is Greater than the People in Power* (2012, 190) that "History is made on the streets not on the internet." Ghoneim still understands perfectly well the role of the Internet in revolution. "If you want to liberate a society, just give them the Internet" (Sutter 2011). Whereas the Internet was an unbeatable method of mobilization, the actual history of the revolution took place in the streets and the squares where protestors/bodies became the most potent antiregime weapon.

Social and virtual media played an important role for me as well during the early days of the revolution, when I was in the middle of the academic quarter at university. Glued to the television and my computer screen, I followed the events as they unfolded minute by minute. Continuous communication with friends and family in Egypt by phone and my own research helped fill the gaps left by Facebook posts and texts. Though I was able to follow the events virtually as they unfolded, I was not physically present in the square, did not put my life in danger, nor did I sleep on the hard asphalt floor or experience revolution the way the women in this book talked about it.[2] I made the choice of remaining in the United States to explain the uprisings to a western audience. My choice presented me with a conundrum at the inception of this project that continued to make me hesitate to engage in this research—and this was that I had not been present in Tahrir during the first eighteen days of the revolution. Though being Egyptian myself with many friends and relatives who participated in the protests, I was not part of the cohort of Tahrir. I initially viewed this as a nonstarter for a research project that tackled women's revolutionary participation, yet my conversations with many of the women I grew to know in fact helped me rethink this.

Perhaps my lack of participation during the protests can be helpful to studying them. Instead of feeling limited by not being in Tahrir, this could actually enable me to be more attentive to the details of the experiences of my informants, unhampered by what could have been my own eyewitness experience. Although I do not claim objectivity, this book primarily relies on *their* accounts, is written through *their* eyes, and records *their* own emotional and physical experiences. Ultimately, however, the results of research projects are a collaborative effort between the researcher and her interlocutors.

*   *   *

The People of the Midan, 2011–2015

The "midan" is often translated from Arabic as a square, piazza, or plaza—a space. It is a focal point in urban design that allows the traffic from streets and boulevards to pour into, for people to gravitate to, and to represent national and historic significance. To modern Egyptians who often navigate its heavy traffic to get to downtown Cairo, the symbolic significance of midan al tahrir or Tahrir (meaning liberation) Square, however, transcends any architectural or urban planning functions. Since its renaming from Isma'iliyya Square by the revolutionary government of 1952, Tahrir Square and its modern downtown environs symbolized the liberation from British occupation, as well as from Egypt's royal Ottoman regime. Meant to provide a better entrance to the burgeoning political and economic life unfolding in midtown Cairo, promised by Nasser's government, Tahrir Square proclaimed the right of ordinary Egyptians to access their country's resources and urban spaces (Elsheshtawy 2016). The midan affirmed in architectural form the 1952 slogan, "Egypt for all Egyptians."

Given the historical symbolism of the midan, it was the natural place of choice for a group of activists to call for a flash protest on January 25, 2011. Yet, neither the members of the April 6th Movement nor those who belonged to the group "We Are All Khalid Said" could have imagined that their protest on National Police Day on January 25, 2011 was to usher in an all-out uprising. At the age of twenty-eight, Khaled Said's life violently ended at the hands of two undercover policemen who brutally beat him. Khaled's skull and bones were so crushed that his face was almost unrecognizable. A photo of his disfigured face went viral amid a wave of anger and protest on social media. The senseless murder acted as a catalyst for the protests against the police on National Police Day, slated to be celebrated on January 25.

The activists, who used social media to mobilize for their protest, had hoped that people would, at the most, join their neighbors and perhaps go out to protest around the major cities. At best, they imagined that small protests could somehow converge into main squares like midan al tahrir. The organizers did not anticipate that tens of thousands would pour into the streets to answer their call for a "day of rage." Cairo was not the only site of revolt. People rose up in protest in other cities all over Egypt: Alexandria, Beni Suef, Mahalla, Port Said, and Suez, as well as Mansura. By the end of that cold winter day on Tuesday, January 25, 2011, it became apparent that the protestors were staying put. They were not budging till their demands were met. They were in it for the long haul. In Cairo, makeshift tents and plans to prepare Tahrir Square as a site for prolonged protest began to take shape. By the twenty-eighth of January, a campsite was already in place as more and more people joined the throngs.

Undercover police and hired thugs presumably tasked with harassing and inciting violence and fear infiltrated the lines. The turning point came on the second of February, when an unimaginable scene unfolded as if from a tale from *A Thousand and One Nights*. The protestors who lived these events and those who watched them unfold across television broadcasts from their homes saw the unraveling of the Mubarak regime. The "Battle of the Camel"—named as such because thugs on camelback armed with swords and machetes, came flying into the mass of people in Tahrir, brandishing their weapons and attacking the demonstrators. This was considered a pivotal day in the history of the uprising. The protestors assumed the regime was retaliating against them for occupying Tahrir Square. Twenty-five people were arrested, as eyewitness accounts placed them in Tahrir Square carrying weapons. To this day, however, the data is inconclusive about who the real masterminds behind this incident were. Despite this, the "Battle of the Camel," was described as the day the tides turned against the regime (Fathi 2012). Leaving serious casualties, with eleven dead and six hundred injured, the incident heralded the ultimate popular disinvestment in a leader whose promises seemed empty and whose presidential bravado in his last address to the crowds was nothing more than an act of desperation. Finally, only eighteen days later, on February 11, Mubarak stepped down, thus marking the beginning but not the end of the uprising.

A Gendered Timeline of Revolution

When historical events are gendered, as in the timeline provided at the beginning of this book, the centrality of women and gender in the revolutionary years leading to Abdel Fattah Al Sisi's presidency becomes clear. Events read with little or no attention to gender dynamics result in incomplete and often distorted history.

After the twenty-fifth of January, and despite the state of insecurity that prevailed in the country, women's numbers in the protests continued to swell. By January 28, eyewitness accounts asserted that women made up half of the numbers of protestors. These assertions can be easily corroborated by simply perusing the countless photographs and footage of Tahrir square during the uprisings. Women's presence was crucial and not incidental to the protests and contributed to the quick results brought about by the sheer magnitude of people demonstrating against the regime. Placed in the hundreds of thousands, some even said in the millions, the protests in Egypt unleashed the strength of the collective. The presence of women in the midan and elsewhere demonstrated that this was no ordinary protest. It proclaimed the inclusiveness of political action as a collective visceral reaction to regime dysfunction, injustice, and ineptitude. During the Battle of the Camel, women reported back from Tahrir Square. Their voices could be heard over the wavelengths of media outlets describing the scenes unfolding in the square. Bold, unafraid, they reported back to news channels around the world. Yes, some admitted, they were afraid, but they were not leaving the midan; they belonged in the revolution, and they were ready for what was coming.

As the days following the end of Mubarak's regime revealed, there were tensions between the representatives of the protests and the old male elite who approached the council of armed forces seeking resolution. A group of men, aptly calling themselves "the council of wise men"—since no women were included—made the first attempts to negotiate with SCAF (the Supreme Council of Armed Forces now in charge of the country). In the midst of the upheaval caused by various political and interest groups vying for control, women were sidelined. On March 8, a march commemorating International Women's Day, organized by a group of feminists in Tahrir, was attacked. Between the heckling and the groping, the few hundred women and men who were there became acutely aware that this was a premeditated and organized attack on them.[3] The incident signaled the violence and thuggery that was to follow in the next few months. Only the very next day, on March 9, the military cleared out the square, burning tents, arresting and beating protesters. They began conducting virginity tests on female protesters, threatening them with accusations of prostitution and rape. This was followed by excluding women from the invitation to participate in deliberations about the new constitutional amendments. In July of that year, the Supreme Council of the Armed Forces (SCAF) dealt yet another blow to women's presence in politics when it canceled the 12 percent quota for women in the anticipated parliamentary elections.

In response to the blatant discrimination against women, the Egyptian Coalition for Civic Education and Women's Participation was established to unite NGOs and women's groups under the same banner. More than 454 NGOs came together, spurred on by the need to protect women's interests in the ensuing conflicts. By the end of the year, the results of the parliamentary elections were announced. Unsurprisingly, women won only 1.97 percent of the seats.[4] The cancelation of the women's quota by SCAF with no precedent and no lead time for women to prepare was, of course, a serious setback to many women candidates. Yet another obstacle was the new voting list system implemented by the military government, requiring political parties to include women candidates. No other stipulation was put in place to ensure that qualified women would have a chance at being elected. Consequently, most parties placed women at the bottom of their lists, which meant that the voters did not give women serious consideration.

For the observers of women's rights in the country, this was the culmination of a series of offenses against women. Military violence targeting women protesters, virginity testing, and threats of rape and public shaming by army officials and allegations of drug use and prostitution in the protest camp, as well as the attack on the women's march on International Women's Day all pointed to a state system not only insensitive to gender issues but intentionally limiting women's political participation and their physical presence in the public sphere. The military's readiness to go to these lengths to restrict women's presence in the political process did not bode well for the resistance groups that formed coalitions during the events of the uprisings. Time would eventually show that SCAF had its own plans for how the revolution was to eventually go forward.

Before the first year of the revolution came to a close, the violent confrontations of the "Cabinet Clashes" in December claimed the lives of more than seventeen people.[5] Once more, but on a wider scale, women were publicly violated during the protests. Military soldiers advanced on female protestors like Azza Suleiman and pounded them with batons. Many others including activist Ghada Kamal and physician Farida el Hessy were kicked and dragged by their hair across the midan. They were arrested and brutally interrogated. The "blue bra" incident involving a young woman who lay unconscious on the asphalt floor as army soldiers stomped on her chest and stomach with their boots made headlines in the aftermath of the violence.[6] It was now clear and beyond a doubt that the military were targeting women, to make a deliberate statement about the lack of sanctity of female bodies that do not deserve patriarchal protections. To the male centric state apparatus, the women of the midan had no honor—a claim that was meant to discredit the revolution all together as a perversion and a circus run by dishonorable men and women.

Women's response to these violations was swift and resounding. They organized the "Million Woman March," which brought thousands of women and men to the streets to protest military brutality, especially against women. This led the protestors to rename the march as "The Daughters of Egypt are a Red Line (not to be crossed)." The protest made an indelible mark on public opinion and regained some territory for women in political deliberations. It obligated the largest patriarchal power in the country, the military, to reconsider its violent policies against women.

The presidential elections came to an end in May 2012, announcing a new president to the Egyptian people. Mohamed Morsi, the Muslim Brotherhood's (MB) candidate for office, was sworn in only a month later. In accordance with MB policies that recognize the importance of the female vote in elections and mobilization, Morsi appointed Pakinam Al Sharkawi, a professor of political science as his special assistant for political affairs. Al Sharkawi touted the standard gender ideology of the MB and so was regarded as an arm of the new government and not an ally for women in office. She soon made statements reinforcing the conservative gender agenda of the Brotherhood which, despite the considerable contributions of its female members, nevertheless continues to consider them as nonvoting members. When Morsi attempted to put forward a constitutional referendum to grant the presidency immunity from accountability, this renewed the protests, and clashes ensued. Pakinam El Sharkawy was drawn into the midst of these conflicts as Morsi appointed her the head of Egypt's commission on the status of women to the United Nations in 2013. Her seemingly unquestioning support of Morsi's bid for autocracy and his less-than-egalitarian position vis-à-vis women placed her under scrutiny when her UN speech was heavily criticized for its complacency and lack of a solution for gender disparity.[7]

The following year, 2013, brought more dissatisfaction with the Muslim Brotherhood president, although some alleged that the deep state was behind the infrastructural problems the country was facing. A youth coalition calling itself Tamarod (rebellion) began a campaign to collect signatures for his impeachment. General El Sisi warned President Morsi against further alienating the populace. Protests between supporters of Morsi and the popular front resulted in continued violence and thousands of casualties. Sexual harassment against women increased as horrific public assaults of women became commonplace. Various initiatives by activist women and NGOs addressed the issue from within a community-based approach, such as Tahrir Bodyguard and Nazra, although the state seemed to remain impervious to the issue. By July, General El Sisi asked for a popular mandate to take matters into his own hands and depose Morsi. Millions took to the streets in response to his call, and he proceeded to arrest the now-former head of state. The massacre of a pro-Morsi sit-in of nearly six hundred people, in a camp in midan *rab3a al 3adawiya* marked the bloodiest yet after the Maspero killing of twenty-eight Coptic protestors, signaling once again that violence and destruction were yet to be a thing of the past.

Violence erupted as prodemocracy groups and Morsi supporters clashed with the police. The clashes between protestors and a number of terrorist incidents claimed by ISIS strengthened the calls for El Sisi to run for president. A law criminalizing protests took effect immediately, fueling a police campaign to clamp down on public displays of dissatisfaction and to arrest those at the heart of the protests. Fourteen teenage young women members of the Muslim Brotherhood cadets were arrested in Alexandria while leading a pro-Morsi demonstration. They were tried in an Alexandrian court and received suspended sentences for one year. The young women were the subject of debate and introspection as questions about justice, age, and gender occupied public opinion and social media. They epitomized the conflict between progovernment and pro-MB groups, spotlighting the struggle over defining fact and fiction in the country. Gender once more defined the crux of the political debate and the struggle over power and domination.

While these debates raged on, however, Mona Mina, a Coptic activist, was elected secretary general of the Doctor's Syndicate. She was the first non-MB member to head the syndicate in years, indicating a shift in trends regarding women's leadership. Hala Shukrallah was elected head of the Constitution Party, becoming the first woman to head a political party in Egypt. Some improvements were also made by including twelve women out of a total of ninety-nine members of a constitutional committee to redraft the constitution. Long-time feminist,

Hoda Elsadda was one of the women entrusted with this task. Her activist contributions as university Professor and a founder of the Women And Memory Forum were instrumental in the difficult negotiations that ensued in the committee (Elsadda 2015). The 2014 constitutional committee's draft was passed by a 98 percent approval at the beginning of 2014. On the third anniversary of the revolution, however, violent clashes erupted once more as protestors opposed the lack of political inclusion, absence of freedoms, and social justice. Frustration with the temporary government mounted amid terrorist attacks in the Sinai, shootings at protestors, and the death sentencing of more than six hundred members of the now-banned MB group. The April 6th Movement responsible for a large part of the mobilization of the revolution was also banned and accused of espionage. By June 2014, presidential elections took place, declaring Abdel Fatah El Sisi president by 96.9 percent of the vote.

While El Sisi's popularity in the country gained him favor with many who saw security as prerequisite for democracy, the revolutionary men and women whose life's struggle was freedom and justice did not. Egypt's jails continued to overflow with activists, now considered undesirable elements in society. While the shootings that claimed young lives went unpunished, campaigns asking for a return to morals shifted the focus and placed the onus on the citizen. Despite small gains for women such as the reinstitution of the parliamentary quota for women, the appointment of women judges to the Egyptian judiciary, female ministers to the cabinet, and the anti-sexual harassment law, many issues remain unresolved as Egypt once more reelects President El Sisi for a second term.

*   *   *

The focus on revolutionary women like Noha, who was quoted at the beginning of this introduction, may risk singling out women as a "special" topic of study. Given that knowledge still continues to be produced in a discursive realm almost entirely dominated by an androcentric logic that defines politics through a masculine lens, the risk of isolating gender as a phenomenon can be overcome through attention to the complex and fluid sociopolitical processes at the heart of historical transformations. Wedded to conceptions of power and strength as determinants of prominence, impact, and outcome, in my view, conceptions of revolution, revolutionary action, and participation must be problematized from other vantage points than the masculine. Rememory allows us to make such an intervention because it provides a window onto the lived experience of revolutionary women—not simply as nostalgic memories of historical events but as both discursive and corporeal interventions into revolutionary history and practice.

In the wake of a revolution, social and political processes still continue to delimit women's participation. These forces are played out to a large degree on women's bodies. Violence and its threat still continue to demarcate the boundaries for women, not despite but almost certainly because of the tremendous role they played on January 25 and beyond. Noting how these processes interweave to reconstitute women's corporeality reveals how these systems operate, intersect, and hone in on nonmasculine bodies. Alternatively, the corporeal is not a passive mass. Animated by desires for democracy and social justice, women use their bodies to negotiate public space, often attempting—not always without success—to overcome the repressive measures that stifle political action. State control, Islamism, neoliberal market changes, the military establishment, and sociocultural patriarchal systems impose boundaries on bodies that dissent—however power defines dissent. Repressive as well as dissenting forces are inseparable; these are forces that produce sociopolitical transformation.

Women's rememories of revolution make filmable the conditions that hone the gendered body as a galvanizing force—simultaneously occurring in the spaces of protest as well as in the retelling. (Re)constituted in revolutionary narrative and (re)articulated in revolutionary rememory, desire and civil disobedience are reignited in a process that links both discourse and the corporeal. Taking into consideration these powerful transformations, this book analyzes gendered corporeality in the Middle Eastern and North African contexts by reconsidering the relationship between bodies and memory, governmentality and neoliberal transformations in Egypt, and the emerging forms of violence, dissent, and identities in the region.

Bodies are instruments of "corporeal archiving." As such, they convey meaning as they are simultaneously inculcated by transmitted knowledges. Bodies also perform memory-embodying social transformation as they repeat experience and create new historiographies.

*   *   *

Feminist scholarship has analyzed the familiar discursive tropes that often represent women from Muslim-majority countries, the Middle East, or women in general. Today, postrevolutionary agendas have appropriated the history of revolution and invest considerable efforts to silence revolutionary voices and activism. The following book aims to unravel these tightly woven structures of knowledge by adopting a counterhegemonic lens that unsilences the cacophony of nonmasculine revolutionary voices. The book's chapters are thematically arranged following a spiraling format. A gendered linear timeline is provided at the beginning of the book for reference. The reader will sometimes experience the full range of events of the Egyptian uprising in one chapter, coming back again to the same time span or a slice of it in a following chapter. A number of the stories of revolutionary rememory will sometimes stop only to be picked up again at the end of the chapter or in a subsequent one. Chapter 1 discusses the discursive context in which women's revolutionary action intervened. Telling women's stories must, at some point, critically engage with these discursive spaces because they shape how women's stories are heard, understood, and archived. Chapter 2, "Gender and Corporeality in Egypt: A History" traces the history of women's corporeal dissent and political participation across Egypt's modern history.

In chapter 3, "Gender, Class, and Revolt in Neoliberal Cairo," women from across the sociopolitical spectrum recount the stories of their participation in the uprisings. Analysis of the state's neoliberal reforms sheds light on the challenges as well as the gains for women. The focus here is on the link between neoliberalism and gender and the state's regulatory systems. The state manages a dual system of internal control through managed chaos while simultaneously projecting an outward image of economic and political stability. Systems of state ideology construct a culture of disregulation, instability, and fear in the context of neoliberal market changes, economic ambitions, and liberalizing pressures from global lending organizations such as International Monetary Fund (IMF) and World Bank. To repress and intimidate dissent, the state acts not only as the agent of control but also as the force that unleashes random violence and condones pandemonium. The bifurcated policy of inward chaos and outward calm centers on the body and its regulation, where nonmasculine bodies are targeted by state agendas. Women's stories from a cross section of Egyptian society give a clearer picture of the ways they have dealt with the impact of neoliberal reforms. The stories told here are particularly significant because they illustrate that despite the diversity in backgrounds and privileges or lack thereof, all these women converged in Tahrir Square during the pivotal days of revolution.

Chapter 4, "The Lived Experience of Women's Struggle," draws the reader deeper into the lives of the women who were at the forefront of protests in the midan. Through their own narratives of revolution, revolutionary women delineate the material dimensions of their bodies. Deeply personal, the accounts reveal the relationship between gendered bodies and the political process. In these narratives, women redefine themselves through their social and revolutionary roles. They are the mothers, the wives, the sisters, the lovers, but they are also the revolutionaries, the activists, the artists, and the women who organized and planned sit-ins, the protests, and those who wrote catchy chants and led demonstrations. Fifty-year-old Amal, who had migrated to Cairo with her husband nearly twenty years ago from rural Beni Suef; twenty-five-year-old Yasmin, who lives in Cairo's cosmopolitan neighborhood, Zamalek; Dalia, a member of the Muslim Sisters (the women's branch of the Muslim Brotherhood); forty-seven-year-old Yara, who heard about the call for protests on the twenty-fifth from Facebook; and the many others who describe their experiences as they took their place among the throngs of people who swarmed Tahrir Square.

In chapter 5, "Bodies that Protest," I focus on how gender lines are redrawn by means of repressive policing through physical and verbal emasculation. At the core of this process are women's bodies, which navigate this tension between the physical and the social, producing meaning in the process, while simultaneously being reproduced. The chapter discusses various ways women's bodies became deployed as weapons of social discipline during the revolution, of shaming, and of the fragmentation of revolutionary lines, as well as the focal point of liberation and protest. The case of the virginity tests, the "girl in the blue bra" stomped on by army boots in the square, the so-called "Virgin Trials" where female cadets of the Muslim Brotherhood were tried and sentenced on charges of violence and mayhem, and similar cases where women's bodies are sites of conflict are but a few of the examples. The chapter ends by arguing for the ways women's bodies transform the terms of gender ideology. Through a collective act of rememory, the women's march against state violence renvisioned the body of the girl in the blue bra as a warrior. A section of this chapter also provides an analysis of the politics of gender in the Muslim Brotherhood.

Chapter 6 looks at violence as specter. Highlighting the disruptive presence of women in midan al tahrir as it changed established frames of dominance, analysis of violence makes visible how gendered bodies are imbricated in the necropolitics of the state. Organized violence and public sexual harassment of women, raids on alleged gay weddings and baths, and the security state's open hostility to burgeoning masculinities are but some examples that point to the measures systems of control implement to instill obedience and discipline in their populations. A number of accounts unfold as the chapter develops. I explore the case of a woman known as "The Lion of the Midan," Naglaa, whose account illustrates how the experiences of women during the first eighteen days in Tahrir Square transcend gender boundaries. The cases of Hend Nafea and Shaimaa al Sabbagh—two young women revolutionaries whose stories epitomize the rearticulation of state power over space and political action, crystalize how female bodies negotiate the politics of dissent in Egypt. Twenty-five-year-old Hend Nafea is in exile in the United States, escaping a court verdict of life in prison, while Shaimaa al Sabbagh, aged thirty-one, was shot by state police as she laid a wreath of flowers in memory of the fallen revolutionaries in Tahrir. She is buried in Alexandria, where she was born, and where her five-year-old son and husband mourn her death. The chapter also examines how public discourse and state policing magnify sexually nonconforming bodies as the deviant other of the authentic heterosexual Egyptian. Linking queer sexuality to the revolution, a media program manifests all as deviant and undesirable. Throughout the book, as in this chapter, nonmasculine bodies defy social and political repression, and despite the dire outcomes, continue acting as sites of dissent and revolution.

The book ends with chapter 7 looking at the politics of forgetting but also noting how the act of rememory can rekindle corporeal dissent in virtual ways thus signaling new beginnings. The final chapter takes note of the forms of resistance emerging among the youth of Egypt in the virtual world of the Internet as groups come together to discuss sexual taboos and to provide each other with input and support.

Revolution, the people's ultimate call for change, is a historical event that must be freed from androcentric bias. As an expression of revolt, revolution, and in particular its manifestation in Egypt, was galvanized by multiple voices and bodies. The vast ranges of the revolutionary body, from young to old, poor to rich, rural to urban, and the ranges of genders, religions, and political and cultural identities not only lend credibility to the uprisings but were also its very defining character. Any conventional androcentric reading of revolution that fails to capture these vibrant articulations in its historiography, ultimately silences the very essence of its character. Therefore, recentering the gender narrative of the uprisings is of particular significance to this study—particularly given the conflicting discourses that vie to frame these important historical events and to obscure women's role during the revolution of January 25.

Notes

1. The term *umma* denotes the entire community of Muslims beyond national boundaries.

2. At the time, I was teaching and giving talks about the uprising in the United States. I gave twenty-two talks to various audiences across the nation in 2011 alone.

3. Watch the reports by participants of the march about what happened here: التحرش بالمتظاهرات في ميدان التحرير.mov, https://www.youtube.com/watch?v=3WLM02cDy4g.

4. Nemat Guenena, "Women in Democratic Transition: Political Participation Watchdog UNIT," 2013, http://www.un.org/democracyfund/sites/www.un.org.democracyfund/files /UDF-EGY-08-241_Final%20UNDEF%20evaluation%20report.pdf.

5. The reason behind the protests included the appointment of Kamal Al Ghanzoury, who had been previously appointed by the Mubarak regime as new prime minister in place of Essam Sharaf, who resigned two days before. Clashes erupted once more after young activist Aboudy Ibrahim's savagely beaten body was thrown out of the People's Assembly gate onto the streets by security forces. This was perceived as an incendiary act by the state.

6. Liliana Mihaila, "Cabinet Clashes Remembered, Egypt Ended 2011 with Street Fighting That Left Many Dead," December 15, 2012, http://www.dailynewsegypt.com/2012 /12/15/cabinet-clashes/.

7. Thouraia Abou Bakr, "The Multi-Talented Pakinam El Sharkawy," April 23, 2013, http://www.dailynewsegypt.com/2013/04/23/the-multi-talented-pakinam-el-sharkawy/.

WOMEN of the MIDAN

1 Telling the Stories of Revolutionary Women

Scenes from an Uprising, Cairo 2011

Scene One

She stood—barely five feet in height—with her feet planted squarely on the ground, facing what seemed to be an endless dark blur of *amn markazy* security men in their black uniforms and helmets. Her face was framed in a bright hijab that accentuated her youthful features. She could not have been more than seventeen years of age. Yet her voice bellowed powerfully out across Tahrir Square without a microphone for all to hear. As she called out short, rhythmic couplets to the crowd, they answered back, repeating word for word the slogans she chose to shout:

> *Huwwa Mubarak ȝayiz iḥ?* (repeated twice)
> What does Mubarak want?
> *Kul' šaȝb yibus rigliḥ?* (repeated twice)
> All the people to kiss his feet?
> Then, staring straight into the eyes of the security forces cordoning off the street, she raised her arm in the air with her index finger pointed upward and shook it from side to side as she continued:
> *Laa ya! Mubarak! Miš ḥanbus.*
> No! Mubarak! We won't kiss [your feet].
> *Bukra ȝlik bil gazma'n dus!*
> Tomorrow, we will step on you with our shoes!

Scene Two

A small crowd of women and a few male supporters took to Tahrir Square on March 8, 2011, to commemorate International Women's Day and reaffirm women's commitment to the revolution. As the group stood in the middle of the square, it seemed as if the turnout was less than expected. A few minutes of waiting for others to join soon confirmed the reality that the thousands of women who were part of the uprising preferred to stay home that day, despite the various efforts to mobilize them. Instead, there was another group who showed up, their voices audible even from a distance as they approached. *Could it be possible?* the women thought to themselves. *Are they really chanting for women to fall and for the revolution to live?* Almost immediately their questions were answered; about a thousand men showed up, with a few carrying signs ridiculing the women's march. They went directly for the small crowd of women gathered at the center of the square. Crude illustrations of men drooling at women, signs ordering women to go home, verses from the Quran that were strategically chosen to accuse women of neglecting their duties and obligations as females, seemed almost alien in Tahrir Square, which had just witnessed one of the most vocal movements in the country for freedom and democracy. As the exchanges between the two groups turned confrontational, it became apparent that the male-led group was bent on stopping the women's march.

A young sheikh, wearing the traditional *gibba wa kuftan,* was carried on the shoulders of men in the antiwomen march. The "sheikh" held pages from the Quran in his outstretched hand, thus invoking religious doctrine as the ultimate authority against the female turnout. Only minutes after they appeared, the men encircled and isolated the small groups of women who were in Tahrir calling for solidarity and quickly started to grope at them. A few male supporters who rallied with the women's march were physically assaulted. "The same men who invoked Islam and brought the sheikh sexually harassed us!" cried one of the women in the march.

Scene Three

> It was a very cold night in Tahrir a few days after the 25th [of January] but we were determined to occupy the square no matter what. We had no idea how to go about setting up camp or organizing the place. None of us knew anything about that. Us women had never done anything like this before. Some had sleeping bags, others just a blanket, and most of us had nothing at all—having decided to do this [camp out] at the last minute. Many of our Muslim brothers were there, they told us what to do. They set up the campground, making beds for those who did not have anything, putting up makeshift tents from bed sheets and clothing. They organized us into rows, designated areas of the square, even made out schedules for us so some slept while others kept vigil. They treated us all the same, never taking notice of who was veiled or not. They slept next to us on the ground and refused to leave even when their commanders recalled them back. We were exhausted and beaten and if it weren't for them we would not have pulled this off.
>
> —*Sanaa, an activist woman from Tahrir describing the early days of encampment in the square*

Recentering the Gender Narrative

Despite women having participated alongside with men in the pivotal days of revolution in 2011, neither media coverage nor academic scholarship afforded them equal attention. Accounts and analysis of revolution remain androcentric at best, analyzing the events from a patriarchal vantage point that privileges the male gaze and normalizes masculine politics. As a rough example, in the most extensive bibliographic list on the Arab uprisings published by the Project on Middle East Political Science (2015) only sixteen articles referred to gender in their titles, and twenty-six referred to women, with a total of forty-two entries out of 888 articles, amounting to only a fraction of the total. I take this one example as a relative indicator of the dearth in scholarly articles dealing with women and gender-related issues and the marginal importance afforded them in the literature on the Arab uprisings.

Language describing the uprisings points to the normalization of the male gender in all aspects of the revolution. Public discourse, magazines, and journals show little effort to be gender inclusive when describing the protestors. Even when mentioning the demonstrators who were killed, males are the only ones mentioned. Feminist Nawal El Saadawi (2013) writes in *Al-Masry Al-Youm,*

> Why have the names of the *shahydat* (pl. female martyrs) of the revolution of January 2011 fallen from the dominant power's deliberations?
> Is it because they are women?
> Or because they are poor and their names are not known?
> Is it necessary for the *shahyda* (sing. female martyr) *or shahyd* (sing. male martyr) to be of the upper class or a member in the parties that compete over government or a friend of a notable journalist or of a media pundit who owns a satellite channel?
> Is there cheap Egyptian blood that the sand soaks up only to be forgotten by the nation and history?
> The nation is not concerned with the blood that is spilt for its sake with the exception of the valuable blood of those who own history and government and weapons and the media. (Translated from Arabic)

El Saadawi points to the intersectionality of invisibility in Egypt. What does it mean to be an Egyptian with "cheap blood"? Class, connections, socioeconomic status, and most of all gender mark the revolutionary subject—even in the most visceral fight to save the nation—as *cheap.* The nation too, according to her, caters to those who "own history" because the nation itself is framed in androcentric terms by those in power. The fight for the nation, therefore, is also the fight to redefine it. And those who lost their lives—women, men, the poor, the forgotten, and those whose blood is considered cheap—forge the path to reclaiming what belongs to the people.

Writing a gendered account of revolution humbly follows in the path forged by its martyrs and those who persist against coerced forgetting. Relying on what I will call "rememory" and the centering of gendered corporeality at its midst, this account endeavors to reclaim the revolution's historiography from the custodial

grip of mainstream politics. It is not simply about restoring women to revolutionary memory; nor is it about the glorification of women as exceptional though
it is about rethinking the gendered framework of revolutionary historiography,
troubling the normative androcentric lens and subverting the dominance of those
who "own history" to expose revolution's underbelly—its lived experience with
all its messiness, joys, and tribulations. Through women's "rememory" of revolution, a deliberate retelling of these events animates gendered bodies, affording
them a re-experience. Rememory thus opens the doors to what is visceral, to the
corporeal archive of revolution, and this is how these women rewrite revolution.

While a predominant focus on women has its own ramifications, the epistemic privileging of masculine politics results in an incomplete and skewed
interpretation of events. Clearly, women's experiences may differ from men's,
but they may also parallel them. Therefore, accounting for how these differences
evolve and impact the course of the uprisings is crucial to understanding these
events. Like their male counterparts, many women spent nights in the midan,
some alone, others with their children huddled against them for warmth. They
marched and shouted the slogans of revolution, *thawra thawra hatta an-nasr;
thawra fi Tunis thawra fi Masr* (revolution, revolution till victory, revolution in
Tunisia, revolution in Egypt); *il sha3b yurid isqat il nizam* (the people demand
the overthrow of government). They stood fearlessly on the front lines while
the state pummeled them with tear gas bombs, and many, despite government
repression, continue to this day to work toward the realization of the revolution's
aims, *3ish, hurriya, 3adala igtima3iyya* (bread, freedom and social justice). Yet,
in the accounts of the first eighteen days of the revolution and the subsequent
months and years that followed, women remained only a marginal group that
was referenced for color—all too common in public discourse and unfortunately
in academic discourse as well. When women were not written out of the record,
their inclusion in revolution lore served particular agendas, be they militaristic,
Islamist, or western orientalist.

Subverting the "Glocal" Hegemonic Lens

Feminists have long since challenged the androcentric bias of knowledge production (Anderson 2004, Fricker 2009, Haraway 1988, Harding 1996, Hooks 1994, Moraga & Anzaldua 1983) yet dominant local and global discourses unfailingly frame
women's sociopolitical backgrounds in ways that rationalize systems of control.
In conventional representations of Middle Eastern women, this androcentric logic
continues to be exacerbated by a history of colonialism, oil war agendas, and the
neoliberal capitalism of the World Bank and the International Monetary Fund's
development imperatives. Persistent images of women from the developing regions
of the world as monolithic, and disempowered; victimized by culture and religion
still have currency today. Aside from a few notable exceptions (Abu-Lughod 2013,

Al Ali & Pratt 2009), feminist analyses are sorely needed that take into account Euro-American military interventions in the Middle East and how neoliberal forces sustain a rhetoric that rationalizes specific social and economic transformations. There are various paths a feminist trajectory may take when concerned with the fluid dynamics of power. One way to do so is to focus on issues of subjectivity and subject formation, in which case context and history are of particular significance for tracing their embeddedness within metanarratives of modernity, postcoloniality, nationalism, and neoliberal economic shifts. By taking into account the processes that shape human subjectivity and desire, our trajectory can at once deal with context, cultural relativity, and knowledge production, while paying equal attention to the formation of selves and persons whose desires and motivations lie at the nexus of larger discourses of modern history. Chandra Mohanty (2003) tasks the scholar of gender in postcolonialist and Muslim majority countries in particular with the challenge of undoing the dichotomous positioning of Muslim women vis-à-vis western women. To Mohanty, debunking homogenizing efforts that lump all women of the developing world into one large, oppressed collective are of paramount concern. To do so, she contextualizes the struggle of women everywhere—but particularly those from the global south underscoring their specificity by means of intersectional approaches.

To "tell women's stories," (Abu-Lughod 2013), it is necessary to address these discursive tropes in knowledge production about "the other" woman (here understood as the third world, Arab, Middle Eastern woman). Revolutionary women's rememories produce a counternarrative to the dominant universalizing and androcentric coverage of western media and local official discourses about the revolution, its participants, and its spectators. However, narrating these accounts of ordinary yet extraordinary women's lives cannot be a task of direct translation; nor does it purport to be more than reconstructive, imaginative, and incomplete. After all, rememorying is necessarily dependent on one's imaginative powers and ability to resurrect embodied past events. Nevertheless, in narrating these accounts, I am attentive to how discourse reproduces power and power relations; that knowledge production is not arbitrary, and that documenting lived experience is a praxis that is necessarily both ethical and grounded in a critique of knowledge. This research agenda, I believe, is closely related to what the ethnographic process in this contemporary, increasingly globalized world must contend with—an awareness that field research is ultimately intertwined with power dynamics embedded in issues of cultural representation. To begin examining these issues, the next section will analyze the framing of the Arab uprisings within the western media lens shaping events according to the grand narratives governing global conceptions of center and periphery. What news and events find their way into the international media and why? Who get to be the players, the heroes and the villains in these representations?

Shaping Revolutionaries and Revolutions

While the Arab uprisings came about as a result of complex social, political, and economic circumstances, various competing powers vied to control how these events came to be represented. Given the current concerted effort in some Arab countries such as Egypt to erase the memory of revolt, it is of particular importance to start here—with a discussion of the discursive assertions of power over how the uprisings are represented. While the uprisings initially attracted a significant amount of attention, there are fewer and fewer references today to these events in the media and public discourse, other than to point to the disruption and chaos the uprisings unleashed on the region. Local and western media reflect conflicting yet sometimes converging interests in controlling how the struggle for local freedom and sovereignty are represented. In the material that follows, I trace how these interests frame gender politics in the revolts.

Gender is often evoked as a marker of civilizational progress, as a barometer that tests the level of progressive politics taking shape in the Arab world or as a symbol of tradition, nationalism, and cultural and religious authenticity. Principal examples of cases cited to support processes of culture-centric, Orientalizing epistemologies include the case of Samira Ibrahim versus the military, which exposed virgin testing; the case of the protestor now dubbed "the girl in the blue bra" and the sexual harassment and assault on women in Cairo's streets. Emotionally and politically charged, these cases therefore highlight core issues that define how the lines of gender are drawn, the powers that vie to control the dissenting body, and how resistance takes shape in the face of oppressive regimes. Media coverage of the Arab uprisings exposes these themes of power and resistance spotlighting the ways they intersect with women's bodies.

A few news outlets observed that women took to the streets "in droves." The emphasis, however, was placed on the marvel of a so-called unprecedented phenomenon of women's political participation in a region often described as beset with a conservative and backward gender ideology that denies women "voice." As reports of this "feminist" participation of Arab women gained some momentum, the general public was pulled into the discursive web of an age-old Orientalist pattern. A pattern that paints all women in Muslim-majority and Middle Eastern societies with one brush, dehistorisizes them, purports them to be generally oppressed, and sees only a feminist western trajectory for the liberation of dispossessed others. While such hegemonic constructs are all too common in the media they are often echoed in academia uncritically reinforcing western political interests in the region.

Locally, however, the media in Egypt representing state interests, questioned the integrity of the revolutionaries and particularly women, often impugned their motives, and described them as women of loose morals. This multiple appropriation on both global and local levels recalls the "double colonization" that scholars such as Chandra Mohanty (2003) describe in their work. The "double" refers to the simultaneous labeling by "glocal" hegemonic discourses. Women in politicized areas of the world (countries that play a key role in global/western politics) are on one hand often cast in the role of the dispossessed by international interest groups, while on the other as the inauthentic westernized other by local patriarchal power. These dichotomous discourses result in further complicating and undermining women's efforts in the public sphere (Hoodfar 2001). Often women's groups have to go to great lengths to mobilize because they must navigate the perceptions that come with this paradoxical positioning.

The events that began with the uprising in Tunisia in December 2010 succumbed—as has much of Middle Eastern and North African (MENA) historiography—not only to the hegemonic discursive western lens but also to local distortions of the patriarchal privileged elite. While scholars after Edward Said (1981) laid out the genealogical processes of Orientalizing European knowledge production that shaped how the MENA and Muslim-majority countries are viewed, a more contemporaneous analysis of these processes is still needed. This is exemplified by the disconnect that emerged between the events unfolding on the Arab ground during the uprising and their representation in news and media coverage. This divide in knowledge production prompts a more serious look at the constructs of knowledge that are the product of cultural translation (Hawas 2012) and those that are nurtured by embedded discourses of Orientalism (El Mahdi 2011).

Fashioning a "Spring" from the Same Old Fabric

The so-called "Arab Spring," hot off the presses, was and continues to be represented as a predominantly young revolution. The term *Arab Spring* is itself a reflection of the implied belief of the momentary awakening of Arabs—the implication being that the Arab past was lived in slumber, only to be reawakened through revolution to the rapture of democracy. While the relationship between democracy and Arab cultures and societies has always been an elusive one, the struggle to achieve political autonomy from western intervention responds to historical shifts and is not the outcome of a slumberous Arab disposition. The Arab world shares a long and diverse history of revolution and revolt against colonialism and oppression. In Egypt alone, the history of revolution spans decades, notably including the 1919 revolution against the British, followed by the 1952 revolution. A history of revolt has been documented across the Arab world with Algeria in 1954, Lebanon in 2005, and in particular the Palestinian revolts against Israeli occupation from 1936–39, then 1987, followed by 2008.

Young people indeed dominated the visual drama of color and movement recorded by photographers and filmmakers. Despite evidence to the contrary, where the participation of older generations, women, and religious groups testified to an organic uprising against intolerable living conditions that affected all society (Winegar 2012, Singerman 2013), young people were often viewed as the only proponents of the uprisings. In Egypt, the young men and women of the April 6 movement, such as Ahmed Maher and Asmaa Mahfouz, occupied the imaginations of millions of spectators through video clips that went viral. The media frenzy that followed the first few months of the uprisings were less a testimony to the actual events and more of a reflection of reactionary local government press releases that dismissed the revolutionaries as "a bunch of disgruntled youth." Observers of the uprisings soon saw the inaccuracy of these depictions, noting the diversity in population makeup of the revolutions across Arab countries, which the participants themselves insisted on highlighting to the world. They recognized that public social unity in displays of religious, gender, and class solidarity were central to the ideology of the revolutions, but more so, pivotal to the credibility that they sought to establish to counter dismissive official accounts of their efforts.

Accounts of the early years of the Arab uprisings also emphasized the role played by young people—for other reasons. On one hand, the idea of revolution itself as transformation and new beginning in the Arab region relied heavily on a stereotypical understanding of the region as a politically stagnant and traditionally backward conservative culture. Such views represent enduring discourses of Orientalism, with reasoning that fails to take account of the impact of colonialism, western intervention, and global neoliberal trends. An uprising of youth against a conservative patriarchal system was also a trope that was seen to challenge Arab norms. While age and masculinity define the latter forms of patriarchy, this particular brand of inequality was not distinguished from its western counterpart. Depicting the revolutions as "youthful" took precedence over the complex political and economic circumstances that gave rise to the protests. The demands of various minorities, such as the Coptic community, for instance, readily faded into the background of the portrait painted of the youthful rebels. Any thoughtful treatment of the impact of wider international interests in exacerbating local conditions was rendered superfluous, in favor of more flavorful reporting. On the other hand, the idea of "rebels without a cause" was more readily palatable to a western audience, where various cultural and social values embraced the notion of change as youthful and progress as the prerogative of the young.

Young people did indeed begin a mobilizing effort that galvanized millions of people across the Arab world. Theirs were also the highest numbers in the streets and squares of Arab metropolises, jails, and tragically, the morgues. Yet although these may be accurate facts, the discounting of all other constituents of the revolution is not only historically distortive but reflects politically and culturally centric trends. These modes of representation that undoubtedly fall back on Orientalist formulations continue to remain lucrative as a rationale for global inequities.

There were journalistic attempts at bridging the East/West divide and assuming less of a default position of the knower. *Ms.* magazine, for example, carried out excellent reporting that problematized the meanings and specificities of political participation for women. *Time* magazine headlined, "Silent No More: The Women of the Arab Revolutions" by Carla Power (2011), which ridiculed the "shock" of w media at Arab women's political participation. Despite these critiques, the press continued their routine reporting, uninformed by the history of women's organizing in the Arab world, whether against colonialists or later to establish feminist and nationalist organizations. The media's lens on women was framed by two main assumptions. The first presumed that Arab women have had no historical experience with political action; the second assumed that these women, like their revolutions, have awakened to western notions of liberation, that is to say, feminism. Paying no heed to the role that class, race, and education play in Egyptian society, Laura King (2011), a reporter from the *Los Angeles Times*, maintained that "women, long considered second-class citizens, say they have found an unexpected equality on the front lines of the demonstrations against President Hosni Mubarak." Then she went on to say, "women have proved themselves to be adept grassroots organizers, taking up visible tasks such as carrying out identity checks and searching bags of women entering the square."

Reports continued to expound on how the revolutions were a split for Arabs from their conservative past. An indicator for this: a kiss planted on a man's cheek in public. In an article titled "Egypt: Why the Kiss Picture Is So Radical" (2011), Garance Franke-Ruta, who was at that time politics editor of *The Atlantic* online, focused on a scene captured on camera in which an older woman planted a big kiss on the reluctant face of a soldier in Tahrir Square. Franke-Ruta explained this to her readers by writing, "Women in Egypt don't normally hold hands in public, let alone kiss strange men. As a picture of compassion between combatants, the image of a plump Egyptian woman kissing a green-eyed soldier on the cheek during protests last week was *a powerful statement of national unity*" (Ibid., italics added). Then she elaborated on the conservative nature of Egyptian women by alluding to veiling practices. Taking veiling as a marker of conservative behavior among women, she went on, "Young Egyptian men may dress in the international style of jeans and soccer T-shirts, but they go home to families where women wear headscarves. An estimated 90 percent of Egyptian women wear the hijab, and more deeply religious women cover not just their heads and ankles, but even their hands, wearing black gloves along with their black face veils, headscarves and abayas (or long cloaks) year round." The author deals the concluding statement: *"In short, when it comes to women in public life, Egypt can be pretty conservative. It's not Saudi Arabia or Iran, but it's also not Lebanon."* (Ibid, italics added). Such sweeping generalizations about entire populations framed many an analysis about the revolutions, in this particular case, taking a kiss as a demonstration of an "unprecedented" social expression of affection never before witnessed in a conservative society, where revolution has relaxed public displays of affection and removed barriers between the genders. The underlying binary construct between conservative and progressive modes of behavior (or traditional versus modern) further distorts this example of cultural mistranslation. A public kiss by an older woman planted on the cheek of a younger man obviously intended as a maternal and ironically somewhat of a patriarchal show of affection (older woman enjoy status over younger men in Arab societies) is translated as an indicator of the erasure of conservative boundaries and the emergence of a new brand of liberation.

Just as liberation from conservative social mores is defined in modernist terms, so is women's political participation. Feminism, understood as the natural progression of democracy—only because this is how it transpired in western history—is another example of the kind of western-centric thinking and analysis that deals with women's issues in nonwestern societies and cultures. In an article that foresees a Middle Eastern feminist revolution, Naomi Wolf (2011) claims, *"feminism is simply a logical extension of democracy*, the Middle East's despots are facing a situation in which it will be almost impossible to force these *awakened* women to stop their fight for freedom—their own and that of their communities"* (italics added). Wolf's reasoning that this generation of women will not stop participating politically since they have experienced the power of mass protest is not without some merit. She overlooks the fact, however, that women have been protesting for decades in the Arab world. Moreover, Wolf sees feminism as a logical development of democracy. Third world women have been debunking these claims since the 1970s by asserting their own culturally specific pro-women discourses that do not necessarily produce western hegemonic forms of liberation. Feminism therefore cannot be understood in these contexts as a "logical" extension of democracy. The logic spoken of here is simply a western one.

Fraught with generalities and lack of attention to special and temporal contextual analysis, the assumptions that drive reporters to write what they write, are based on normative constructs that posit the Orient as the backward antithesis of western civilization. In this binary opposition, the implicit hierarchy, which views western civilization as the single most human trajectory to progress, dictates how these reports imagine the future for a democratic Arab region. Accordingly, women in the Arab world have "awakened" to feminist consciousness, and a feminist transformation is Arab women's "logical next stage after the revolution"

(Ibid.). Relaxed social formalities and public expressions of affection are taken as indicators of positive change, as is the notion that Arab women could actually succeed at political action because they carried out simple organizing tasks like bag checks. Though these are by no means the only ways women protestors in the Arab world were appropriated by international media outlets, they do represent a general, almost formulaic structure that dominates knowledge production about this region and women's issues in particular. They are part and parcel of a historically rooted but also very current systematic body of knowledge. This knowledge reproduces an Arab, Muslim, Middle Eastern "other." When this other is reduced to a one-dimensional, pliable subject matter, it can dully rationalize political and economic policies at whim. Homogenization, dehistoricization and essentialism, as well as the unproblematic application of a western-centric lens, facilitates and justifies a range of actions, from appropriation of resources to geopolitical restructuring, as well as the redrawing of boundaries and the establishing of new power alliances.

The Struggle over Representation

The glocal lens notwithstanding, a considerable number of my interlocutors were keenly aware of these dynamics of "misrepresentation." Several women I spoke with had been interviewed on many occasions by reporters, researchers, and graduate students. Some had become adept at interviews, often guiding our conversation in ways they thought would interest me. One of the women mentioned that she was often on television, another recalled how several foreign reporters spoke to her and took photographs of her, and another confronted me about why I approached her in particular, accusing me of perhaps finding her of interest because of her rural roots as others have. Being involved in political work heightened their awareness of issues of representation, making them particularly cautious about who was writing about them, for what purpose, and for whom. Aside from security concerns that became an issue after Mohamed Morsi assumed office, many women who were involved in revolutionary activism assumed the role of my teacher. For that I was grateful. Noha, for instance, whose opening words to me corrected me, "I am not an activist; I am a revolutionary," wanted to be understood with no ambiguity right at the start of our conversation.

Aziza, a woman I spoke with in Giza, said to me, "Do not waste your time with me. I am not an interesting woman, and I do not deserve to be mentioned in your book. There are others who have done more than I who should be included."

Pointing to their growing discomfort with being in the spotlight, some women always began with a disclaimer: "I don't know much but . . ." Their self-effacement and nuanced awareness of how their efforts could potentially be misconstrued only strengthened my resolve to bring their stories and what they stood for as revolutionaries and activists to the pages of this book.

While these problems arose with how the media represented the women of the midan, let us now turn to research and scholarly publications to assess the extent of their contributions to the gendered historiography of the Arab uprisings.

The Revolution Shall Be Gendered

Scholars of Arab societies and politics have written extensively about the Arab uprisings—what they were, why they emerged, and what they achieved or didn't achieve. Many analyzed the impact on the region's geopolitical contours—all important contributions that must be considered (Lynch 2013; Sowers & Toensing 2012; Korany & El-Mahdy 2014, Bayat 2017). The bulk of the literature, however, addresses the events of the Arab Spring—itself a controversial, distortive term that unfortunately became naturalized as a label for the Arab uprisings and their aftermath—largely from a default male perspective. Often unproblematically emphasizing normative masculine-centric knowledge about the public sphere of politics, with little attention to such feminist scholarship that long debunked default ways of understanding these spaces as Carol Pateman, *The Sexual Contract* 1988; Wendy Brown, *Finding the Man in the State*, 1992; Ruth Lister, *Citizenship in Theory and Practice* 1997; and Suad Joseph, ed. *Gender and Citizenship in the Middle East* 2000 as a separate phenomenon and not as part of the events of the uprisings.

A small but growing number of scholarly books have chosen to focus on gender in the Arab uprisings. The majority of the work takes the form of edited volumes, with very few monographs that treat gender in revolution with a more sustained approach than a chapter. Only a select few have dealt with the events following the uprisings of 2011 from a gendered perspective, for example, Al Ali (2012), Hatem (2011), Hafez (2012), Singerman (2013), and a special issue edited by Andrea Khalil (2014) in the *Journal of North African Studies*, also published as a volume. Edited volumes include El Said, Meari, and Pratt (2015); Hasso and Salime (2016); Khalil (2014); Olimat (2013); and Sadiqi (2016). These compilations explore various important topics that range from the analysis of constitutional discourse (McLarney 2016) to social media and sexual harassment (Skalli 2013) to body politics (El Said 2015) and gender and the reshaping of identity (Abouelnaga 2016).

While each of these contributions and several others provide vital discussion of issues relevant to the topic of revolution and women's participation in the political sphere, more attention needs to be directed to include women's accounts and their lived experience within the context of historical and sociopolitical analysis of the Arab revolts.

The most recent book by Shereen Abouelnaga (2016) takes a critical literary approach toward theorizing women's identity and agency postrevolution. In particular, Abouelnaga argues that analysis of women's agency should neither be approached anachronistically nor viewed as an abstraction. To her, agency should be understood as a lived, fluid, and evolving experience. The lived experience of agency needs to be simultaneously grounded in the larger history of the nation as well as in the microhistory of the individual. Reading the revolution as a "text," she positions the female body as a discursive oppositional force to the status quo. This is in addition to the various forms of expressions of resistance manifested by revolutionaries, whether musical, artistic, verbal, etc. The body signifies to her, therefore, a medium of gendered intervention, which seeks to rewrite women's social and cultural narrative. Abouelnaga also discusses women's memory as a form of countering the dominant patriarchal narrative. I agree with her view that the body as well as memory are important components of resistance and indeed occupy an essential focus in revolution. Yet, the scholarly record on societies of the Middle East and North Africa has tended to fall short in theorizing the gendered body other than to focus on its victimization.

Specific topics, for example: women's dress and veiling practices, oppressive sexuality norms and rituals (often in relation to Islam), female genital mutilation/cutting (FGM/C), and reproduction and family planning have for decades dictated the parameters of a very limited field of study. Few if any studies have considered the body within contexts of protest and revolution in relation to the wider sociopolitical structures of power that discursively engage the corporeal form. Foregrounding the gendered body as the point of intersection of sociopolitical, cultural, and historical investment illuminates how it is at once produced while also acting as an agent in the construction of discourse.

In my view, however, and as this book will show, both the body and memory are inseparable in the ways women have intervened in the uprisings. They are mutually dependent upon and entangled in each other. As this book argues, women rewrite their bodies and their revolutionary agency through rememory and vice versa. Bodies and revolutionary subjectivity are the impetus for memory, but memory—fluid and open-ended—in turn imbues the corporeal with "life force," if you will. While Aboulnaga's critical approach is a much-needed one, especially in light of the various attempts at grappling with the gender aspect of the revolution, what is still missing from much of the theoretical and macropolitical analysis of the uprisings is the lived experience. Centering the lived experience of women in revolution is imperative to theory. The experiences of the women whose accounts are narrated in this volume drive the theoretical and paradigmatic discussion. Without these accounts, we remain mired in abstraction.

Two short accounts intended as journal entries from Tahrir Square provide a crucial perspective of the personal in the events of the first eighteen days of revolt. The first is an e-book published soon after the beginning of revolution in Egypt, written by Nariman Youssef, called *Tahrir: 18 Days of Grace* (2011); the second is Mona Prince's *Revolution Is My Name: An Egyptian Woman's Diary from Eighteen Days in Tahrir* (translated by Samia Mehrez) (2014). Both offer a unique account of women's experience in the square at a time when there was a dearth of writing about women's daily encounters with state repression and revolutionary action during the first few days of the revolution. Nariman, a young Egyptian woman educated in Edinburgh and working as a translator, reflects on the emotive reactions to participating in the protests. Mona, a writer and professor of English literature, offers a starkly realistic memoir of her days in Tahrir. Her book takes account of the sense of community and the conflicting reactions of people in protest, as well as the tensions between generations and political viewpoints. More of these personal accounts are needed to redraw the gendered parameters of the events of the uprisings. It is, however, rather limiting to view the first eighteen days of revolution as the epitome of the complex political and social processes that continued to take place after these pivotal days. As the timeline provided at the beginning of this text demonstrates, much develops following the days after Mubarak stepped down. While the initial eighteen days are of significant historical importance, it is not at all accurate to assume that the first eighteen days in Tahrir Square can represent the historical developments that occurred in the subsequent years. The following monograph pays close attention to this shortcoming in revolutionary history by interviewing women who were actively involved in the uprising across a spectrum of several years that stretched from 2011 to 2015 while tracing the gendered steps of the Egyptian uprising across the course of this time.

Conclusion

Attention to women's personal lived experience during the revolution is essential to providing a more meaningful analysis of the Arab revolts. *The Women of the Midan: The Untold Stories of Egypt's Revolutionaries* focuses on women's narratives of the revolution from diverse cross-sections of the population. It sheds light on women whose marginal social and educational privileges do not normally grant them access to the printed word or to public media. The ordinary women who left the comfort of their homes, their factory stations, and their rural villages to face the barrels of army guns and tanks were driven by various motivations and a myriad of revolutionary desires. Not assuming that their activism is feminist or even political, the following chapters explore women's desires in uprising. Whether to bring a better life for their families, to incite political change, to fulfill their feminist aspirations, or simply to see justice and equality for all, their hopes and their dreams inspire the writing across this book. The stories they tell about their days in protest and resistance, their thoughts as they left their homes to join the mass protest, and the rich tapestry of their lives are woven together to illustrate the tenacity and diversity of these Egyptian women in the face of repression. Their testimonies bear witness to the drama of revolution as it unfolds. They counter ingrained constructs regarding gender, women, and sociopolitical action in the Arab region. These women became a voiceless sea of faces that media cameras and reports failed to recognize as a heterogeneous mass of people, with unique histories, political trajectories, and challenging realities that they each sought to transform. Given that women were integral to the revolutions that took place in the Arab region, disproportionately representing them in the literature, homogenizing them, overwriting their voices, and imposing our theories over their desires in what will one day serve as a record of a major historical event for future readers and specialists is distortive and leads to a skewed androcentric and hegemonic historiography of the Arab uprisings and the region as a whole.

In regions of the world that are (re)particularized by neocolonialist discourse as antimodern, extremist, and misogynist, ignoring or misrepresenting women's role in society has especially dire consequences to scholarship and public discourse. In the particular case of nonmale genders, their diversity in the region, their active participation in society, and the political or social orientations they espouse are areas of scholarship that need to be highlighted and brought into the center of any narrative about the Arab world. *The Women of the Midan: The Untold Stories of Egypt's Revolutionaries* highlights how marked/gendered bodies redraw the parameters of state and government control, patriarchal hegemony, and the dominant discourses of Islamic organizations over the public political sphere. While the intervention of women's bodies into spaces that exclude them challenges these forces, the struggle, as well as its retelling, hones the body in multiple ways. The accounts of revolutionary women reflect these fluid processes of subject-making where identities, personal dispositions, political activism, and citizenship are constituted through a fluid process that is mutually produced through resistance and subjection. These continuous but inconsistent struggles take place not only within the specific context of revolution but also within the wider historicity of neoliberalism and global politics.

The struggle of revolutionary women continues in the process of retelling, in recounting, and in rememory—a struggle through which the boundaries of women's bodies become redrawn in revolutionary lore. Complicating these processes that write and rewrite on women's bodies is the act of telling their stories. Dominant, often western discourses produce this struggle through familiar tropes that reduce the complexity of women's revolutionary activism in the Arab region into a linear, temporally specific, and western historical parody of feminist experiences. Gender is once again evoked as a marker of civilizational progress and as a barometer that tests the level of progressive politics taking shape in the Arab world. These representations affirm the western liberal feminist narrative and validate gender ideologies that do not take into account local moral and cultural specificities. The stories that revolutionary women tell here mirror the effects of a struggle that is also constituted by a long history of dissent. It brings into focus the web of relationships Arab gendered bodies are enmeshed within as they push the boundaries of political participation and practices of citizenship.

The account of women revolutionaries in *The Women of the Midan: The Untold Stories of Egypt's Revolutionaries* captures how women's bodies are marked in the rhetoric of power to reproduce and rationalize dominant ideologies. Yet, women transcend the boundaries of gendered discourse and rework its terms to manage new forms of participation and resistance that transform social values and embodied political subjectivity.

2 Gender and Corporeality in Egypt
A History

I COULD HEAR the sounds of children laughing and yelping in joy outside as we sat down to talk in her office. The sounds never fail to cheer me up, and cheering up was needed on this day of remembering. This was the month before General Abdel Fattah Al Sisi was to become president. I was in Egypt in April, watching in amazement as identical posters of his decorated military bust were hung on every streetlight on bridges, highways, and street corners. "Where did the revolution go?" I asked her. She told me where, as she leaned over to talk to me.

> "You are making me remember. I had started to forget. We all have," she sighed. "We have all lost hope and we have all *kabarna dimaghna* [meaning we have managed to forget by focusing on other things] and our daily lives have taken us away from the revolution and its goals. We made ourselves forget the price that others have paid during the days of *Mohamed Mahmood*.[1] Whenever I ran into an injured person who lost an eye or a leg, I would find in them a strange determination to continue what we started. I used to be ashamed of myself because sometimes I was tired and weak. But I would always draw strength from them. Even now when everyone has taken part in raping and violating the revolution, I still try to cling to their image perhaps in the hope that I would find the strength to continue but despair pulverizes me."

I have to admit this was hard to hear from Mervat, who is known to be one of the most dynamic organizers of the revolution. In the silence that followed, the sounds of the children in the playground outside seemed very far away, even though they should have been louder. Her words were grim, spoken with such feeling that my eyes got cloudy and I blinked to clear them in front of this woman who has witnessed some of the worst scenes of injury and death. I looked down at the floor, partly to compose myself but also to avoid seeing the anguish in her eyes. Reluctantly I raised my eyes to take another look at Mervat. She was a petite woman with a gentle, round face and large, expressive eyes. Looking older at this moment than her forty years, Mervat's usually colorful and flamboyant nature was replaced by a hunched, somber mood. She clenched and unclenched her fists, absent-mindedly turning her head to watch the children outside.

I cleared my throat. "Mervat, how did it all begin for you? Were you there in Tahrir Square from the beginning?"

"No, I wasn't, actually. I am one of those people who began to get involved *after* the famous first eighteen days."

Interested and surprised by this, my attention turned to what was happening in front of me now. Her mood visibly lightened. First, she displayed subtle changes in posture. Pushing her shoulders slightly back while straightening herself up, Mervat then began chronicling her revolutionary journey, telling me with a growing animation in her voice about how she got together with her best friend after watching the news every day and hearing from family members who were daily in the midan. She learned that help was needed—medical supplies, food, drink, and blankets. They both pooled their resources, and what they couldn't pay for themselves, they collected money to buy. In the span of a few days, they had filled a car with supplies. Mervat and her friend Rania drove the car toward Tahrir Square, but they were stopped by the authorities and searched. To their horror, they watched as the soldiers picked up the boxes of bandages, disinfectants, and blankets and threw them off the bridge into the Nile River. Angry but trying not to show it, the two women composed themselves, for fear that they would be arrested. To their surprise, they were released, so they got back in the car and drove away as fast as they could. The incident, although disappointing, did not deter Mervat and Rania. They returned to the midan again and again. Over the course of a week, they smuggled a few bags of supplies at a time. This continued over a period of two months, but by then they were completely involved in the demonstrations in the midan.

Mervat and Rania soon realized that there was so much more they could do than just demonstrating in the midan. As they led marches to Tahrir from their neighborhood, they met more women who were interested in organizing. Realizing that connecting with other women would achieve much more than the two of them together, they started to think about ways to mobilize more women, so they focused first on their neighborhood. In evening meetings, they'd invite specialists to talk about political participation, the history of feminist groups in Egypt, government, and elections. When they developed a critical mass, they knew they were ready to establish themselves as a women's group, and so it all began.

Building the Blocks of Corporeal Dissent: A Discursive History

Though the record of women's participation in political dissent in modern Arab countries is well documented by feminist scholarship (Badran 1996; Baron 2005, among many), during times of crisis such as wars, national struggles for independence, or revolution, gender issues are usually relegated to the margins (Lazreg 1994; Fernea 2000). Therefore, it comes as no surprise that just as they had previously experienced in the revolution of 1919 against the British and the 1952 revolution against British occupation and the land-owning elite, in the aftermath of the 2011 revolution, Egyptian women's groups still faced marginalization. Throughout shifting sociopolitical and economic conditions, women continued in their struggle to gain a foothold in the changing terrain of Egyptian politics.

My aim in this chapter is to trace the various dynamics that have traditionally constituted these setbacks, while paying special attention to the circumstances that contributed to the building blocks of women's protest work in Egypt. I situate the gendered body in the middle of these dynamics to elucidate the relative importance of its act of bodily protest in the Egyptian uprising. Bodies that are historically at the center of debates of honor/shame, of power/disempowerment, and of inclusion/disinclusion respond to calls for political action differently than male bodies. Non male bodies (albeit non normative bodies) inculcated with discourses that render them vulnerable to social, cultural, and religious norms follow their own choreographies of protest.

The constraints that women have historically navigated to arrive at that moment of revolt are the focus of this chapter. To gain an understanding of the lived experience of revolt as a gendered subject, we must problematize the body, as it is constituted historically as well as theoretically. How bodies are gendered in protest is also central to this experience of revolt and of the rejection of state and patriarchal control. It is important not to view these experiences as simply "awakenings." This risks obliterating the long history of dissent in Egypt, where gendered bodies have been honed through social and political measures and where, in turn, they have incited change and transformation. The following pages place the negotiations that write women's corporeal protest in Tahrir and elsewhere within their constitutive history. These negotiations are subsequently rekindled in the narratives of revolutionary women recounted in the rest of this book. Women's groups during the revolution also evoked the legacy of the feminist role models in Egypt's history.

A women's advocacy group called the Voices of Egyptian Women, led by two activist women, Nazli Shahine and Fadia Badrawi, organized a powerful visual and informative campaign with *Baheya ya Masr*, started by Inass Makawi, to encourage women to participate politically. One of their most powerful messages was raising awareness of the long history of women who led the way to revolution. The group created large banners depicting the faces of historically notable women such as Queen Hatshepsut, Hoda Shaarawi, Dorreya Shafiq, and Shahinda Maqlad, which were carried by women protestors. The importance of this history was not lost on women in the revolution. It helped galvanize them and provided them with an empowered sense of dignity that sustained them even when things were challenging. This history is at the center of this chapter.

Ottoman Harems and Modern Living

Centuries of war, colonialism, and depletion of resources invariably transformed Egyptian society. These transformations are often historically paradoxical when it comes to women's bodies. In the nineteenth century, Muhammad Ali Pasha (1769–1849) modernized Egypt's infrastructure yet simultaneously institutionalized Ottoman traditions of gender segregation and a new market economy, which had mixed effects on women. He began his policies of modernization and reform with the establishment of a strong bureaucratic state system unrivaled in Egypt's modern history. Various systems of state control were strengthened during his time, within which the institutionalization of male power and the hegemony of the religious establishment became entrenched. Well-established religious institutions such as Al Azhar University furthered its historical proprietorship over the articulation of personal status laws that were to govern women and the family (Cole 1981).

The introduction of modern education in the nineteenth century by the Pasha was intended to establish a labor force capable of carrying out his plans to industrialize Egypt. This initially excluded women, though in subsequent decades, women would become encouraged to obtain a modern education and to bring up their children according to modern values. Yet, during British colonialism, this also ushered in a national educational system that was divided across class and gender lines (Russell 2004).

Though modern medicine provided immeasurable health benefits to both men and women, it relied on bodily regulation (Fahmy 1998; Hatem 1997), inculcating through its methods an internalized submission to surveillance and western scientific authority. While most women enjoyed the benefits of these modern developments, they were paradoxically subject to laws that allowed little space for change or negotiation. Such contradiction therefore undermined women's opportunities to fully participate in these socioeconomic transformations in their own right as political subjects. Denied the full freedoms that men enjoyed in marriage, divorce, and life security, women were permanently placed under institutionalized patriarchy. The increased masculinization of the state's public institutions alienated women from access to government and leadership positions—a challenge they continue to face to this day.

Family and ethnicity, writes Beth Baron (2005), helped constitute nationalism during the mid-1800s. Since the time of the Mamlukes, the harems of the elite—made up of multiethnic African and Circassian slaves—defined the nature of the elite household in Egypt. Female slaves were considered a prize commodity for shaping the upper Ottoman classes, thus bolstering the Ottoman elites as a racial, genetic, and social pool separate from the local Egyptian population. Consequently, the gradual abolition of slavery in the latter half of the nineteenth century, maintains Baron, helped "Egyptianize" the Ottoman household in Egypt. This coincided with a rising nationalist trend that emphasized bourgeois norms and modern principles of child-rearing. Thus, historical shifts that characterized the transition from Ottoman harem life to modern bourgeois households were played out on the bodies of female foreign slaves and young Egyptian mothers.

The exposure to cultural norms brought about by modernization and colonialism and a gradual shift from Ottoman to modern bourgeois European status symbols caused many upper- and middle-class women to reflect on their contradictory plight as symbols of tradition and culture on one hand and as the embodiment of modernity and progress on another. Though some scholars depict these challenges as dichotomous, it is not clear that privileged women themselves experienced them as such. The memoirs of Egyptian feminist Huda Shaarawi (1879–1947), for instance, depict the events of her life when she astutely negotiated the social expectations imposed upon her (1987). A wealthy upper-class woman enjoying power and prestige, Shaarawi nevertheless often found herself in situations over which she had little or no control, due to patriarchal social customs and traditions. Her desires for modern bourgeois companionate marriage, for example, were thwarted by her mother's plans for her at the age of thirteen to marry an older man who was already married. Although Shaarawi eventually gave in to the arranged marriage, she laid down her rules and through a concerted effort over the period of several years, she managed to bring her husband to accept them.

Shaarawi's biography clearly exemplifies the fluidity of the perceived dichotomy between the modern and the traditional, since she was adept at negotiating the impositions placed upon her and was frequently able to push beyond the limits of her role in society (Shaarawi 1987). There were other challenges facing Shaarawi and the upper- and middle-class feminist movement that intensified in 1920s Egypt. The growing nationalist movement posed one challenge. Although women were socially and politically marginalized, they were still expected to uphold a bourgeois nationalist agenda and to have patriotic political sentiments. This is not to say, however, that women were completely immobilized by social restrictions; other than Shaarawi's case, there were various indications that women managed to outmaneuver their political isolation. Women's role in the 1919 revolution was evidence of this.

The participation of women in the nationalist revolution of 1919 brought public attention to their organizing efforts. Though they had played a significant role in mobilizing and sustaining the protests during the revolution that led to his success as prime minister, Saad Zaghloul's government ignored women's demands for social and political rights. Shortly after 1923, Huda Shaarawi established the Egyptian Feminist Union and continued to call for suffrage. Zaghloul eventually did concede to raising the marriage age of girls to sixteen and to offering more opportunities for women to gain an education. Despite this relatively small gain, it was in changing people's perception about women's public role and ability to mobilize that Shaarawi's efforts were rewarded. The mobilization of women's bodies against the British in the 1919 revolution for independence had already set a precedent that could not be denied. Egypt's patriarchal social system could no longer afford to ignore the demands of women whose feminist consciousness was now ignited.

The struggle for independence, however, was not just the purview of urban women (or the women of the upper classes). The historical record points to women from Menufiya, Mansoura, Beheira, and Alexandria who put their bodies and their lives in harm's way to fight European colonialism (Al Naggar 2014). Women from the villages of Ghamreen and Tata were especially ferocious in their resistance against the French army in 1798—a fact that earned them quite the reputation as valiant combatants. In Alexandria, women and children defended the battlements of the city, taking up positions in its old towers (Cole 2007). They took part in the attack against the French garrison in Mansoura, where large numbers of men and women ended up losing their lives, while in Damanhur and Rahmaniya, women took away their food provisions and abandoned their homes rather than submit to the French or supply them with rations. They put up a fight wherever they could. An army officer reportedly recounted how a peasant woman gouged the eyes of an aide-de-camp with a pair of scissors, only to be shot. French army soldiers often note in their memoirs that the villagers who marched to defend their homes were composed of armed women and men with lances and pistols (Cole 2007). Likewise, in the fight against British occupation, women's role was critical in a number of armed confrontations, as in 1807 in the popular resistance in Rosetta (Al Naggar, ibid.).

Women's resistance against colonialism from the eighteenth to the twentieth centuries demonstrated their ability not only to mobilize and to raise funds but also to act as a corporeal force that galvanized society against a common enemy. Similarly, various attempts at mobilizing women to create a unified feminist front have met with some success in the last few years in Egypt, since the recent revolution. The Egyptian Feminist Union was reestablished in the same year as the 2011 revolution and enjoined more than a thousand feminist groups in the country. The new coalition hopes to reinstate the feminist struggle for equal rights at the top of the political agenda. E.F.U.'s history thus far has mirrored quite clearly the repercussions of gendered political discourse and the patriarchal limits imposed on women's role implicit in notions of modernization and social progress. Yet despite these efforts to bring the female constituency together in an attempt to strengthen society and to shift the boundaries of gender privilege in Egypt, women's bodies continue to remain encoded in class hierarchy and to reflect class and socioeconomic privilege.

The impact of privilege on women's mobility however, varied historically. Before the turn of the nineteenth century in Egypt, women of privilege faced social restrictions that largely affected their mobility, yet women of the lower socioeconomic class, at least initially (toward the end of the eighteenth century), enjoyed some measure of autonomy and financial independence. In this latter group, most Egyptian women did not have to observe harem living, nor were they compelled to take on new, modern markers of social status. For quite some time, women in the underprivileged classes could run small businesses, manage their own income, and participate with some measure of freedom in social life. Their bodies were neither stigmatized nor considered the space where their family's power and heritage marked their claims. Yet, less than half a century after this, in turn-of-the-century Egypt, Juan Cole (ibid.) surmises that an ideological divide would characterize class difference. Having little to gain from westernization and finding the new modern adoptive cultural codes difficult to access or digest, the lower classes were more inclined to resist these perceived impositions by staunchly guarding their traditions and beliefs. In so doing, many of them found a newly articulated Islamism more palatable and easily identifiable with their own values and traditions.

Though in reality, social change can be far more complex and nuanced, Cole maintains that the general social trends of the time saw a bifurcation in Egyptian society along class lines. While the middle and upper classes turned away from harem life to the West for a handle on progress and financial opportunity, the lower classes maintained a strong hold on their Islamic faith, adopting Ottoman forms of gender segregation that had previously been of no particular importance to them, as a form of "Islamic" life. Cole concludes that this created a cultural as well as an everlasting ideological class divide in Egyptian society. Consequently, many women whose businesses were not eliminated through competition with larger business found themselves pushed toward a segregated and limited existence and increased dependency on their male counterparts.

The history of women's bodies reveals a long engagement with privilege and hierarchy that continues to this day with new implications. In Tahrir Square, the accounts of women from the months of revolt indicate that their lines defied class and privilege. Among these protestors, collective solidarity transcended any religious, class, or urban/rural boundary. This became clear to me as well as I started gaining access to revolutionary networks. Women from very different backgrounds introduced me to each other and I found myself enmeshed in warm and unaffected relationships that transcended established social boundaries. The connections between women revolutionaries bridged large expanses of Cairo's neighborhoods, including religious and socioeconomic levels. This is not to say that class differences did not exist in Tahrir. To this day in Egyptian society, women's bodies encapsulate not only class hierarchy but also the social and cultural metaphors that a western education and access to global capital can make available to Egypt's elites. These social markings on the gendered body had an impact on how people—especially women—were treated by security forces in Tahrir and are echoed in some of the accounts that will come up in the following chapters. Class did indeed play a role in Tahrir Square—one that often protected upper-class women from brutal treatment by the police and which some protestors navigated to extend this protection to others who were less privileged.

Aside from mirroring class conflict, women's bodies have often reflected the changing discourses of social reform projects. Muhammad Abduh (1849–1905), one of the leading figures of modernist Islam, for instance, supported education for women and called for the legal reforms of traditions harmful to women and the family, such as polygyny. Abduh's views, however, were staunchly opposed by emerging Islamist voices of the Muslim Brotherhood around the late 1920s. Hassan El Banna (1906–1949), founder of the Muslim Brotherhood, called for a strict gender ideology whereby women's and men's roles were viewed as different and complementary, with men having authority over women. Differentiating between women's and men's bodies, El Banna's religious discourse emphasized the biological nature of each and the materiality of the corporeal form. He was a strong advocate of gender segregation. In 1940 he wrote *Risalit al Mar'a al Muslima*, "Letter to Muslim Women." Meant as a reminder to Muslims of the role of women in society, the letter reflects El Banna's civilizational anxiety brought about by western cultural invasion, the result of which he describes as "the shadow of a revolutionary and vicious wave" (El Banna 1980) spreading in Egypt and other Islamic countries. This wave of westernization, he maintains, is led by those who wish to emulate Europeans and who take advantage of the flexibility of Islamic laws (ibid.). To El Banna, women's increased physical presence in the public sphere was at the root of this trend, hence the need to reinforce the tenets of Islam regarding women's mobility. Once again, women's bodies become the pivot around which the struggle for identity politics is played out. El Banna recommends in his letter that women remain in the home—even to conduct their prayers in its privacy, so as to prevent the mixing of the sexes, which is the root of all evils such as crime, the breakdown in the family, and indeed, the loss of honor.

Despite El Banna's segregational rhetoric regarding women, he did mentor Zeinab Al Ghazali (1917–2005). She recounts in her memoirs how she regarded him as the ultimate guide or imam of God and eventually pledged to him her commitment to Islamic *da'wa* (which literally means *invitation to Islam* but encompasses the movement to spread Islamic teachings, in this case from the Brotherhood's perspective). Al Ghazali became one of the Brotherhood's most avid members and founded The Muslim Ladies Association in 1936. Al Ghazali, who incidentally had been a member of the EFU, did little to resolve the modern/tradition paradox that marked its debates on women's bodies. Instead, Al Ghazali echoed El Banna's views, employing a naturalizing discourse in her gender agenda. Women's bodies, in Al Ghazali's rhetoric, were seen as necessarily reproductive. As mothers and teachers to the future generations, she envisioned more of a domesticated role for women, versus a direct public role for men. Both the Muslim Brotherhood and its offshoot, the Muslim Sisterhood, as it was later called, developed an ideology that was in distinct contrast to the West and its perceived disregard for authenticity and gender norms. Al Ghazali's views are particularly important to Islamist women in the Muslim Brotherhood organization today. Her legacy is one that presents an Islamist alternative to a western "feminist" approach for women, yet the lack of a vision for Muslim women outside of the roles prescribed for them by El Banna and Al Ghazali's own plans for the da'wa movement restricts its applicability today. Though she was imprisoned for six years, during which she recounts in her memoirs how she was harassed and tortured, Al Ghazali remained steadfast in her devotion to the demands of the movement (Al Ghazali 1988).

Dissenting Bodies and the Nationalist State

The socialist revolution of 1952 posed a challenge to the dominant Islamist approach to gender. Drawing on socialist ideals for its programmatic agendas, the revolution led by Gamal Abdel Nasser (1918–1970) sought a social and cultural system that would allow all Egyptians equal access to resources. Nasser's secular regime rejected a natural discourse that engendered difference. In a public speech, Nasser's account of a meeting with an Islamist leader epitomizes his views about women's bodies. Despite being a staunch patriarch as a father and husband in his own family, he refused to assume responsibility for his own daughter's bodily comportment. He preferred instead to use humor to dismiss Hassan Al Hudaibi's (who in 1953 would have been the Supreme Guide of the Muslim Brotherhood) views on veiling in Egypt. The incident took place during a meeting between the two to discuss Islamist issues. According to Nasser's account, Hudaibi's first agenda item was a Muslim Brotherhood proposal to enforce veiling on Egyptian women, to which Nasser responded famously, "Your daughter is studying medicine and she does not wear the veil. If you can't impose the veil on your daughter, what makes you think I can impose the veil on 10 million Egyptian women?" (YouTube 2012).

Interestingly, during Nasser's retelling of this story, a male voice from the crowd is heard shouting, "Tell him to wear it himself!" (meaning the veil), at which the crowd, including the Egyptian leader, break out in laughter. Despite the humorous exchange, this short anecdote tells the story of women's bodies in dramatic proportions. From Huda Shaarawi's famed removal of the face veil in 1923 to this speech thirty-five years later, veiling had become so uncommon that men roared with laughter at the idea of mandating the *hijab* or the *tarha*, which is the term Nasser used in his speech, meaning *scarf*. His usage of the word *tarha* to me seems deliberate, as it secularizes the religious terminology of hair covering by referring to a scarf, rather than the weighted term *hijab*.

This incident also highlights the changing meaning of veiling over a period of time. Not only have the meanings attached to the veil changed, but the general disposition to the idea of covering women's bodies also shifted with the changing political and socioeconomic context. It clearly illustrates how the socialist state under Nasser, although patriarchal, is nevertheless committed to social equality and the inclusion of women in rebuilding the nation and regards veiling as a woman's choice. Despite this, however, women's bodies and the prospect of covering them or uncovering them remains the purview of the patriarchal state, and any demands to the contrary are dismissed.

In this case, Islamists who were heavily persecuted by Nasser's secular government during that time sought to extend their influence on female bodies. This recurring dynamic that places women's bodies at the heart of opposing political agendas continues to trade in women's agency and virtue in Egyptian history, as noted by historian Mervat Hatem (1994). What is also interesting about the incident cited here is the nod to female agency, where the limits of male patriarchy can be discerned in the way Nasser acknowledges quite conveniently that neither he nor the Supreme Guide can tell their daughters what to do with their bodies— if only in terms of veiling.

The socialist state had more pressing issues to ponder, such as education, social welfare, health care, and government social services. With access to these opportunities, women eventually gained the right to vote and assumed government positions for the first time in modern Arab history. Their numbers swelled in the labor force in response to calls for industrialization, and they registered in equal numbers to men in universities around the country. Women ran for parliament in 1956. In the following year, two women became members of parliament, Rawya Attiya and Amina Shukri. Attiya, who came from a political family (her father was a member of El Wafd Party) and served in the Liberation Army, is remembered as the first woman parliamentarian in Egypt.

Rawya Attiya's (1926–1997) long engagement with political activism requires more than a mere mention here, as it is a remarkable history of women's protest and embodied struggle for social justice. Her story demonstrates that despite being the linchpin in larger political struggles, women's political bodies constituted by contending discourses simultaneously constitute the space of protest. Rawya grew up in a political household, as her father, Shams El Din Attiya, was the Wafd Party's general secretary of the Governorate of Gharbiyya and a personal friend to former vice president El Nahas Pasha. Shams El Din played a significant role in his daughter's life. At the young age of eleven, she visited him in prison while incarcerated and this was an important part of Rawya's childhood recollections (Goldschmidt 2000). This was in 1936, when protests had broken out in Cairo against the nominal independence granted to Egyptians by means of the newly ratified Anglo-Egyptian Treaty. She recalls in an interview how she and her classmates carried Egyptian flags and marched through Cairo's downtown streets. When they arrived at Qasr al Eini Street, however, security forces had arrived to disperse the protest. A stray bullet caught her in the arm, and she fainted. Huda Shaarawi, who happened to be close by, witnessed what had happened and took her to safety to the headquarters of the EFU. Having met Shaarawi at such a young age and then later Safia Zaghloul, whom she visited frequently, marked a turning point for Attiya, who maintains that she "was raised politically" by the two women (Magdi 2009).

In the early 1940s, like many other known activists, college life further politicized Attiya. Soon after she was admitted into Cairo University to study history, she gravitated toward student organizing, becoming a member of the student executive association. When demonstrations broke out again against the British, the police encircled the Cairo University campus to quell student demonstrations. Attiya was assigned to smuggle out the student leaders, whom she disguised by wrapping them in bandages and gauze. She drove off with them in an ambulance van and returned right away to the blockaded university to pick up more students. This went on until she had smuggled out all fifty of her compatriots to safety (ibid.). Attesting to her fearlessness and her ability to think creatively under pressure, these stories must be read against the general social status and gender roles of women in Egypt during the 1940s. Although many women contributed to *al 'amal al watani* or nationalist activism at that time, few were so physically engaged with deliberations of this kind by putting their bodies in harm's way and confronting armed police.

After graduating with a university degree in history, Rawya went on to pursue other degrees: a diploma in pedagogy, another in psychology, a diploma equivalent to a master's degree in journalism in 1951, and a degree in Islamic studies. She later worked as a journalist for six years, during which time she was mentored by some of Egypt's celebrated journalists: Mustafa and Ali Amin, Musa Sabry, and Hosn Shah.

Soon after President Nasser nationalized the Suez Canal, however, the Tripartite Aggression that was led by Israel, France, and Britain in 1956 pushed Rawya into nursing and military training. She donned the overalls and trained with the military school in Giza. When she was deemed ready to conduct operations, the military sent her with a group of nurses with supplies and revolutionary leaflets to Port Said to egg on the resistance during the Suez War. As it was not customary for women to travel alone, she often had to disguise herself as a man to avoid being identified during these trips. Attiya managed to complete ten missions to Port Said. Subsequently, she was promoted to the rank of captain in the Liberation Army, taking on the task of organizing the refugees who had to flee their homes in Port Said due to the air raids. As part of her duties, she trained more than four thousand women in military medical care.

It was therefore not unexpected that Rawya Attiya would be one of eight women who presented themselves as candidates for parliament in 1957 when Gamal Abdel Nasser made parliamentary membership open to women. This election campaign, however, was no small feat for a first-time runner who was a woman embarking on a whole new role in Egyptian society. What made her campaign even more challenging were her opponents: six well-established men, among whom were Ahmed Foaud, the director of the Egyptian Central Bank, who was a personal friend of President Nasser's; Abdu Murad, a lawyer; a well-known businessman; and several others who lacked neither experience nor clout. In her account of her campaign from her memoirs (ibid. 2009), she recounts, "I was thinking about how to run this electoral battle knowing that the other candidates had already visited their constituents and held conferences with them. I felt they had revealed their cards."

Her astute assessment of her competition led her to follow a completely different approach. Rather than ride in long, dark sedans and dress in sophisticated outfits, as her competitors did, which alienated the people, Attiya drove herself in an open jeep, wearing her army fatigues. She would just walk through the neighborhoods on foot. "People received me with *zagharid wal tabl wal zamr* [an expression meaning great joy: literally ululations, drumming, and flute music]. Everyone was happy to see me as the first woman to enter the elections. And I started to feel that I was pulling the rug from under the feet of the male competition." Despite the enthusiasm surrounding Rawya Attiya's campaign, however, the general sentiment of society regarding electing a woman for parliament was not favorable.

Even with these reservations, Attiya proved a worthy opponent in the electoral process. Threatened by her popularity, her main competitor, Ahmed Foaud, called on his friends from government. Foaud and his supporters wore *galabiyyas*, Egypt's traditional dress, instead of their expensively tailored suits, thus following Rawya's strategy. When President Nasser refused to intervene and endorse his friend and colleague, Foaud took a different tack. This new development will illustrate the pressures on women as newcomers to the election system and the kind of electoral politics they must have had to navigate. It all began like this: Rawya Attiya was summoned to a meeting with Magdi Hassanein, the head of the election committee of her district. At the meeting, she was surprised to find that her opponent, Ahmed Foaud, was there as well. In an interview, she relays the conversation between herself and the two men as an exact dialogue— so important are those memories to her. Hassanein tells her that she was brought to his office so they could give her advice for her own benefit. They expressed their concern for her well-being and safety, given how "vicious" the competition was going, and she was advised to quit the elections. Rawya replied, "We are seven candidates. Why am I the only one being singled out?"

"Because you are a woman," replied Hassanein. "You will not be able to win. There is no hope for you."

"And if there is no hope for me, why am I here?" came her retort.

"Because of the fatigue and disappointment we are trying to spare you. In addition, the treasury is available to compensate you for your expenses, so take what you spent" (2009). Rawya then recalls how she adamantly refused to be "bought" and to step out, to which the other man reminded her that the election was in two days and that if she remained in the race, no one would win. Her response was that she would look forward to the repeat election.

The results were tied, but in the retake Rawya Attiya won the election, despite attempts at slandering her in the press as an American spy. She became the first Arab woman ever to be elected to parliament. It was a victory on many levels for Rawya and for her constituents—certainly for setting the path to women's political participation. Attiya was a force to be reckoned with in parliament, calling for the reduction of working hours for women laborers, since they worked two shifts, one in the workplace and one at home. The issues she continued to tackle concerned the family and its well-being, especially with regard to the effects of polygamy. She called for the abolition of polygamy and prepared a new law to that effect. Although most urban representatives approved of her proposal, it did not find appeal among parliamentarians representing rural interests, who perceived it as an imposition and a limit on their reproduction which would consequently limit their labor force (Zevi 1959).

Rawya Attiya served in parliament for only two years, but her record is impressive. She went on to occupy various important positions in the country, such as the head of the Red Cross where she continued to help army vets and their families. She also chaired the Society for the Families of Martyrs and Soldiers (Goldschmidt 2000). Her proudest moment came as she was visiting a bombarding unit in Port Tewfik in 1968, where President Gamal Abdel Nasser said of her, "I believed in the struggle of Egyptian women from the example of Rawya Attiya" (Magdi 2009).

Opportunities for leadership positions in Egypt's budding socialist government were available for a certain cadre of women. Over the years, well-educated, highly qualified women who were self-made and not born into privilege became increasingly visible in the political arena. Hekmat Abu Zaid (1922/3–2011) for example, born in a small village in Assiout called Sheikh Dawud, was a university professor. She had received her master's and then a doctoral degree in educational psychology from the University of London. Abu Zaid was appointed as minister of social affairs and implemented policies to make education accessible to all, regardless of gender, class, or financial ability. She continued to pursue these goals even after she returned to her university career. There were many other women who were prominent activists but did not occupy formal positions in government. Marie Assad (1922–), who dedicated her life and career to social development, worked tirelessly to eradicate FGM. Others like Amina El Said (1914–1995), who was the first woman editor of a major journal, *Al Mussawar*, later starting a women's magazine, *Hawaa* (meaning *woman* or *Eve*), forged their activist path outside of government. Soheir Al Qalamawi (1911–1997) was a renowned author and the first woman lecturer at Cairo University and later a parliamentarian. Both were middle-class women who were affiliated with the EFU and were dedicated feminist activists.

The increase in women's public participation was not a direct result of a predictable progression of modernization. As we have witnessed elsewhere, modernization did not necessarily adopt a gender-sensitive agenda. In general, feminists have had legitimate umbrage at liberal modernity's androcentric biases that define the default subject/citizen as male. This gender-centric orientation rendered the social contract—whereby citizens define their rights and obligations to the state—as detrimental to women, according to Carol Pateman (1988). By means of the "social contract" in western liberal contexts, she argues that women had been prevented from casting their votes, since law and custom viewed this as unacceptable. Moreover, the "employment contract" restricted women's access to employment and entry into unions, while the "sexual contract" exploited women's sexual and reproductive labor by means of marriage. While a modern socialist regime in Egypt encouraged an increase in women's participation in the labor force, women's political participation was to be hampered by setbacks that paralleled those they faced in other contexts. The industrialization of Egypt's economy and the emphasis on local production required the participation of both men and women. This prompted a significant change in the state's approach to women and gender issues by singling out gender equality in the constitution of 1956, Article 31 affirmed that: "All Egyptians are equal under the law in public rights and duties, without discrimination due to sex, origin, language, religion, or belief" (McLarney 2013). The state also legally enshrined women's rights in the constitution and in labor laws and strongly acknowledged the challenges that women faced to balance social and public work with family duties. Clearly assuring women that the state will "facilitate" this process, Article 19 states "the State facilitates for women the reconciliation between her work in society and her duties to the family" (ibid.). Women were granted benefits such as maternity leave for a period of three months—which was a leap forward in contrast to Labor Law 48 of 1933 that only protected women from heavy work during pregnancy (The Solidarity Center 2010). Encouraged by these changes, numbers of women in the labor force swelled in virtually all fields, according to Leila Ahmed (1992), who notes that although the sectors of education and health absorbed women workers in large numbers, they were found in technological specializations as well.

The government's reforms did not revisit the so-called Personal Status Laws that governed family life and limited women's access to rights at home. Once again, women's bodies were claimed by domestic laws that precluded their full participation in the public sphere. Moreover, as the regime became increasingly more authoritarian, systems of government assumed responsibility for various aspects of the feminist struggle and in the process appropriated the growing feminist voice in the country. Mervat Hatem labels this turn in gender politics in Egypt as "State Feminism" (1992). Meanwhile, the nationalist agenda focused on the issue of population control as a window into socially engineering society and shaping the family as a reproductive unit. Women were at the heart of an emerging rhetoric around birth control, which linked the lack of resources, poverty, and the unyielding problem of illiteracy to rampant population growth, according to Omnia El Shakry (2007). The regulation of women's bodies and especially rural bodies became the principal occupying factor of the regime's plans for modern development. By characterizing feminine corporeality as the core of the issue, however, these new measures for social engineering and modern restructuring reduced the complexity of national and international problems to a gender problem.

Though the new regime's implementation of social development projects, new legislation, and opportunities for women to participate in governance were improvements on the past, there were still limitations. During the period of the 1950s and '60s women who envisioned a more egalitarian society were moved to protest. Foremost among these women was Dorreya Shafik (1908–1975), who, along with a group of other women, deployed her body to confront state gender repression, leading a hunger strike during Nasser's regime to demand that women earn equal political rights. Shafik was committed to the feminist struggle, but as the state eventually subsumed feminist groups under the umbrella of "State Feminism" (Hatem, ibid.), she was placed under house arrest and prevented from continuing with her activism (Botman 1999).

The controversy surrounding Shafik's hunger strike and her activism helped shape women's resistance in new and interesting ways in Egypt. The history of hunger strikes as peaceful resistance elsewhere is well documented. Gandhi's seventeen fasts as individual protest against a range of causes including his own countrymen's infighting and British colonialism are integral to India's resistance history (Ganguly and Docker 2008). The suffragette movement in the United Kingdom also deployed hunger strikes as an effective mode of resistance against imprisonment during the turn of the twentieth century. Fear of liability, or worse, martyrdom inspired the practice of force feeding by prisons that often resulted in serious health and psychological damage (Mayhall 2000). In Ireland, anticolonial resistance against the British deployed what was an Irish traditional custom of conflict resolution that brought attention to injustice and shamed the injurious party. Hunger strikes were a powerful corporeal statement that raised international awareness of the plight of the Irish. This was indeed a successful measure that also built on the experiences of suffragettes, though not before it took the lives of hundreds of Irish fighters and activists (Murphy 2004).

These experiences that put the body into the service of one's political cause illustrate how corporeal dissent works in incarceration. In these cases, depriving the body of its essential nutrients until it is reduced to devouring its own organs simultaneously denies the state its sovereign power to exercise control over the citizen's body. Thus, hunger strikes reverse what Achille Mbembe describes as, "the ultimate expression of sovereignty resides, to a large degree, in the power and the capacity to dictate who may live and who must die" (2003, 21). By refusing to sustain one's body, a hunger strike is the ultimate form of peaceful resistance because it defeats the very tenets that rationalize the state's power, the right over life. Although Dorreya Shafik did not go on a hunger strike under duress in prison, she herself was not a victim of colonialist or state brutality (she did organize against the British mandate in Egypt as well as against the state), Dorreya Shafik, however, was a woman committed to the cause of gender equality, to a fault. She staged a hunger strike in the office of the head of the press syndicate in objection to the absence of women in the first constitutional committee after the 1952 revolution. She was joined by a group of women, and they all embarked on what was to become an eight-day fast. However, this was to become an uphill battle and not just against hunger.

For the duration of the hunger strike, the women occupying the Journalists' Syndicate's office were photographed, interviewed, and subjected to excessive scrutiny, ridicule, and hearsay. They were accused of being "*al 'abithat*" (from *'abath*, meaning *idol play*) by literary giant Taha Hussein, who had once supported Shafik's efforts. There was hate mail, yellow press, and gossip accusing them of eating in secret, of debauchery, and generally of staging the entire event to attract attention. This public campaign, surmised Cynthia Nelson (1996), was designed to undermine women's credibility as a political force at a time when the regime was still trying to gain credibility for itself. They could not afford the embarrassment or the negative press that would imply that the state could not take care of its citizens. Shafik received a written statement from General Naguib (who was the first acting president since the revolution) consenting to her demands. This marked the first victory for these feminist agitators. What Nelson writes about these transactions is highly reminiscent of the events following the revolution of January 25, 2011: "The public discourse surrounding this hunger strike clearly reveals that Dorreya Shafik and the women protesters had not only maneuvered the women's rights issue into the forefront of public consciousness but also challenged Naguib and the military rulers with an embarrassing and confounding situation. This was the moment of deep schism between those who favored a return to civil rule and the reestablishment of parliament and those who, fearing that the old power groups would return, favored surrendering all power to the military junta" (Nelson 1996).

Nelson's summation of the events in 1954 parallels similar events that took place in Tahrir in 2011, when women's bodies were framed by the military as deviant to discredit the political claims of revolution. In an environment that was both transitioning and unstable, nonmale dissenting bodies are constituted as unruly and contentious, otherwise "carnivalesque," after Bakhtin (1941). Carnivalesque bodies represent the garish and loud expression of resistance that inverts (and ridicules) the illusion of stable control imposed by power. Since women's bodies are the very surfaces on which struggles for control of the public sphere are played out, in the Egyptian case, deploying the female body in protest was a profound act. Therefore, Dorreya Shafik, her compatriots and the women who followed in their footsteps in 2011 decided to reclaim their bodies in acts that clearly challenged the regime's sovereign power.

Liberalizing the Economy and Women's Bodies

With Gamal Abdel Nasser's death in 1970, the presidency passed on to Anwar Sadat (1918–1981), who drastically reversed the course that Nasser had placed the country on. Egyptian society experienced yet another wave of change, this time one that ran counter to the socialism of the previous regime. The new political landscape touted economic liberalization, free-market capitalism, deregulation, and privatization. "Open-door policy" and the influx of foreign capital into the country shifted the course of the lives of ordinary Egyptians. It ushered in an era where the state's role as provider and as economic producer began to taper off. A paradoxical reality soon developed with the growing liberalization of the country's economy. To procure international loans in the form of western aid and encourage investments from global capital, the state became heavily invested in maintaining and projecting an image of internal stability and the internationalization of Egyptian society to the outside world.

Anwar Sadat's nascent liberalization policies did little to alleviate poverty, however. With the increase in unemployment and lower wages, the gap between rich and poor widened. The "bread riots" of 1977 were an act of dissent and of desperation. Witnessing the growing wealth of a small percentage of the population who openly displayed their power and affluence while food subsidies for basic staples were cut prompted Egyptians to take to the streets for two days. The state deployed the military to quell the demonstrations, resulting in the injury of eight hundred and the death of eighty people. More than a thousand were taken prisoner. Facing this public act of no confidence in his leadership, Sadat sought instead to forge alliances with dissenting groups to combat leftist dissent. During his presidency, Islamists gained a stronghold in society and emerged as a contender for power. Sadat often bartered women's rights in return for appeasing militants (Hatem 1994). This was a strategy that proved difficult to maneuver, since it posed a strong challenge to his attempts at introducing laws for women's protection in the event of divorce.

Women's bodies were at the heart of his regime's sociopolitical climate. Whether as bargaining chips in a bid for power by a secular government or Islamist opposition or as markers of the Islamization/westernization of society, women's bodies also continued to reflect persisting dynamics of class and socioeconomic disparities in Egyptian society. While those from backgrounds with access to western education and culture followed a comportment that was essentially western in both fashion and outlook, such corporeal dispositions paralleled the growing shift toward Islamism and tradition. Women's bodies sported what became known as, "Islamic dress" or *al zy al islami*. Donning the hijab became popular as an essential part of this new Islamism. A covered female corporeality became a marker of the Islamization of the Egyptian streets. This was not a new phenomenon, as it mirrored the earlier decades of the twentieth century, when bodily comportment followed a range of dispositions largely along Islamic and western lines.

The new phenomenon of veiling, however, had contemporary implications reflecting different priorities that varied according to class, urban/rural status, and educational level. The lines that separate these motivations behind veiling are not always linear, consistent, or predictable. During the initial period of *infitah* and as its socioeconomic dynamics continued, veiling and Islamization increasingly began to cross class and education lines. Suffice it to say that during this period of *infitah* or open-door policy between 1973 and 1981, the practice of veiling (aside from the motivation to be committed to Islamic teaching) spread across society not only as a new form of piety but also as a method of coping with cultural change, according to Arlene McLeod (1993). Veiling enabled the mobility of the female body to navigate the new spaces that were opening up as a result of globalization and increased contact with the West as well as the internal migration of rural families to urban centers and external migration to oil-rich Arab countries where veiling is almost hegemonic (ibid.). Upward social mobility brought about by rapid profit from new business opportunities also introduced an element of social anxiety. Families who shot to the top of the social ladder upon their return from the Gulf, were often mindful to remain committed to Muslim customs and traditions and to their roots. Veiling in those instances was a marker of both authenticity and piety.

In the midst of growing Islamism, an Egyptian woman who was born to a rural family in the village of Kafr Tahlah in 1931 published an explosive novel entitled *Al Mar'a Wal Jins* (*Women and Sex*). It recentered women's bodies in the midst of public debate—but this time from a woman's perspective (1972).

Nawal el Saadawi graduated from Cairo University with a degree in medicine in 1955. She subsequently went on to receive a master's degree in public health from Columbia University. El Saadawi was the epitome of a generation of women compatriots of the 1952 revolution, whose lives were transformed as a result of the opportunities afforded them by socialist reforms of Nasser's regime. They gained access to government grants to travel abroad called *minha lil kharig*. These grants were based on previous government grants put in place by modernizing systems of governance during Ottoman rule. Recipients often occupied key positions in universities, government, health, or the arts upon return to Egypt.

Women and Sex was a frank account of the abuse of women's bodies, from an intersectional perspective. El Saadawi took to task tradition, religion, patriarchy, government, class, and capitalism to make visible the injustices that were committed against the female body. With a special focus on female genital cutting, she makes inroads in presenting a counterhegemonic lived experience of women's bodies. In the first of a series of autobiographies, she writes in her book *A Daughter of Isis*, "When I was six, the *daya* [a term used for midwife] came along holding a razor, pulled out my clitoris from between my thighs and cut it off. She said it was the will of God and she had done his will. . . . I lay in a pool of blood. After a few days, the bleeding stopped. . . . But the pain there was like an abscess deep in my flesh. . . . I did not know what other parts in my body there were that might need to be cut off in the same way" (1999).

The practice of female genital mutilation or cutting (FGM/FGC) placed women's bodies at the center of national and international debates around issues of Islamism and liberalism. The uproar against FGM/FGC demonstrates how the history of women's bodies in the developing world is never entirely played out on local platforms. Bodies become the point of intersection of global and local discourses of power and are produced through these processes as well. Global forces, whether colonialist, imperialist, global capitalist, or human rights organizations, intersect with local Islamism, nationalism, feminism, and patriarchy and take place at the level of the female body.

Nawal el Saadawi's own career attests to this process of what she calls the "glocal." She lost her job as director general of the Health Education Department following the release of *Women and Sex* (1972) because it immediately framed her as a threat to the status quo. To maintain internal stability and to undermine progressive elements in society, Sadat curried Islamist favor in return for ceding control of the Egyptian street to conservative and pietist trends. El Saadawi's work and outspoken opposition to Islamism disrupted this delicate equilibrium, and her views on issues of sexuality ran counter to his new law, *qanun himayat al-qiyam min al-ʿaib* "Protection of Values from Shame." Following a directive from President Anwar Sadat in 1981, El Saadawi was arrested and jailed for two months.

The indictment of Nawal El Saadawi epitomizes the centrality of female corporeality in the political and social transactions maintaining the structures of power in Egypt. Sadat's condemnation of El Saadawi played well into his agenda of exchanging control of the public space in return for Islamist control of the private sphere of the family. This is not to say that such bargaining was not without its complexities. Sadat approved of his wife Jehan's plan of introducing new family laws for the protection of divorces, for instance. Whether he introduced new legislation to reset the terms of his political arrangement with Islamist groups is not clear, but his support of Jehan's public role did not endear her to Islamists and conservatives, who did not see a place for a woman in public office and certainly not as a strong influence on the president. Her efforts to put in place laws that guarantee a divorced woman's right to be notified of her husband's marriage to another woman and to have custody of her children and marital residence were met with great opposition by many and even by feminists who saw the reforms as imposed from the top down.

Despite his attempts at courting the favors of Islamists, however, Sadat's presidential career and indeed his own life ended at the hands of a group of Islamist officers in 1981. Taking issue with his gender reforms, which they perceived as directives from his wife, and following a wave of arrests, Islamist militants took it upon themselves to put an end to Sadat's endeavors. This is not before he had left an indelible mark on gender issues, forms of public piety, and bodily comportment. In interviews with Sadat's killers, some cited a woman's body at the top of their list of triggers for carrying out the shooting. (Though the rationale for carrying out the attack is far more complex, the corporeal symbol cannot be ignored.) The woman was Jehan Al Sadat. The single image of her dancing in the arms of American president Jimmy Carter at a ball in the White House is considered by some as the tipping point leading to the assassination of Anwar Sadat (Guenena 1986).

When Saadawi herself was placed on a death list in 1991 by Islamist militants for allegedly insulting Islam, she resolved to leave for the United States, where she accepted a teaching position at Duke University. In 2002 a lawsuit was filed against her to annul her marriage on the basis of claiming that she was an apostate. The timing of these attacks on El Saadawi's activism coincided with increased international attention to women's issues and especially FGM in Egypt and the Middle East. The United Nations' world conferences on women had spearheaded campaigns to focus on women, extensive deliberations within which El Saadawi was involved. She had served as United Nations advisor for the Women's Programme in Africa and the Middle East from 1979 to 1980. The fourth World Conference on Women took place in Beijing in 1995, where FGM was a pivotal issue. The year before this, the United Nations Conference on Population and Development had taken place in Cairo, demanding that women be afforded the right to their bodies. El Saadawi spearheaded many of the local Arab efforts to present women's case in the UN. She was by now a familiar face in the proceedings, and her international renown did not escape the attention of local officials who were invested in preserving a positive front to the international community.

In the wake of the UN Population Conference held in Cairo in 1994, an incident embarrassing to the Egyptian government became internationalized through CNN, bringing indirect attention to anti-FGM activists like El Saadawi. CNN aired a graphic and disturbing report of a young girl being subjected to an unsanitary clitoridectomy procedure—all captured in real life on camera for visual consumption. The controversy directed much undesired attention at Egypt, which had originally banned FGM in 1959 but then had subsequently revoked the ban. Only a month later, motivated by the urgency to contain the scandal, the health minister issued a law that banned FGM except in medical hospitals. The new law was criticized by feminists for medicalizing a violent practice against women rather than eliminating it altogether. In 2008 FGM eventually became outlawed as a practice. This has had little impact on its wide prevalence, statistically estimated as mutilating 80 to 90 percent of Egyptian female bodies.

The controversy surrounding the genital cutting of Egyptian females in which El Saadawi and others were embroiled acquired a religious dimension as well. Gad-Al Haq-Ali-Gad al Haq, who was then Sheikh al Azhar, declared female cutting as a religious requirement. He was countered by the Mufti (government-appointed position of a legal religious expert empowered to make decrees), Muhammad Tantawi, who asserted and later issued a *fatwa* (religious decree) declaring the practice as un-Islamic and corroborating this by publicly disclosing the fact that his daughters were not cut.

This highly intersecting picture of FGM epitomizes the recurring context within which women's bodies and women's right to make decisions regarding their bodily practices take place. Government ministries, Islamic scholars, feminists, liberals, and international organizations all vie for a seat at the table to discuss what women can and cannot do with their clitorises. Local debates escalated between liberals and feminists who view FGM as a violent practice on women's bodies on one hand, and groups of Islamists who support the notion of female cutting as an Islamic "requirement" on the other (a debatable fact). While other Islamic scholars and adherents held contradictory views to these assertions, finding cutting un-Islamic but also acceptable, the contours of the female body begin to be drawn in debate. As international human rights claim the civilizing role against FGM and the state in Egypt seeks to appease dissent among liberals and religious pundits alike, women and feminist groups' stakes become marginalized and ignored.

The effects of FGM on women's bodies and how it impacts their physical and mental health is well documented (Rahman and Toubia 2000), yet the controversy itself and the conflicting discourses of FGM had an additional role to play that also impacted women's bodies. Saadawi's campaigns to free women's bodies from such abuses, for example, brought her into the complexities surrounding women's bodies in the country. El Saadawi came into a full confrontation with local government and Islamist groups in Egypt. This in turn resulted in attacks on Saadawi by these parties, pushing her toward finding refuge in international settings where her notoriety gained her currency. This has unfortunately framed her work as "grounded in 'modern' or 'western' medical and feminist thought," as Leila Ahmed writes, elucidating that "the consciousness informing her text is anchored in western thought and indeed is inconceivable and indecipherable without this body of work" (Ahmed 1989, 41). Indeed, Nawal El Saadawi continues to be a controversial figure, like the gendered bodies she describes in her famous novels; however, she has long labored against these discourses that seek to oppress them. Yet, she herself is very much the product of these discourses as well.

Neoliberal Change, Gender, Corporeality, and the State of "Dis-regulation"

Hosni Mubarak (1928–) became president of Egypt upon Sadat's assassination in 1981, remaining in office for thirty years until the January 25 revolution of 2011 presented him with little choice but to step down. At the outset of Mubarak's presidency, pressures by conservatives and Islamist groups caused the repeal of laws dubbed "Jehan's laws." But as his regime continued in office, women's issues once again gained attention through the renewed efforts of his wife, Suzanne. The new presidency was to usher in yet another first lady who was as visible and as vocal as her predecessor, Jehan El Sadat whose influence on her husband's regime provoked much controversy. A presidential decree in 2000 established the National Council for Women (NCW), which comprised a number of the most visible feminists in Egypt. The very existence of the council, which was presided over by Suzanne Mubarak herself, undermined the autonomy of feminists, as the state once again appropriated their political independence in the country. The council was also regarded with alarm by women's groups and NGOs because of the tremendous amount of international donor funds it appropriated (Deif 2004).

In the same year the NCW was established, the new *khol'* law or the law for unconditional divorce was passed. Islamic law (*shari'a*) granted women seeking divorce the option to dissolve their marriages, provided they returned whatever possessions their husbands had given them during their marriage. It was a relief to thousands of women who had unsuccessfully pursued divorce through extensive and debilitating court proceedings. Critiqued because of its links to Mrs. Mubarak—although many legal experts and feminists worked tirelessly to develop the law for several years—the law raised massive objections. Other laws encouraged women's political participation, such as those providing them with 12 percent of seats in parliament. For the first time in Egypt's history, women were appointed by presidential decree as judges. Tahani al Gibali became a judge in 2003, followed by thirty other female judges. This came as a blow to the General Assembly of the Egyptian State Council of Judges—made up entirely of men—who almost unanimously voted to bar women from the judiciary.

With regards to women's rights, therefore, the Mubarak era made some progress, although the regime is marked as yet another effort to neoliberalize Egypt's economy that had detrimental effects on women. This is attested to by the conditions of extreme poverty among the struggling groups of society and the deterioration of government public services. The Structural Adjustment Policies (SAPs) of the 1990s had a long-term impact on the Egyptian economic and social structures, especially in rural areas, which increasingly became more Islamized. Once again women's bodies became flagships of Islamist power, while the deregulation of government services had an even larger impact on patriarchal structures in society. These changes beckoned an era where patriarchal bargains, which previously held long-term benefits for women, no longer held appeal for them. In what follows, I explore these changes more closely as they lead in some direct and otherwise indirect ways to the Egyptian uprising of 2011.

Neoliberalism and Gendered Corporeality in Egypt

The Egyptian state had attempted for decades prior to the uprisings to assuage global market forces, aid and development agencies, local and regional contenders, to fulfill the economic ambitions of its ruling elites. Outwardly, it appeared as if the state was doing so well, since Egypt was touted as an International Monetary Fund (IMF) success story (Pfeifer 1999), a "world's best improved in doing business" by World Bank (World Bank 2010), and its privatization program ranked fourth in the world for its success by IMF (Osman 2010). In the past two decades, such testimonies characterized the representation of economic and political conditions in Egypt and other Arab countries such as Morocco and Tunisia as great victories of neoliberal reform. Described by experts as a free-market economic philosophy that relies on the deregulation of governmental and market supervision to release capital from profit constraints, the neoliberal turn was spearheaded by Ronald Reagan and Margaret Thatcher in the 1970s.

Though the intense drive toward privatization, tax reduction, and deregulation in western neoliberalizing states has never yielded the trickle-down effects that were initially promised, the doctrine has since been marketed globally as the answer to stagnant economies, joblessness, and debt. In developing countries like Egypt, "The neoliberal program" writes Tim Mitchell (1999) "has not removed the state from the market nor eliminated 'profligate' public subsidies. These achievements belong to the imagination" (31). Mitchell maintains that neoliberal policies in Egypt have had detrimental effects on poor households; on the quality, nature, and rate of agricultural production; and on the industrial output of the country, but what about the effects on women? How have gendered/"othered" bodies fared with the policies of deregulation as they experience what David Harvey (2005) has labeled the "creative destruction" of former systems of governance? How do patriarchal gender relations function under the shift toward deregulation? What conclusions can be reached if we place the gendered body at the intersection of neoliberalism, patriarchy, and gender? And what role did these political economic changes play in mobilizing women to take to the streets to protest government? From a history of neoliberalization policies to the impact on gender relations and outcome for women and the labor force in Egypt, the next section lays out the socioeconomic background for understanding women's participation in the Egyptian uprising.

Tim Mitchell's description of Egypt as the "Neoliberalism of your desires" (1999) is not alone in its frank condemnation of the shift toward Structural Adjustment Policies (SAPs). It is, however, unique in its rendering of how tales about phantom states of stability and prosperity are woven in Egypt from chaos and poverty. Neoliberal "rationalities" of progress frame how SAPs are envisioned and applied as rubrics of success. Aimed at reducing state intervention in market activities, social services, and the deregulation of trade and industry, SAPs act as requirements that qualify developing economies for seeking international loans brokered by the World Bank and IMF. These policies can be viewed as the prime methods by which neoliberalism has become hegemonic. Karen Pfeifer et al. (1999) describe the impact of Structural Adjustment Programs as follows:

> SAPs encourage the globalization of investment, and finance and trade, eroding national sovereignty's hold over economic policy and favoring transnational corporations and foreign private capital. The early stabilization phase of restructuring invariably induces recessions, with a sharp fall in investment and a rise in unemployment and poverty. Then follows legal liberalization of land tenure, investment and labor laws, and finally privatization—the divestiture of public assets and enterprises. These policies frequently favor the owners of land and capital over urban workers and rural peasants. Furthermore, SAPs rarely make good on their "trickle-down" promise of enhanced growth and efficiency in the long run (14).

On January 25, 2011 and in the immediate years that followed, thousands of women took to the streets to protest forms of political and economic oppression which men experienced as well. Neoliberal market reforms dictated by IMF and World Bank in the 1990s had changed the structure of the rural patrilocal family (Bach 1998). The impact of these changes on gender roles and relations were significant.

The idea of the extended family as a production unit was replaced with the nuclear family through a series of land reform laws. The land reform laws of 1992 directly restructured the rural patriarchal unit by limiting access to land. Through eliminating the freeze placed on land rent by the earlier socialist Nasserist regime, landlords now had the power to increase rents on farmers, in some cases by several fold. The direct impact of limiting land caused an immediate spike in the unemployment of young men who, faced with the necessity of supporting their families, started a wave of urban migration to the cities, especially Cairo. The large numbers of rural migrants seeking employment in urban centers were initially absorbed by a building boom in the city, but this was short-lived. As labor saturated the market, wages and jobs were hard to come by. Many of these young men were left to creatively manage their livelihood, which did not always lead them to legally sanctioned employment. Men who were able to find employment in countries of the Arab Gulf and Saudi Arabia left their families behind in large numbers to look for work.

In the meantime, these drastic socioeconomic transformations were to have dire consequences for women. They either struggled to take care of their families with absent fathers in the city or they joined their husbands in the city or in countries of the Gulf. Many women struggled to make ends meet, taking odd jobs that provided little in terms of social services or guaranteed employment. It is therefore unsurprising to find that 22 percent of Egypt's families are women-led (World Bank 2002). Rates of poverty are higher for Egyptian women than they are for men, with the numbers showing higher rates of poverty in rural areas. Research points to a higher probability of poverty for women in Egypt than for men. In urban areas, women are likely to be poorer than men by 2.3 percent and in rural areas by almost double at 4.79 percent (Odekon 2006).

This dark picture—albeit darker for women—encapsulated here for the sake of brevity, illustrates the last decades' dire repercussions on Egypt, arising from governmental corruption and reliance on foreign aid. More important, it points to the varying experiences of men and women as they negotiate the impact of "neoliberal reforms." The demise of patriarchal ties and the obligations that patriarchal systems imposed on both genders were replaced by a culture that was antithetical to the values and traditions of many rural Egyptian families—a fact that was detrimental to the survival of support networks that often compensated the very poor in the absence of state support. A principal consequence of these socioeconomic changes is the turn to religious groups for support, especially in rural areas. Lest this become a simplistic rationale to explain away the turn to religion, it is important to note that material gain is often a pathway to recruitment to religious organizations and movements in a poverty-stricken environment (Wickham 2002). As state subsidies progressively receded from individual lives, medical care, education, and employment fell to Islamic and Christian religious organizations whose numbers grew exponentially over the years.

The social and economic disempowerment of the male head of the family in rural traditional areas had repercussions for women as well. The direct undermining of the patrilocal extended family household denied older women control over the labor of younger women and the comfort of being served in old age. In fact, rural areas in Egypt are witnessing a growing number of elderly women who are left homeless due to the lack of patriarchal provisions for them. The weakening of family values that guaranteed older women economic protection and status by their living male relatives leaves these women more vulnerable to social stigma. Younger women, who often relied on other women for comfort and support in the extended household, also found themselves in nuclear households, separated from other women in unfamiliar urban centers where they were isolated. Despite the amenities and privacy provided by apartment living, which could enhance bonding between the spouses, these women found themselves more and more removed from the means of production and social networking of the large household or village, thus undermining both their status and their ability to negotiate with the patriarchal system (Bach 1998).

With the turn of the second millennium, working-class Egyptian women who had reached adulthood and were now more educated, modernized, and religiously inclined than their mothers, had to make a difficult choice. They either had to forgo the patriarchal benefits that their mothers had enjoyed and face a future that was increasingly isolating or change with the changing times and rely on themselves while simultaneously upholding some of the values of the patriarchal arrangement, which entailed the respect of males, elders, and older counterparts. These constraining circumstances were largely behind my informants' reasoning for joining the protests in January 2011.

In the fieldwork data collected for this project, working-class women who struggled with poverty and lack of government support consistently remarked on the challenge of working endless hours in return for barely sustaining wages— never experiencing a feeling of stability or having the ability to afford the basic needs of their children. It is therefore unsurprising that women factory workers were behind the labor protests in Mahalla that shook the foundation of the neoliberal economic structure in the country. The stories of two of these activists will be covered in the chapters that follow as they bring into view the economic and social challenges that motivated hundreds of thousands of women to lead marches and even incite demonstrations all across the region. Despite their labor activism efforts, however, a number of my informants talked about feeling insecure—even ashamed and put upon by members of their own families despite their hard-earned contributions. Even in middle age, a number of the women still struggled to afford a place of their own in the less expensive reaches of Egypt's new urban centers such as the Sixth of October City.

On the other hand, there were those revolutionaries who were both economically and socially empowered by neoliberalism, despite continuing to remain limited by their gender identity in the public sphere. Their stories too will be the subject of the following chapters. Considered part of the privileged elite, these women nevertheless sprang into action, putting their resources into the service of the uprising. Some organized daily meals, medicine, and emergency supplies to the protestors; others put their lives in danger and engaged as "frontliners." One young woman described how she singlehandedly started an NGO to protect women against harassment. Others worked for large corporations, enjoying the benefits of high income and privilege brought about by neoliberal institutions.

David Harvey, whose *Brief History of Neoliberalism* (2005) is considered today a treatise on the subject, developed a working definition of the economic and political practice that, since the 1970s, has assumed global dimensions with varying degrees and effects. To Harvey, the neoliberal turn that galvanized the economies of Britain and the United States in 1979 under Margaret Thatcher and Ronald Reagan respectively was predicated on the premise of "deregulation, privatization and withdrawal of the state from many areas of social provision" (3).

While neoliberalism clearly took on a different trajectory in healthier economies in the West, the context in developing countries presented a wide variety of hit-and-miss attempts at deregulation. Often resisting pressures from global organizations like World Bank and the International Monetary Fund (IMF), for fear of fomenting rebellions, many struggling world economies stepped up the militarization of their policing and brutalized their populations to prolong their regimes. By any means not a unique feature to these economies, the neoliberal state—according to Harvey—despite its emphasis on deregulation, freedom, and individual entrepreneurialism, often takes on policing and militarizing functions to secure and guarantee private property and the functioning of currency, markets, and market exchanges. While such states often operate repressive systems that rely on the threat of violence and abuse of citizens to perpetuate control, they simultaneously rationalize their exercise of force through neoliberal discourses of legitimation. Though violent and abusive of their citizens' rights, neoliberalizing states such as Tunisia and Egypt are touted as "success" stories and of having even "resilient" economies whose "reform" strategies have succeeded in economic growth (Pfeifer et al. 1999).

From Discipline to Control: How Bodies Experience Deregulation

The importance of controlling the body is central to new formations of governance under neoliberalism, according to Michael Hardt and Antonio Negri's analysis of globalization and capitalism in *Empire* (2000). Focusing on capitalist forms of control in modern and postmodern societies, they begin from a Foucauldian paradigm of biopower to consider how populations are shifting from being societies of discipline toward being societies of control, postbiopower. State subjects interiorize attitudes towards social integration and exclusion of difference. "Power is now exercised through machines that directly organize the brains (in communicating systems, information networks, etc.) and bodies (in welfare systems, monitored activities, etc.) toward a state of autonomous alienation from the sense of life and the desire for creativity" (23).

Though specific to the West, Hardt and Negri's historical saga of *Empire* provides some understanding of the Egyptian case, for it explains how people's bodies are implicated in heightened policing and increased militarization of society. It also helps shed light on how systems of repression and control become globalized to sustain global capital and political interests in developing countries. Demonstrators in Egypt were often photographed with tear gas canisters showing "Made in the USA" clearly emblazoned on their metal siding. This is because technologies of control often become accessible to autocracies supported by western governments in the form of aid, military exchanges, and/or training local military and secret police in the West. For example, in addition to the military aid package it receives annually, in Egypt under Sadat, Egyptian security units acquired more than 25 million dollars, as well as training and highly advanced equipment from the CIA (US Central Intelligence Agency) (Kahana and Stivi-Kerbis 2014). Similarly, the SAVAK, Iran's infamous secret police under the Pahlavis, were also trained and equipped by the CIA (Ambrose and Brinkley 2011).

Heightened militarization and securitization of developing countries not only sustain tyrannical regimes but also rationalize the imposition of austerity measures and deregulation—a fact that makes visible the link between global and local measures that control and manage the body. In developing economies, a number of scholars have argued after Harvey (2005) that neoliberal market changes, economic ambitions, and SAPs stipulated by world international aid organizations such as the IMF and World Bank (Bach 1998; Dahi 2011; Farah 2012; Harvey 2005) often result in systems of governance that ultimately resort to control for quelling local resistance. Deregulation under conditions of poverty, illiteracy, and weak infrastructures is not only unrealistic but exacerbates the already dire living conditions of the very poor. When these conditions escalate, they often lead to the rise of police states, armed militias, and rampant violence, as in the case of Sierra Leone (Conteh-Morgan 2006). The cyclical nature of these transactions is often predictable as, in response to increasingly dissenting populations, deregulating states often shift budget priorities from services to security. Violent repression of dissent, mock elections that amount to falsified results, and subversive police systems that resort to torture and corrupt illegal means of punishment are but a few of the markers of neoliberalizing transitions that Egypt has shared with developing countries in similar predicaments.

The Egyptian government shifted the economic priorities of its funds—sorely needed for its population—into establishing extensive systems of intelligence called *amn al dawla* or State Police Apparatus. A fortress-like building at the center of Cairo is home to this extensive bureaucracy of repression that ensured the longevity of the regime, regardless of its functionality. The government was to conduct its plans for deregulation and the introduction of neoliberal "reform" by dispossessing those already destitute and by violently clamping down on dissent. The Egyptian Emergency Laws put in place back in 1967 extended the dominion of the police, giving them the right to detain individuals and to try them in military courts. This allowed authorities to shut down newspapers and apply more censorship. The 9/11 attacks on New York and Washington further rationalized the use of brute force and the denial of human rights to suspects, who can be tortured and extradited with no legal ramifications (Shehata 2004).

Dismantling the Patriarchal Bargain

Though brute force on people's bodies was central to the scheme of deregulation, the perpetuation of undemocratic governance, and the sustenance of corruption, it could not be effective without (dis)regulation that inculcates fear and insecurity. Other techniques of control target the filters that people employ to organize their responses to the world. By means of a matrix of regulation and repression, the state targeted social structures and support networks essential for the survival of communities, such as systems of gender and patriarchy. Paradoxically, the state sought to perpetuate its power through metaphors of paternalism, thus denying masculine heads of families their normative patriarchal idioms and appropriating them for itself. In the development of state systems in the Arab world, state leaders often assumed kin structures and kin idioms, thus creating "state patriarchal forms," according to Suad Joseph (1994). In Arab patriarchy, masculinity is not only predicated upon age and gender but also upon the assumption of protection and sustenance of family needs. Therefore, state systems that appropriated the power but not the obligations of patriarchy appeared unjust and ineffective. Despite this, Hosni Mubarak clung to the role of the disciplinarian father, repeatedly employing paternalistic metaphors, even when millions congregated in squares all over Egypt demanding his resignation.

In the 1950s and '60s, Egyptian metaphors of identity were honed in masculine tropes. Epitomized by attributes of humor, gallantry, and honor (El-Hamamsy 1982), the concept of "*ibn al balad*" did not resonate much with the Egyptian of the new millennium. The decades of continuous unpredictability, deskilling through the lack of proper education, unreliable state services, and denial of basic human needs, even efficient transportation, contributed to a state of loss and disillusionment that severed not only a connection to the "*balad*"—meaning Egypt—but more seriously a connection to the self as a potential agent. Many protestors, including this young woman, a filmmaker, described it as such. "Before January 25 I didn't have faith that my voice could be heard.

I didn't feel like I was in control of my future. The metaphor used by Mubarak that he was our father and we were his children made us feel as though we lacked any motivation. The revolution woke us up—a collective consciousness has been awoken" (Al Jazeera 2011).

The state ran its well-oiled machinery of political control under its paternalistic umbrella, restricting individual freedoms by means of the emergency law that allowed security police to conduct random roadblocks, arrests, and investigations that always carried an implicit potential of turning violent. It was this potential for random violence—not just the act of violence itself—that inculcated within the individual Egyptian a subjectivity of silence (Abul Fadl 2011). Young men in particular, and males in general, became the target of random state violence, torture, and humiliation. Young men were pulled off the street, simply for the act of walking. They were denied the various resources their parents might have enjoyed: education, health care, and government jobs.

Young Upper Egyptian poet Hesham al-Gokh (2010), dubbed prince of poets, writes in his poem *Goha*:

> It is an awful feeling to sense that your country is a weak thing
> your voice is weak
> your opinion is weak
> that you would sell your heart and your body
> that you would sell your pen and your name
> (but) they would not bring you the cost of a loaf (of bread)

The state as father was a myth that was dismantled in the midan. As demonstrators held up the soles of their shoes in the direction of the giant screens broadcasting the image of Mubarak the night he stepped down, they were shattering the myth. The dismantling of state paternalism had a tremendous impact on the protestors. It allowed them the freedom to see themselves for the very first time as potent actors and enabled the hopeful possibility of a "return" to the ideals of the ibn al balad that were stifled by years of prohibition and despair. To this end, the rebirth of the "true" Egyptian now finally freed by the country's youth headlined the success story of the uprising. Reclaiming Egypt in Tahrir Square on February 10, 2011 may have only been a symbolic rather than systemic change, but its impact was transformative.

When a women's march was attacked by male protestors in Tahrir on International Women's Day the protestors' conviction in the return of the true Egyptian, the honorable and honest ibn al balad was shaken, which shattered the shiny veneer of revolution for some. Sexual harassment stood for all the things that ibn al balad did not. It signaled the fragmentation of the people as a community and undermined their newfound solidarity in Tahrir. While rates of the street harassment of women in Egypt are close to 90 percent, not a single known case of harassment was reported from Tahrir Square during the first days of the uprising. This reinforced the belief that the uprising brought back the true Egypt, where men respected women and protected their honor. Nahla, one of the protestors who was in the square the day the women's march was harassed, describes it as follows: "We honestly believed that our revolution had transformed everything overnight. Despite knowing that change cannot be so swift, we desperately wanted to believe that it could. When we were attacked in Tahrir, my mother said to me, 'What did you expect? Did you really think that you could change people?'" This is what made the attack on the women so difficult to accept.

Despite the rebirth of ibn al balad, immediately after the events in Tahrir and other urban centers in the country, one alarming fact after another pointed to attempts at marginalizing women from political participation. One indicator of this was the naming of the very first people's group to take initiative for opening negotiations with the SCAF as the "Council of Wise Men." The group included such prominent male figures in Egypt as Secretary-General of the Arab League Amr Moussa, businessman Naguib Sawiris, and lawyer Ahmad Kamal Abul Magd. Although this raised flags for various observers, many argued that the council did not represent youth either. The naming implied that this was a levelheaded group that arose in response to chaos. But the speed by which these male alliances were forged in the first weeks of the revolution took women by surprise. They were excluded from the committee on constitutional reform and were left out of the constitutional changes that were put in place by the committee. This blatant exclusion of women from the Egyptian "spring" led many to question the uprising itself; put succinctly by one woman activist, "It is simple, this revolution means nothing to me if women's rights are not honored!"

So why this shift in the attitude of the hegemonic masculine public? Is it as simple as saying that women were used only to be discarded and told to return to their homes? How can we seriously consider this a possibility when the events of the uprising have made it clear that women are capable and deserve the recognition and inclusion that they call for? Examining the sociocultural dynamics behind this inclusion/exclusion of women in the political sphere questions how this contradiction has, in recent years, characterized the nature of gender relations in an Arab country such as Egypt. What happened to the "patriarchal bargain" (Kandiyoti 1988), which scholars of gender in the Middle East have astutely used to analyze women's negotiations with patriarchy? The events of the uprising have revealed that changing notions of masculinity have observably shifted the terms of the patriarchal bargain both freeing women and young people from its hold but also putting them at a disadvantage in the absence of alternative forms of support.

Given the mutual productivity of masculinity and femininity in Arab culture, to understand the attempts to marginalize women from postuprising politics must entail a reexamination of masculinity. Suad Joseph (1988) discusses in her work on connective patriarchy in Lebanon how Hanna, the brother, constructed his masculinity by feminizing his sister Flaur and vice versa. She points out an important dynamic in the production of gender, sexuality, and power, one that is mutually constructed through idioms of honor and shame and ultimately reproduces Arab patriarchy. We can understand from this that patriarchy is mutually produced through femininity and masculinity. Relations between the two siblings studied by Joseph were emblematic of male/female development along Arab patriarchal norms of that time and context. On the other hand, what was observed in Egypt within the context described previously, is the construction of a problematic masculinity. Whereas love characterizes the male/female relationship in Hanna and Flaur's family, hate is the sentiment expressed by the young man to his beloved who subjected him to much suffering and humiliation. To an Egypt that is addressed as a mother and a loved one Hesham al-Gokh writes (ibid.):

> You make me hate your black eyes and my days passed
> You are not my beloved from this day onwards
> My beloved is dead!
> ......
> All who tell you they love you, are hypocrites
> When I told you I loved you it was hypocrisy
> Love means two (people) who are building
> Not one who is building and hundreds who destroy
> Love is a condition
> Love means an open space in the hearts of lovers to lovers
> It means that the poor sleep warm at night
> Love means a letter to all those who are imprisoned
> Why are they imprisoned?
> It means to live with a goal
> For a mission
> It means I feel my value in you

The degree of feeling, depth of hurt, and years that lack hope, security, and justice impact the connective state of patriarchy that Joseph describes. Al-Gokh does not turn his back on love, nor does he tire of his beloved. Instead, he explains to her that under these destructive circumstances, he cannot bring himself to love her. Feeling shunned by his beloved, the young man is alienated from his environment. He is defeated, unappreciated as a man by the very thing he holds dear, his own country, whose black eyes no longer hold appeal. In fact, she is dead to him. What happens to the young man then when he is raised to believe that he, like the generations of patriarchs before him, is entitled to his beloved's affection and care, only to discover that these are no longer available for him? A far cry from ibn al balad's honor and strength, he has nothing to give or take but hate. In the absence of the privileges of the past, patriarchy becomes synonymous with hate.

The experiences of the young man described in Al Gokh's poem are not universal in Egypt, although they represent the sentiments of growing numbers of disenfranchised youth in the country. Moreover, even the threat of the loss of masculine privilege in a patriarchal society shapes the kinds of masculine behaviors and experiences in society. Various forms of masculinity exist along age, class, and power lines in Egypt. R. W. Connell (1995) classifies four different kinds of masculinities, with each having varying degrees of access to patriarchal benefits. He calls them hegemonic, complicit, marginalized, and subordinated. Males who are marginalized or even subordinated have minimum access to patriarchal dividends and are associated with the least attributes of hegemonic masculinity. Under hegemonic masculine systems, homosexuals for instance are associated with females according to Connell's model and are therefore denied patriarchal benefits.[2] During the protests, male demonstrators were often described as homosexuals by pro-Mubarak supporters. The word homosexual, *khawal*, can often be heard on videos taken of security police taunting protestors. The threat of the loss of male privilege has such dire consequences that it is often used as a threat in violent confrontations with police.

It can be assumed from the mutually constructed relational model offered by Joseph that gendered identity under patriarchy is mutually produced. Accordingly, the more males are subordinated, denied patriarchal benefits, and associated with females, the more extreme their gender differentiation from females. Gender differentiation from females is often played out on nonmasculine bodies. It can take the form of violence, sexual harassment, public shaming, and physical segregation. Women's bodies become targeted to maintain systems of patriarchal benefits and avoid emasculation by hegemonic masculinity. Consequently, violence, abuse, and sexual harassment of women is the outcome of masculinity built on hate and deprivation. In a similar vein, Sandesh Sivakumaran (2007) maintains that sexual violence is often necessarily perpetrated in public to redraw gender boundaries and privilege:

> Sexual violence against women in conflict frequently takes place in public, in front of the victims' communities and their families. On an individual level, there is the added aspect of public humiliation and shame, an added stigma. There is also little chance that word of the rape will be kept quiet. Public sexual

violence is also, then, a way of communicating to the rest of the community, of spreading fear and vulnerability throughout the area. An entire community may feel compelled to flee; indeed this may have been the very purpose of the public nature of the sexual violence in the first place. The power of the perpetrators is vindicated, on show for all to see. (p. 268)

In the absence of political freedoms that guarantee legitimate means of opposition to the state, dissent takes shape by violating those who become objectified and bargained with in power discourses, to avoid state regulation and punishment. Passive resistance is commonly a demonstration of overwhelmingly oppressive conditions (Scott 1985). Few studies have linked these forms of noncombative resistance with gender and gender violence. Growing violence against women in neoliberal contexts has been captured by some scholars who show how gender ideology is shaped under conditions of neoliberalization and deregulation (Battacharya 2013). Under conditions of repression nonstate actors who are silenced and criminalized often take subversive measures to influence the status quo. Attacking women in public to shame the state that violates and emasculates them is one such tactic. Another strategy encourages trends that limit women's public action to demonstrate social influence. Women are often victimized and marked as the "other" in struggles for political control and to tip the scales in favor of one party or other. They become economically disempowered, silenced, and invisibilized from public spaces and political processes of decision-making.

This situation is exacerbated by changing values of masculinity that are rendered infirm and marginalized by repressive "security" measures. Neoliberal market economies further limit access to resources while simultaneously perpetuating myths of social mobility. Frustrations emerging from the withdrawal of state subsidies and services are complicated by global discourses that mark Arab youth as "terrorist" and "violent." Young males in overpopulated countries like Egypt where youth constitute more than 24.3 percent of the total number of citizens are often both criminalized and marginalized by state police (Central Agency for Public Mobilization and Statistics 2016). Rising levels of police violence were of major concern to the protestors on National Police Day that was designated as the first day of demonstrations for that reason (Ismail 2012).

Conclusion

This chapter traced the gendered bodyscape in Egypt since the turn of the twentieth century to the present. Probing the contours of the corporeal through an intersectional analysis that takes account of the historical, social, economic, and political it clarifies not only how neoliberal transformation, patriarchy, and gender operate on a local level but their global connections as well.

The corporeal lies at the nexus of these forces and consequently at the heart of forms of discipline and control. It is therefore embroiled in shifts in national projects, the politics of empire, the global financial market, and changing patriarchal norms.

The revolution of 2011 ushered in radical changes to people's consciousness and corporeal awareness. The sheer magnitude of the mass protests in the millions was in itself a unchoreographed corporeal statement of revolt. Arguing for the need for theoretically unpacking the dissenting body, the preceding chapter embeds the corporeal within the very forces that seek to construct it. Through this gendered corporeal reading of Egyptian history, one can discern the role that the physical body has played in sociopolitical transformations, not only as a recipient of policies that control and discipline it but also as a platform of resistance and individual dissent. With this historical background, the book goes on to elaborate on how the gendered body comes to be a signifying agent of collective action and of transformation.

Patriarchal forms of politics clearly play a role in defining gendered corporeality during Egypt's modern history. This has been discussed in this chapter beginning with Ottoman modernization schemes, to nation-state building and the neoliberalization policies of Egypt's deregulating states. Despite the dire consequences of neoliberal policies on poor households, agrarian production, and the public industrial sector in Egypt, these shifts have only been framed as "successes," which upon closer examination reveal their ramifications to the citizenry in general and the body in particular.

As gender lines are redrawn by means of repressive policing through physical and verbal emasculation, public masculine behavior increasingly seeks to assert masculinity by differentiating itself from femininity. By targeting women in public places through violent harassment and assault, male perpetrators project their own disempowerment by brutalizing women. Women's bodies become a platform on which masculinity violently differentiates itself from the feminine, thus seeking to redeem its lost privileges. The fact that harassment is a public act is not coincidence. Sexual harassment is public because it is meant to be a public demonstration. Traditional male patriarchy that teaches honor and protection of femininity would seem to be challenged by such vicious male acts. Paradoxically, these acts of public violence against women aim at regaining a sense of lost power by males marking women as the weaker sex, sexual objects to be pillaged, touched, and humiliated. "Marginal masculinities" differentiate themselves as the opposite—the stronger sex, the sexual actor, and the plunderer who exercises power over those who are seen to transgress. As nonmale genders become the target of these burgeoning forms of masculinity, religious discourse also emerges as a contender for defining gender and gender relations. Historically, the deployment of religious text has targeted women's bodies, whether seeking their seclusion, genital cutting, or protection from harm; these discourses also contribute to the framing of the issues around corporeality.

By contrast, women's corporeal dissent challenges the premise upon which these acts of violence are based. This is because the feminine body restructures the public space and claims visibility, thus vying with marginal masculinities and the politics of erasure. By understanding how corporeal politics are shaped and how they shape the public sphere of politics, we can perhaps articulate a gendered corporeal epistemology that enables and reaffirms women's efforts over the last decades.

Women in the Arab and Middle Eastern regions have had to contend with masculine politics that prioritize public issues and shape the outcomes of political endeavors. The importance of foregrounding women's role in building the new political sphere in the country at this point in history cannot be underscored as an indicator of the future direction the Egyptian sphere of politics will take. Whether women's role in politics, the labor strikes, or their organizing energies in Islamic activism—not to mention the campaigns for the abolishment of discrimination and denial of rights through women's rights NGOs and the like—these various forms of social and political activism will have to galvanize into a solid women's front in the country before they can be openly acknowledged. What that entails is a rethinking of patriarchal politics and women's historical negotiation with its tropes. In other words, a critical reexamination of the "bargain with patriarchy" that Kandiyoti so astutely described and a new-on-the-ground dissection of masculinity in Egypt as a necessary constituent of the patriarchal bargain. Women in Egypt today are faced with the question, is bargaining with patriarchy still useful as a negotiating tool? And what are the alternatives available for women to shape the future of their nation?

Notes

1. The five days in November 2011 when confrontations between the authorities and the protestors resulted in many deaths and injuries.
2. Under classical patriarchal systems, however, women may acquire patriarchal gains when they bargain with patriarchy, according to Kandiyoti (ibid.).

3 Gender, Class, and Revolt in Neoliberal Cairo

Bᴙɪɴɢɪɴɢ ɪɴᴛᴏ ꜰᴏᴄᴜꜱ how neoliberal "reform" and its processes of deregulation discussed in the previous chapter are lived by Egyptian women, this chapter discusses the effects on the wide range of women from the working class to the middle and upper classes. Whether contrasting or paralleling or simply complicating neoliberal ideologies, the stories of the women who joined the revolution in Tahrir Square in 2011 reveal the sociocultural dimensions of neoliberal restructuring, the shifts in gender relations, patriarchal values, and social organization in the last decade and how these tie into the events that have taken place from 2011 to the years to come.

"This Revolution Was about Us": Zeinab

"I am a woman who was raised in a poor home," began fifty-four-year-old Zeinab. "Nothing has changed to this day. I pay four hundred L.E. (in 2015, this was about fifty US dollars) a month in rent for a room for myself and my children in Saft El Laban. I was on my way today to *lagnit al i'asha* [Committee for Living Support] to request 125 L.E (US$15.80) for *ma'unet al shitaa* [winter stamps]. After taking three different modes of transportation and standing in a long line, they told me that I needed to bring a different application form other than the one I had that showed a welfare number from the Department of Statistics," she told me. She was not complaining to me or asking for help. Zeinab shared her problem in the spirit of sharing but nothing else.

She was a short and strong-looking woman. The hands that rested on a purse across her lap were calloused and tough. They had seen many years of hard work. She looked at me with eyes that missed nothing, from behind eyeglasses that had tiny diamonds in the corners. As she continued her account of the journey that took her to the midan, she paused to mention that her son was one of the revolutionary "stars" of the media.

"What is a star?" I asked her.

In response to my question, she held her cell phone out to me to show me its background picture. It was a photograph of the cover of a leading magazine, showing a young boy running amid what appeared to be explosions. "This is my son, Mohamed. He was only ten at the time. I took him to the midan with me every single day."

"Were you not scared for him?" I asked.

"No, I was not scared for any of our lives. God is the protector. We went as a family; my husband, who was in wheelchair, and my daughter, who was a student in *i'dadia* [middle school] also came with us. This revolution was about us. Do you understand me? How could we not go?"

I understood what that meant. This revolution provided its participants with a sense of ownership, probably for the first time in their lives. After years of civic disempowerment, being able to express one's needs to others, stating one's problem in a public forum and openly calling for justice made each person in the protests feel the same as Zeinab, as if the revolution was about them personally. She continued:

> "My family is from Upper Egypt," Zeinab or Om Mohamed, as she is called by her friends and neighbors per tradition, continued, "even after our family moved to Cairo so that my father could get more work opportunities, he didn't stop cursing our poverty. He worked hard but could barely afford to make ends meet. As for me, I decided to educate myself by myself. If my father could not afford to put me in school, I could teach myself how to read and write. And somehow I was able to do it; I read my brothers' schoolbooks and could read the newspapers. From the little money I was given to buy groceries, I set aside a few piasters to buy the opposition newspapers. I also read *Al Ahram* [the national "official" Egyptian paper] and liked Ahmed Ragab, who wrote about how Sadat eliminated government subsidies. Sadat oppressed his people, so they rebelled against him. It wasn't just the people, even *al amn al markazy* [Central Security Forces] and many women joined those riots. Shortly after that, there was the case of Suliman Khater; they arrested him and placed him in a military prison and they tortured him to death. People cheered for him, and they called for his release. There were many protests across the country. I was only sixteen. My brothers and I joined the university protests despite the widespread arrests."

Om Mohamed is referring to the Bread Riots of 1977, when Sadat removed government subsidies on basic foods. Suliman Khater's death in prison is sometimes cited as the spark that ignited those riots, although, as in the case of the 2011 uprising with the killing of Khaled Said, there were far more general conditions that affected the Egyptian people that galvanized the masses. Khater was an Egyptian soldier who opened fire on Israeli tourists, killing seven of them. After his arrest, he was found dead in his prison cell, which some surmised was the result of an assassination by the government to avoid an international incident with Israel. The Bread Riots, however, were the working class's spontaneous uprising against Sadat's compliance with World Bank and IMF recommendations. What was clear from her rememory of these events, however, is that Zeinab was politically aware and involved in political action at a young age. From what she described, she continued to be politically active, even after she was married and had children of her own.

Of the women I interviewed, only a few shared Zeinab aka Om Mohamed's politically active history before the 2011 uprisings, yet many described socioeconomic constraints very similar to hers. Like Zeinab, they saw their fathers as the main breadwinners, who failed to give them equal opportunities like those afforded their brothers. This disparity based on gender is a commonly cited problem for young women and is often regarded as the main cause for the higher rates of illiteracy among females in the Arab region. In the absence of sufficient income in patriarchal cultures, families often prioritized their sons over their daughters to go to school. The rationale being that young boys grow up to be men who will, in turn, take care of their families, while girls ultimately leave with their husbands and become their responsibility, not the family's. Girls are assigned domestic chores that help their mothers and provide support for the male members of their families to find income-generating opportunities in the public sphere. Poverty keeps young girls from school. Ideologies that persist in linking girls to the domestic and to biological reproduction rationalize these pragmatic choices as well. In Egypt, the percentage of the population over age fifteen who are illiterate are 56 percent female but almost half that rate for males at 33 percent (UNESCO 2002).

Other women I spoke with also described how they struggled to have interests other than the domestic, and even many more talked about how marriage and children kept them from following political news. All of my interlocutors, however, described a transformation that was brought about by the uprising of January 25, albeit in different ways. Take, for example, Naglaa, a forty-year-old government worker, revolutionary, mother, and daughter who lives in Egypt's sprawling new metropolis in the Sixth of October City. Like Zeinab, her family migrated to the Caireen metropolis. In Naglaa's case, however, she moved from the coastal city of Alexandria, escaping social stigma and looking for work after her husband left her.

A Poet, Not a Revolutionary: Naglaa

"I am originally from Alexandria . . . but moved to Cairo nineteen years ago because of some . . . problems." That's how Naglaa began her story. Not wanting to pry, I listened to what she chose to share with me and was grateful at that moment that she agreed to meet me at all. It was only after several persistent phone calls from me and a long exchange of text messages that I half-convinced her to agree to chat. (I say "half-convinced" because she was not completely sure that her story was in any way exceptional and suggested that there are others who are far more important to the revolution than she.) I have been interviewing activists in Egypt since 2011, but in the summer of 2014, few activists who took part in the revolution three years earlier wanted to reopen the subject. Egypt had slowly fallen into an uncomfortable numbness once more, and the dust had settled for now in Tahrir Square, where it all began.

A few months after our first meeting in her office, Naglaa told me the "whole" story. She explained, "I had nothing to do with politics prior to the revolution. I am a poet, a romantic who likes pictures of roses, blue skies, and rolling waves. How did I end up in squares and street protests?" She shook her head in puzzlement at her own life.

Naglaa grew up in what she described as a "good home" and attended a local language school (semipublic schools where a second language, often English, is taught). Her father often traveled to Arab countries, looking for work opportunities, while her mother worked as an accountant for the *ghazl we'l nassig* (textile) industry. She grew up learning from her mother that a woman has to perform her traditional duties in the household, that she had to be feminine and physically appealing. Naglaa was an avid reader and wrote romantic poetry. She dreamed of romance and finding someone one day. When she was eighteen years old, she married a man with whom she was madly in love. She saw in him the future she dreamed about. Two children later and a few years into the marriage, her husband announced he was leaving for Qatar to pursue work. After he left, she never heard from him again. Soon after that, Naglaa and her mother received terrible news. Her father, who was working in Jordan at the time, had passed away. Though he had often sent money home in the past, it had dwindled down to a few hundred pounds per month and then stopped altogether. To their chagrin, they learned he had a family in Jordan. It was they who inherited everything, while Naglaa and her mother were only left with more bills to pay.

The labor migration of male heads of families has been increasing exponentially since the government lifted restrictions on migration in 1974 in an effort to liberalize the labor market and usher in neoliberal policies. With the numbers initially quadrupling in 1974, rising to almost four million Egyptian labor migrants in 2007, mostly to Arab countries (Zohry 2007), the impact on Egyptian families was tremendous. Although migration can be commonly seen as a source of upward mobility for the working class, a boom for the economy, as well as a deterrent to inflation (Singerman 1996), the effects migration has had on Egyptian families and gender relations can be observed to this day, as in the case of Naglaa. In the 1970s, with Sadat's open-door policy, remittances from migration drastically improved the public image of his administration as it initially implemented structural adjustment policies. Soha Abdel Kader has documented the impact of migration on working-class and rural families as such: "The emerging diversity of household types includes an increasing number of households headed by women as well as those containing multi-generations.

There are also households that remain closely linked even though the members are split as a result of migration (multi-spatial households)" (2001, 20). Yet, according to Abdel Kader, the reshuffling of gender roles in the family paradoxically has an empowering effect on women, who are often forced to access male-dominated spheres of labor, thus creating precedence for the inclusion of women in these spaces.

Finding herself with no source of income and two children to support, Naglaa decided to head to Cairo, where nobody knew her and conversations with friends and neighbors would not hint at blame for the disappearance of her husband. No significant work prospects were available for a woman with a *diblom mutawasit* (intermediate diploma), so Naglaa had to be resourceful. She set up a stand selling tea to microbus drivers, next to their parking lot in the Sixth of October City. For a while, she barely made ends meet, but things got complicated when her mother, Nadia, joined them from Alexandria. Nadia overshot her unpaid leave from work and was eventually fired, leaving them with even less income. Determined to take care of her mother and children, Naglaa devised a new plan. With a loan from a relative, she bought various kinds of calculators and small gadgets at wholesale prices and began selling them in Ataba Square, where many students shop for school supplies. There she staked her spot and set up a makeshift wooden stand with the help of her mother and daughter. The three of them took the bus every morning at four thirty from the Sixth of October City to Ataba, carrying the stand and the merchandise. A few years later, they had enough money to rent a storage space for their merchandise, so they would not have to carry much on the bus. This new arrangement came at a good time, as Naglaa's mother fell ill and lost the ability to walk, eventually becoming completely paralyzed from the waist down. Naglaa was shaken and distraught for her mother, but she was undeterred. She took care of her sick mother and her two children while working at her stand in Ataba from dawn to dusk. Nadia, Naglaa's mother, described those days as "dark."

Naglaa continues to be instrumental in supporting the revolution and ensuring that "the blood of those who died will never be for nothing." She had joined the revolutionary April 6 group who were credited with the initial organizational work that mobilized the masses in Egypt's Tahrir Square on the twenty-fifth of January. She was imprisoned three times by the authorities. Her friends tease her about how often she was found in the midst of struggles with the police, either trying to free one of the younger activists or objecting to the violent treatment of protesters. Naglaa took two bullets to her shoulder and one to her leg during the protests. Though the antiprotest laws in Egypt are brutally enforced, to this day, she continues to protest, from commemorating the revolution, to mourning the deaths of the young and old, to demanding the release of imprisoned revolutionaries. If protests are taking place, Naglaa is there.

Like others, including Zeinab or Om Mohamed, whose story we have discussed earlier in the chapter, Naglaa's domestic priorities expanded into politics, allowing both to coexist in her daily life. Zeinab's concern with economic survival, however, forced her to place her political activism on the back burner when she got married because of family demands and lack of funds. Zeinab's husband, who was similarly politically inclined, also needed to focus on providing for their small family. This momentarily distracted him away from demonstrations. "We still read opposition papers, and we were involved in spirit, but it was not till years later that we started to get involved again," recalls Zeinab.

A New Beginning for Zeinab

In 2010, Zeinab and her husband were at *dar al qadaa al 3ali* (Supreme Court), where they were following up on a legal case related to her husband's work. Suddenly, they noticed groups of young people congregating around them. It turned out to be a demonstration organized by the April 6th movement. She approached a young man, and they started talking on the sidewalk. They wanted justice for political prisoners, he told her. "Immediately I felt I understood what they were trying to do. I wanted to stand and protest with them, but the authorities were already forming a cordon [a barrier] around them, so we watched from a distance and then left." That day was a new beginning for Zeinab.

"The government said do not go to Tahrir on the twenty-fifth . . . but I insisted on going! I went on the twenty-sixth!" Zeinab looked defiant as she relived those momentous days, raising her index finger in the air and then pressing it hard against the table to emphasize the point, "*Al hag* [referring to her husband] saw what was happening. He came home and said to me, 'Don't go out. The young people are demanding that Habib Al 'Adly [minister of the interior] be removed from office. The television is saying they were trained in Serbia.'"

> "*Al hag* went to work, and I sat lost in my thoughts. My ten-year-old son looked at me intently and said, 'I am thinking what you're thinking.' I leapt out of my chair. 'Let's go!' I said. "We got on the bus from Saft Al Laban to Tahrir. The streets were empty. When we arrived at Mohamed Mahmood Street, we were met by the security police, who were blocking the road. I turned to a group of young people to my left and asked them, 'What is going on?' They said *we want change* and described how they saw the intolerable situation in the country. There was no talk of a revolution, no deposing of Mubarak or anything like that. We became friends, and we are friends to this day," said Zeinab.

She continued, "At the same time, the government began using violence against the protestors in Suez. One person was martyred. When this happened, the youth asked the people to demonstrate on the 'Friday of Anger.'" It was the end of the month, and Zeinab and her husband were completely broke. But they could no longer tolerate state-sponsored television, so they went out and bought a small satellite dish with installments on spec, so they could watch al Jazeera. When they had access to this alternative source of news, Zeinab felt more inclined to step up her activism, since she was now better informed. State television at the time was still broadcasting the news that these protests in Tahrir were simply disgruntled youth who would soon get tired and bored and go home.

I joined a *maseera* [a march through the streets] from Boulaq al Dakrur to Tahrir. It was organized by Ziad el 'ilaimi and Asmaa Mahfouz. We decided to divide ourselves up. Some fell and others died; we separated, but we could not get into Tahrir. When we arrived at the Qasr el Nil Bridge, we bent our heads to pray and got intensely beaten by the Interior thugs. But while this was happening all over the place, there were so many other acts of kindness that kept us going. People threw water bottles and food out to us from their balconies. The Ministry of Interior was gone by the twenty-eighth [of January]. It was too much for them to deal with the throngs of people, so they left. There were no selfish desires amongst us those days, no struggles over power. We decided to occupy Tahrir Square. The tents came on the twenty-ninth. I brought with me an old bedsheet from home and borrowed a piece of wood from a carpenter who lives near me. I nailed the wood together, spread the sheet, and took my seat under my new shelter. The Muslim Brotherhood, the Salafis, and the April 6th also set up their tents. I was so happy, despite the tragedies that happened around me. People died next to me on the bridge; a small boy died in the square, but these terrible losses only strengthened our resolve.

Zeinab described the first eighteen days of the uprising in Tahrir in iconic terms. "Every person who went to Tahrir during those days had a beautiful dream for this country. Nobody was going out for a picnic and especially not after the Battle of the Camel." This sense of elation among the occupying demonstrators was not universal, however, as some began to get restless, according to Zeinab. "Large numbers of people left Tahrir after Mubarak gave one of his talks, when he talked about his 'children' and 'my people.' Some said we should give him another chance and left the square. Others warned that if we left, he would hunt us down." She described the plots to fragment their unity and to pit one person against the other. She talked about demonstrators who were paid fifty L.E. (less than seven dollars) to pose as the Muslim Brotherhood or part of the April 6th movement and then create trouble in the midan. Despite this, Zeinab and her family tenaciously held on, even when they were beaten and pushed and their tents were dismantled again and again. "The Ministry of Interior beat me. Everyone beat me. But the young people saved me and took me to get medical attention."

With a bemused expression, she recounted the story of Medhat, a rural teenage boy who came to Cairo by himself to take part in the demonstrations. He lost his wallet, and all his money was in it. That same day, as Medhat was running in the midan away from tear gas bullets, he found a wallet full of money on the ground. He picked it up and delivered it intact to the lost-and-found station. "*Shakl al midan, shakl el nas,*" she said, meaning that Tahrir Square was a reflection of the people in it. In this simple example that brings the ethics of the revolution to a very individual level, Zeinab described what the revolutionaries wanted their Tahrir to be: a place where the virtues of honesty, bravery, selflessness, and cohesiveness took shape. It was not a place where economic necessity took precedence over these essential virtues. What dire consequences structural adjustment policies (SAP) had on people's lives were being reversed in Tahrir Square. It was not where individualism, greed, and competition had any credibility. In fact, as the revolutionaries themselves communicated through their chants and various social media outlets, Tahrir Square was the place where the new nation was being reborn.

The chants that Zeinab had both learned and composed in the midan reflected these political ideals as well. She was quite an accomplished *hatifa* (chanter). Unafraid to voice these principles of revolution in a public place two years later, as we sat drinking tea in a café across from the Nile in Giza, she began to recite loudly. One after another, the chants she had memorized by heart spilled out. These were chants about class, about being dehumanized by poverty, and about being marginalized by the government.

- *Humma biaklu hamam wi ihna el ful dawakhna we dakh.*
  (Translation: They eat pigeon while we eat beans that make us and the beans dizzy.)
- *Humma bialbisu akhir moda we ihna binmut sab'a fi uda.*
  (Translation: They wear the latest fashions while we die from living seven in one room.)
- *Yasqut yasqut Hosni Mubarak. Irhal ya'ni is'a inta mabtifhamsh?*
  (Translation: Down with Hosni Mubarak, down with Hosni Mubarak. Leave! It means just go! Don't you understand?)

And then there were the times that Zeinab climbed up on stage with her son Mohamed and chanted through the microphone. Below is a slogan that they both composed together:

Baladi mitba'a mitba'a.
Baladi ishu ya gama'a!
Mitba'a limin?
Mitba'a binizam.
Salamat ya nizam!

(Translation:
My country is sold, sold.

My country! Wake up people!
Sold to whom?
Sold in an organized way (*binizam, nizam* also means regime).
Greetings, oh regime (organization!)

Despite the catchy phrases and the underlying humor that relies on a play on words and irony, Zeinab's slogans mirror a deep-seated chagrin. Her experience with poverty and class difference frames her political rhetoric and finds expression (and a large following) in the slogans and chants she called out in Tahrir and now in the café where we sat.

As she continued chanting in the half-empty space, something very remarkable happened. Right behind Zeinab, I watched as one by one, the chef and his helpers came up from the kitchen to listen to her. She was completely unaware of this as she sat with her back to them, but the men who gathered behind the counter with their arms folded across their chests seemed to be in complete agreement with her. They nodded their heads, whispering among themselves, and remained there until about twenty minutes later, when Zeinab and I got up to leave.

The following year, Zeinab and I got together again over tea. Egypt now had a new president, Abdel Al Fatah Al Sisi, and while he restored the status quo after the Muslim Brotherhood president Mohamed Morsi, Al Sisi was by no means the answer to the revolutionaries' dreams. Political repression was at its worst, according to many, as the new protest law threw thousands in prison and clamped down on civil liberties. Though the country seemed to be more stable, stability was simply a relative term that no one seemed to agree on. Egyptians still struggled economically more than ever before and, on the whole, the revolution was thought of as a thing of the past for some, while for others, it never happened at all.

We started catching up by talking about our children. Zeinab shared first that her two children now want to leave Egypt. "This is our country!" she exclaimed. "We have rights here!" She could not understand why her young ones who experienced Tahrir Square with her during the uprising did not want to remain behind to fight the good fight. Her daughter was expelled from school because she wrote in an examination paper that the police did not protect the people. (Similar stories can be read in Mada Masr, 2014.) Mona, Zeinab's daughter, was about to graduate from high school and start university in the fall. Now Zeinab did not know if that was going to be possible. "The constitution states that there is freedom of expression. Then what are we teaching these young kids?" she wondered.

Zeinab's husband had died from a chronic illness the previous year, leaving them with nothing but his pension, which amounted to a little over seventy dollars per month. More financial constraints for the family seemed to loom on the horizon, and Zeinab was concerned what was to become of her children now. When I asked Zeinab about financial aid or a fund that could ease their money worries for a while, she was emphatic. "I demand my right from this government. My right to live with dignity and freedom. To not need to put out my hand. I want what is mine as a citizen of this country. I want no aid and no fund." Zeinab was visibly angry as she finished speaking. Her situation—as dire as it was, was similar to 27.8 million Egyptians who lived below the poverty line in 2015, according to CAPMAS (Central Agency for Public Mobilization and Statistics). While poverty in Cairo hit 18 percent of its population, it was much lower than other parts of the country. In Upper Egypt, for example, poverty is rated at a staggering 56.7 percent. The report by CAPMAS suggests that poverty rates would be higher overall by 4.6 percent, had it not been for the food and family subsidies provided by the government. Access to these subsidies—if we can take Zeinab's previous experience at the Ministry of Social Affairs' public outlet as an example—was deeply mired in endless bureaucracy and mismanagement, revealing subsidies to be an unreliable form of support for the family.

Rememory against Painful Forgetting

The struggle still continues for Zeinab, as it does for millions of other Egyptians who live on less than a dollar a day. The years after the initial uprising took a toll on people's hopes for a better future. There were no easy answers as Egypt, like other Arab countries that have undergone political change in the last five years, fought to regain its footing. In the meantime, millions like Zeinab and her two children who could not rely entirely on meager state pensions and nominal subsidies had to fend for themselves. What made these challenges even harder for the many demonstrators of the uprising is that they were given no answers. The current regime avoided any public engagement with the issues that drove Egyptians into the streets demanding better lives. Poverty seemed once more to be understood as the burden the Egyptian citizen needed to carry silently. Hardly any mention of the uprising—now reduced to a set of symbolic references—where almost six thousand Egyptians lost their lives (Human Rights Watch), no discussion of strategies, in fact no political participation would be welcome during these dire times of "rebuilding."

"Our efforts over the past six years are not futile, but it produced a new reality. We need your sincere efforts now to develop this state, because countries like Egypt don't develop overnight," proclaimed President Al-Sisi on the revolution's anniversary in 2017 (Daily News 2017). The general sentiment, however, only six years after those momentous events of revolution was to forget.

Memories of the 2011 uprising were hard to evoke in 2014, and even more so in 2015. Following the removal of Mohamed Morsi from office by the military, a wave of uncomfortable relief prevailed among many. While a large segment of the population was supportive of the removal of the MB (Muslim Brotherhood) government, others who supported the MB faced devastation and even tragedy. In 2013, security forces had opened fire on an MB encampment, killing more than eight hundred people.

In the months before the new presidential elections were to take place, I was in Cairo, still gathering data about women's participation in the revolution when, for the first time since the project began, I became aware that people were reluctant to talk. It was not simply that there was fear of divulging facts out of a sense of protectiveness of others, but there was a genuine pain in recalling the events that took the lives of so many while amounting to dire consequences to the democratic process.

Right before I left for the United States that spring of 2014, I stopped by several of my favorite bookstores to purchase a few books and tapes of revolution music to take back with me. When one store after another did not carry what I was looking for, I became curious and asked an attendant. After repeating my questions in three different ways, he finally came up to me and leaned over the counter, whispering, "ya, madam, we don't have these things anymore. Don't waste your time." He would not explain why he had tapes from the 1950s but not from 2011. "It just is." He shrugged. The incident was a harbinger of what was to come, as people's reactions to speaking of the revolution mirrored those to an invitation to a séance. While some people were reluctant to resurrect a ghost for fear of bringing back many painful memories, others reacted strongly against the idea because they were too practical to believe in ghosts and therefore preferred to think that ghosts were a myth. The latter preferred to move forward and not look back.

"But I Live in Imbaba": Hala

Thirty-three-year-old Hala, who described herself as a "journalist in training," appeared to belong to the group who were reluctant to dredge up old memories of the revolution. She too was initially very reluctant to talk to me that year and apologetically suggested I talk to someone else. "Others deserve more credit than me," she said, and after hearing this several times from various revolutionary women, I now understand to mean, "I don't know anything, I didn't do anything, so leave me alone." As our conversation over the phone progressed into an hour and a half, however, Hala sensed that I could perhaps be trusted not to be a government spy or a satellite TV anchor, or simply that I could be someone she could talk to. She finally agreed that I visit her where she lived at her parents' apartment. "But I live in Imbaba," she said hesitatingly, anticipating a reaction from me because of Imbaba's notoriety. I assured her that this was of no concern, and we set a time and date for me to visit with her.

Imbaba is a neighborhood that organically expanded out of what was originally rural land in the northern part of the governorate of Giza. Over the years, concrete buildings began appearing sporadically, despite the threat of legal action by the state. Consequently, the area that to this day is largely denied public services; has little or no access to hospitals and schools, running water, or electricity; and is home to a large population of unemployed youth. In the absence of state police and government regulation, Imbaba acquired the reputation of being an *'ashwa'ia* (shanty town or slum). Confrontations between *gama'at islamiyya* (Islamist groups) in Imbaba and the state in 1992 have framed the area in public discourse as the root of crime and extremism (Dorman and Stein 2013).

I recalled all this as I walked up the narrow alley to where Hala's family lived. It was difficult to imagine how people could thrive in an area where even breathing was hard to do from burning garbage—an activity residents of Imbaba had to resort to since they did not enjoy the privilege of a garbage-collection system. I continued looking for the building, but with no consistent house numbers and with all of the structures looking similar with unfinished exteriors and small entryways off of the dirt roads that have sprung out of necessity, I soon realized the futility of the task. But, as Egyptians say, "*illy yisal maytuhshi*," (one who asks will never get lost), and upon asking one of the neighbors, the correct direction was pointed out to me.

Hala had mentioned on the phone that she was seeing a doctor for intestinal problems, but I could not have predicted how thin and frail she looked. She stood in the doorway to greet me as I huffed up the stairs. When I asked how she was feeling, noting how thin and pale she looked, Hala said, "Thanks to God, I am better now. You should have seen me a few months ago. I looked like a mummy." Aside from having been struck by security police in her stomach as well as the middle of her back while she was taking pictures of a riot, Hala's condition had already been underway before then. Despite many visits to the doctor, they could not diagnose her symptoms of lack of sleep, lack of appetite, and inability to digest food. Hala believes she has post-traumatic stress disorder (PTSD). As it turns out as well, her parents and her male siblings were not very supportive of her activism or of her friends who came to visit. According to her, they believe she is a misguided innocent who was swayed and corrupted by others. Hala has learned not to talk about the revolution at home. She does not bring it up or comment when anyone else does. "It is better this way," she says in a voice that is not without regret.

We sat down in the first room off of the entryway on a U-shaped bench built against the blue washed walls. The upholstered cushions beneath us were covered in bright flowers that cheered up the dimly lit room. It was midday, so the wooden shutters were hinged, filtering a tiny stream of light into the small space.

A curtain was drawn across a side corridor that I guessed led to the kitchen, where her mother later emerged with a tray of tea. Hala said to me:

"You know, I had no interest in politics at all. I knew that there was corruption—you know it is not hard to tell people's interests from their actions, that's all. Then all of a sudden you wake up. This is not my country (you realize)! The most poignant scene: close to the Mehwar road where the epitome of corruption and the slums are. My heart aches as my eyes see the big advertisement signs showing the upscale places and the beauty of the sprawling green lawns. But the reality that exists literally right behind the large billboards is not like that. Those are the slums where we live."

Hala continued, pausing every now and then to sip her tea:

"We lost a lot of people in the revolution. To this day we do not know how many. Being politically active, doing anything remotely political at all can get you killed. I took pictures of a demonstration, they hit me and took my purse and my camera. He [a plainclothed policeman] had a gun in my face. I grabbed it and screamed in his face, "Kill me!" So, he hit me hard across the mouth, then in my stomach, and when I keeled over, he hit me in my back. This was in Ein Shams. Another time, I was in Mokattam, [a remote suburb in a mountainous area southeast of Cairo] reporting in front of the Muslim Brotherhood's headquarters. That year, journalists had come repeatedly under attack both by MB security people and by Morsi supporters. Even though the newspapers wrote about this and the union of journalists objected several times, this violence continued. The incident in Mokattam was on March 3 of 2013, a delegation of revolutionaries went there to object to the beatings of Mervat Musa and Ahmed Domah [who were staunchly opposed Morsi rule]. I was there too with several of my colleagues. The MB headquarters was cordoned off by men dressed in black outfits with facemasks, and they were carrying guns. They were wearing bulletproof vests. *Sobhan allah rabina yidihum il quwa*," she said sarcastically, shaking her head (meaning *may God give them strength*). "These men are supposedly officers in the police force, so why do they wear masks to hide their identities in public?"

A few days later, on June 30, 2013 a protesting mob attacked and set the Muslim Brotherhood headquarters in Mokattam on fire. The protest demanded the resignation of the then president Morsi. Following these violent demonstrations, a committee of revolutionaries and several political parties organized a million person march to impeach Mohamed Morsi because of his perceived failings as president.

That day in Mokattam, however, Hala and several others, including the activist Ahmed Domah (now in prison serving a life sentence) were beaten and threatened by the authorities. She was punched in the face by one of the masked "officers," and several others sustained injuries, which were duly reported in the news. "I had a breakdown after these two traumatic events," she continued. "I was wearing a veil; he [an officer] pulled it off my head and told me to go die. *"Istabahu dam ay had ghir il hara'ir.*" (They legalized the deaths of anyone other than the female cadets of the Muslim Brotherhood.) In Hala's view, the revolution revealed the underbelly of the oppressive apparatus of the state. "The revolution—God save it—exposed a lot of facts. Many masks have fallen."

Regular news of the deaths of young activists with whom Hala worked side by side prompted her to say, "Every drop of blood is valued in God's eyes, and it will not be spent in vain." The pain of rememory was written across her face like a dark cloud of sadness as she told me what had happened to young "Jika," seventeen-year-old Salah Gaber, who fell during a demonstration on Mohamed Mahmood Street in November 2012. Jika was shot in his head and remained on life support for five days until he was pronounced dead. Hala was in Mohamed Mahmood that day too, despite a recent operation. She was volunteering in the midan clinic where young Jika's bloodied body was carried in. Hala screamed in disbelief when she saw him—she had just been talking to him on the phone only a few hours before. The shock and loss of someone so young that she knew well shook Hala to the core, but these losses seemed to keep coming.

Now visibly shaken by her rememories, Hala stares out into space as if she could see these events before her very eyes. She pauses for some time. Tears well up in her eyes. She blinks them away. I do not interrupt her train of thought. Then she tells me about Al Husseini Abu Deif, who was a photojournalist who often worked with her on journalistic projects. An hour before he died, he approached her in the clinic that was set up in front of the El Ithadiya presidential palace, where intense protests against former president Morsi were taking place. Al Husseini asked Hala about the numbers of the injured, wrote it down, and left to report on new attacks on the protestors—part of a topic he was documenting for release that addressed human rights infractions during Mohamed Morsi's rule. He came back with a bullet that rendered him unconscious, and he too was transported to a hospital. His camera, with all the evidence he was gathering, was gone, according to Hala; someone had stolen it. "And there were others and others. Still, I did not witness the atrocities that others recounted. The seventy-two children who were slaughtered like chicken in Port Said and their friends who later died in the protests."

Hala was alluding to the mass murder of soccer fans of Al Ahly Club during a game in the city of Port Said. The perpetrators never came to light. The fans, many of whom were teenagers and college students, were reportedly trapped in the stadium as the gates were shut, preventing their escape. As the lights were dimmed, violence was unleashed. This horrific incident is often cited as an example of regime revenge against the Ultras who galvanized the protests in Tahrir Square during the first days of the revolution.

"God's wisdom. Ahmed Harara lost his eyes." Another pause, then, "Those deaths were messages from God to remind me, to remind us, to never forget the revolution." Harara is considered as an icon of the revolution because snipers shot both of his eyes on two separate occasions when he was protesting. The shots rendered him blind in both eyes. Hala leaned back and rested her head on the back of the sofa, her eyes staring out at the ceiling. She remained like this for several minutes. This was the point in our conversation when I realized that the memories of the loss and death she was resurrecting were no longer for my benefit. The rememories had brought back every feeling, every bit of pain. Still staring at the ceiling, it was as if she was seeing all the ghosts. She was processing what had happened perhaps this was part of her healing process. I like to think it was helping as I felt pangs of guilt at making Hala relive these terrible moments through my probing, however gentle I hoped I was being. I thanked her quietly as I shook her hand and quietly left.

The loss of human life hit many of the activists quite hard. The majority of the activists I interviewed, like Naglaa, Zeinab, and Hala, all had traumatic experiences with the death of loved ones, friends, and colleagues. What exacerbated the sense of deep loss was the growing realization over the last few years that the revolution and their sacrifices did not bring the changes that they had hoped. Corruption and lack of freedoms, in addition to the constant hike in prices, continue to be prevalent phenomena. These issues were an essential part of any conversation I had with my interviewees. While between 2011 and 2013, my interlocutors were somewhat hopeful and reflective about politics and where Egypt should be heading in the next years, between 2014 and 2015, most of my informants became either pessimistic about the future or seemed even reluctant to discuss the revolution at all.

"I Became Nabil": Attiya

There were still those who were neither pessimistic nor reluctant. Attiya, a young entrepreneur who started a hairstyling business, fell into this group. As she painted her life in optimistic terms, she also revealed another dimension to the complicated web that frames women's political participation: religion. Being a Coptic Christian, Attiya's hope to see equality between Muslims and non-Muslims and to feel safe running her business and seeing her husband's grocery shop thrive. But despite the state government's pledge to liberalize the market, it did not follow through with its promises of making the market safe from religious zealots bent on marginalizing minorities and limiting their access to resources. While for some, religion played a significant role that directly impacted the livelihoods of non-Muslim women, for others, dynamics brought about by socioeconomic status affected their lives more. Protestors who were economically and socially comfortable nevertheless suffered emotionally from the perceived failure of the revolution. Yet, unlike some of the women discussed thus far, their lives went on as they did before the revolution. They still went to work, got paid, and returned to comfortable suburban homes that were air-conditioned and had all the latest cable networks hooked to their flat TV screens.

Although she did not enjoy these comforts of suburban living, Attiya's one-bedroom apartment that she shared with her family in Shari' El Sudan in Mohandessein was close to one of Cairo's busiest commercial centers. This was good for her hairdressing business and her husband Yunis's grocery store. The couple were raising their son, George, and working hard to build a life in the urban capital. "I am a dreamer! And I am dreaming of a better Egypt." A better Egypt is what prompted this thirty-seven-year-old to take a bus to Tahrir Square on the twenty-fifth of January. "I was the only one in my family who went down [to Tahrir]. My mother nearly died of fright because of me. I would be in the revolution, and I would tell her, don't worry, this background noise is just the TV!"

Thinking of her family, Attiya shifts to describing her mother and her siblings. After giving birth to three girls, Attiya's mother finally had her wish, a son. Nabil was born to her mother when she was past her prime childbearing years, but she was so happy that she was finally "Om Nabil" that she distributed *sharbat* to the entire neighborhood. Not only did Nabil grow up to be handsome and smart, but he also became the perfect son, Attiya explained. When Nabil graduated from college studying commerce, a friend of his told him that he could find Nabil work abroad. Nabil was excited at the prospect because he always wanted to travel and to help his family as well. To their mother's chagrin, he left for Germany and remains there to this day. Nabil married a German woman and has three children. He came to visit a number of times, but he couldn't make up for his absence much. "So, in a way, I became Nabil. I took care of my mother when my father died, and I made sure that she doesn't need for anything. Nabil sends money from time to time, but it is my work that helps pay for my mother's medical bills and for whatever else she needs."

As Nabil left the family circle to pursue a life abroad, Attiya—the eldest daughter, who was never granted any of the privileges bestowed on her brother—became the sole breadwinner in her family. "I never went to high school. After middle school, my parents decided it was time for me as the eldest daughter to take care of the family and help my mother. We did not have much, but we lived in a tight-knit community of Coptic Christians in *al sa'eed* (Upper Egypt), whose lives revolved around the church. I missed all this when we moved to Cairo and we had to get used to the streets and the transportation." In Cairo, Attiya found herself under scrutiny as she commuted around the city in public transportation, often traveling from one end of the city to another. "I am not veiled and I don't wear long [robes]. In the metro, someone spit on me because my hair is not covered. In the microbus, Quran is playing really high, people stare at me. Back in our village, they paid people to grow their beards and wear *al niqab* [face-veil]. I would not be like that. I am free to be myself, but others do not think that way."

To Attiya, it seemed that although urban living offered her economic opportunity and the ability to build a new life as a wage earner with her husband, it still came with the challenge of having to live alongside a larger hegemonic Muslim population. What made this more challenging was the fact that she was also exposed to new forms of discrimination that she could somewhat avoid in her tight-knit community back in her village in Upper Egypt. Without the safety net of kin and neighbors, she felt vulnerable and exposed in Cairo.

Attiya met Yunis, whose family is also Coptic Christian from Upper Egypt. Like hers, his family moved to Cairo in the 1990s, looking for better work opportunities. At 10 to 15 percent of the population, Coptic Christians are the largest non-Muslim community in Egypt. Yet, these percentages are highly controversial, according to Mariz Tadros (2013), due to the government's lack of transparency in conducting and communicating a census. In 1972 a government census claimed that Copts made up 6.31 percent of the population of Egypt. A spokesman for the Coptic Church challenged that number by suggesting that Copts were 15 percent of the population (Nahdet Misr 2007). Copts have a long and ancient tradition in the country that goes back to the first emergence of Christianity in the region. In the last three decades, however, Coptic Christians have been caught in a tight vise between the state and extremist Islamic militants. Despite Attiya's previous experience of safety among her Coptic community, rural areas in Upper Egypt witnessed violence erupt over interfaith marriages and disputes over commercial interests. Several churches were burned down over the years. In 2011 the Church of the Martyrs in Alexandria was bombed, leaving twenty-one Coptic Christians dead and many hurt, signaling the growing inability of the state to prevail over sectarian violence.

Minorities in the developing world often attract the attention of western countries that adopt protective measures to preserve the human rights of marginalized communities. Marc Michael (2013) argues that western protective measures often prove detrimental to minorities, since western intervention exacerbates differences and magnifies social stigma (Michael 2011). Under neoliberal reforms, states withdraw from social services, thus allowing for the proliferation of charitable religious organizations that eventually challenge state authority and widen the gap between faith groups. Michael (ibid.) writes that the burgeoning of these organizations reinforced by imperial liberal discourse around religious minorities that need to be saved further increased the bifurcation of the population along religious lines.

In the case of Egypt, the state encouraged religious social endeavors, whether Christian or Muslim, and aside from its concern with political Islam, remained uninterested in the ramifications religious development had on national unity. State funding to schools and hospitals saw radical cuts largely as a consequence of structural adjustment policies, compelling each community to build their own.

Religious segregation became all too common as a result, so much so, in fact, that young schoolchildren grew up in religious privately run schools, where they had no opportunity to know or even interact with children of other faiths. In fact, Michael goes on to maintain that Mubarak's regime exploited the threat of sectarian strife to ameliorate its importance as peace and stability keeper. This backfired during the revolution, however, as the burning of churches and the targeting of Coptic Christians signaled the demise of state protection (ibid.).

The largest destruction of Coptic religious edifices took place during Mohamed Morsi's presidency, when about one hundred Christian structures ranging from churches to educational and commercial buildings were set on fire. In many locales, Muslim leaders and members of the community stepped in to help their Coptic neighbors during these horrific events. They helped cordon off a number of the remaining buildings to protect them from vandalism. Despite media attention to these events, however, the government at the time took little or no action to stop the anti-Coptic rhetoric (Egyptian Initiative for Human Rights 2013).

Recent violence against Attiya's community on October 9, 2011 (a day later remembered as "Bloody Sunday") on which twenty Copts were crushed to death, seven shot, and three hundred wounded during a peaceful march brings back memories of earlier events in 2000. During violent rioting in Al-Kosheh village, near Sohag in Upper Egypt, twenty Copts and one Muslim lost their lives, and many more were injured. All of the accused defendants, who happened to be Muslim, were acquitted, which to her meant that Coptic lives were easily dispensable in the eyes of her government. She linked these injustices Copts face to the larger corrupt system in the country that clamps down on human liberties and silences people's voices. An incident from the early days of the revolution where she said a cooperative community was beginning to develop among the demonstrators reminded her of this but also of the power of the people to support one another in the face of injustice.

That incident remained etched in Attiya's memory as an example of how communities should operate and the role Tahrir Square played as a space where this actually took place. An old man stood on a raised platform, calling out to whomever would listen, in the hope that someone could help:

> "In Mohamed Mahmood Street [off of Tahrir, where a number of deadly clashes erupted between security police and the protestors], a man started calling out at the top of his voice so people could hear his problem. He said that he was seventy years old and that he used to own a piece of land on which he built a house. One day, another man seized it, claiming to hold rights over the property. The old man lost his house *and* his land, and now he wants justice. He asked people to help him if they have experience with the law. People often did things like that. They told their stories and the problems that brought them to Tahrir Square. As Copts, we also experience such injustice. My brother-in-law

owns a jewelry store next to a church. The Muslim Brotherhood stormed the church and killed the janitor, the altar man, and set the place on fire. We heard the news on the net [Facebook], and I ran to the church because I was also worried that they would destroy my brother-in-law's nearby shop if they knew he was a Copt. When I arrived, I found that the police had already removed the bodies and locked the church doors. About ten to fifteen days later, I went to see the church, and to my dismay saw all its papers and ancient icons burnt to ashes. But this year [2015], the army took over the rebuilding, and the church is even better and nicer than it was before."

Before we both stood up to leave, Attiya's parting note was an earnest wish. "In Tahrir during the first eighteen days, the cross and the crescent were often raised over the heads of the protestors. I want so much to see those in reality and not just for decoration," said Attiya.

Something about that wish made me pause. It captured the spirit of the revolution in my conversations with the revolutionary women I grew to know. The idealism and the strong conviction in a better future—the dream that still captured the imagination—was the driving force for so many of them. No matter what happened after this, what pressures many of them will be exposed to—some were to end up in jail, others arrested and released—these dreams of a better tomorrow would hopefully prevail.

Despite the struggle in Attiya's life and the precariousness of her livelihood and that of her family, her optimism and her belief in herself as an agent of change were tremendously inspiring. I turn now to those women whose livelihood was directly threatened by the privatization of state-run industries, to see how they fared under deregulation and what their stories can tell us about the uprising and the labor history behind it. These were the women laborers of the textile factories.

Women Factory Workers, Labor Mobilization, and the Revolution

Many have now heard of Israa Abdelfattah and Asmaa Mahfouz, the two young women who, with the help of social media, sparked the beginnings of the January 25 revolution in Egypt. They raised awareness on Facebook about the plight of Egypt's population, they mobilized viewers on YouTube, and drew on cultural and religious idioms to galvanize the revolt of January 25. Yet, few have paid attention to the initial purpose that motivated these so-called "Facebook girls." Gendered media commentary about these two young women often diluted their contributions and attempted to expose them as "fakes" who were corrupt. Israa had cofounded the April 6th group on Facebook in 2008 with Ahmed Maher to incite public support of the labor strikes in the industrial town of al Mahalla Al Kobra, and Asmaa was a member of the same group. The momentum that grew out of their mobilizing efforts and culminated with the 2011 Egyptian revolt of

January 25 had originally organized around the labor movement and in particular the labor strikes. A group of three thousand women mobilized these strikes
three years before in the industrial city of al Mahalla Al Kobra (Beinin and
Hamalawy 2007).

In factory cities such as Mansoura and Al Mahalla Al Kubra, women industrial workers were at the forefront of the mass strikes that exerted the final pressure on the former Mubarak regime to step down. Comprising nearly 24.1 percent
of Egypt's labor force in 2014 (World Bank), women workers hold a variety of
jobs in various sectors of employment. Women factory workers are 43 percent of
those who are employed on a national level (BSR 2010). They have emerged as a
powerful, organized, and highly active group to be reckoned with in the country.
They participated in large numbers in mass strikes, in the occupation of factory
floors, and in widespread demonstrations. Their labor militancy led to the free
unionization of labor for the first time and played a central role in negotiations
for better employment conditions. The site of some of the most militant demonstrations and visible participation for women is the rural industrial city of Al
Mahalla Al Kobra, where several labor uprisings initiated countrywide strikes
since 2006. There, women played a critical role in the mobilization of labor, particularly at the public-sector textile factory of Misr Spinning and Weaving Company (MSWC), *shirket al ghazl wal naseeg* or *ghazl al mahalla* its shortened form.

The role of women's activism in factory labor militancy is of prime importance for the women's rights movement in the country. Women's issues and
demands for equitable treatment by the law regarding access to resources, political participation, and personal status laws have been stalled since the end of the
initial revolts in Tahrir that saw the toppling of Mubarak's regime. This is despite
their impressive turnout, even under fire. With the initial crisis averted, women
have had to protest against their mistreatment by the armed forces and against
sexual harassment in Tahrir. As they regrouped under the umbrella of the Egyptian Feminist Union (EFU) in October 2011, their movement is still limited in its
ability to mobilize and raise awareness among Egyptian women in rural areas.
In my view, women labor activists are central to bridging the gap between the
feminist-leaning urban women's groups and their rural counterparts, thus creating a unified feminist front. Women laborers, though, are careful to distance
themselves from feminism, but that does not stop them from demanding equal
pay. "We don't want anything of the sort [feminist demands], we just want to
have a good salary and a decent life for both of us, women and men," Soad, a
twenty-nine-year-old labor activist told a reporter in 2008 (Morsi 2008). Women
labor activists also have the capability to spur the feminist movement in Egypt
forward because of their labor militancy and experience with labor activism and
unionizing struggles. Several women leadership figures are among those who
have led campaigns and labor strikes. And they have forged alliances and created

networks of support for themselves that can firmly position women's rights on the political agenda in the country despite the challenges. Under the right circumstance, these women labor militants have the potential of invigorating the momentum of Egypt's feminist movement.

Women's labor militancy efforts merit more consideration than they have been afforded to date. By contrast to the large corpus of work dealing with women's labor activism in the developing world such as in Latin America (Brickner 2006; French and James, ed. 1997), Asia (Ong 2010; Barraclough and Faison 2009; Silvey 2003 and others) and Africa (Berger 1992; Meer 1991; Mukurasi 1991 and others), very little attention has been afforded to labor movements in Arab and Middle Eastern societies, with no known feminist or anthropological attention given to women's participation in the labor movement to date. In what follows, I turn to a discussion of the history of women's industrial work and of al Mahalla al Kubra, the main center of labor militancy and the leading textile industrial capital in Egypt.

Home to the oldest as well as largest government sector textile company, Al Mahalla Al Kobra is situated in the middle of the agricultural Egyptian Delta in the governorate of Gharbiyya, where the population was 442,958 in 2006. Originally called the Egyptian Company for Spinning and Weaving in Al-Mahalla Al-Kobra, the "Misr Spinning and Weaving Company" located in the city today employs roughly twenty-seven thousand workers, down from the forty thousand of its heyday. The impressive industrial complex was built by economic reformer Talaat Harb in the neoclassical style of the early 1920s and is considered by many to be one of the core locations that served as a catalyst for the Egyptian revolt of January 25.

What started out as a model of twentieth century industrial production, down to the design of neighboring communities of workers, recreational facilities, and state-of-the-art assembly lines, the textile mill of Mahalla went from being a legend to becoming a symbol of the exploitation of thousands. The processes of liberalization and privatization of the 1990s that continue to this day incited thirty-five hundred to four thousand planned strikes in Egypt in recent history (Beinin 2011). Egypt signed the Economic Reform and Structural Adjustment Program (ERSAP) with the International Monetary Fund (IMF) and World Bank, to privatize 314 publicly owned businesses in 1991. Within the span of ten years, more than 60 percent of Egypt's public sector became privatized. The changes that followed were unbearably difficult to handle for the already economically disadvantaged working class. Under the public sector, workers had enjoyed job security, pensions, free health benefits, and a small but steady income in bonuses. President Nasser had implemented substantial reforms to labor legislation (Laws 317, 318, and 319 of December 1952). This legislation made layoffs more difficult and improved fringe benefits. It also imposed compulsory arbitration on all labor disputes and banned strikes. Workers were adequately compensated and were given annual bonuses and enjoyed benefits. Increased privatization, however, threw the factory workers at the mercy of unscrupulous Egyptian and international businessmen who now enjoyed free rein to layoffs and putting workers on temporary work contracts making firing them easy and more frequent.

The neoliberalization of the Egyptian industrial sector was also gendered. Like many developing regions around the world, the growing poverty of women impacted by privatization and structural adjustment in Egypt was exploited by the new capitalist global world order. As poverty increases, more women are forced to seek jobs at industrial plants that hire women on a temporary basis, pay them lower wages than men, and offer no health or job insurance. In Egypt, the percentage of women workers more than doubled from 10.9 percent in 1981 (917,000) to 22.34 percent in 2006 (5.11 million), according to the Central Agency for Public Mobilization and Statistics (Shukr Allah 2006 in Beinin 2011). These new neoliberal adjustments also reinforced old gender ideologies around the sexual division of labor. In other instances, global capital drew upon gendered discourses that emphasized women's dexterity, nimbleness, and "natural propensity" for monotonous work (Salzinger 2003). In short, as scholars argue, these neoliberalizing measures contributed to a worldwide phenomenon of the feminization of poverty. In Egypt, woman-headed households in 2008 increased to 13.4 percent from 11.8 percent in 1992 (Index Mundi 2012). While 36 percent of woman-headed households are poor, only 28 percent of households headed by men are poor (IFAD).

It is therefore not surprising that on December 7, 2006, having been denied a long-anticipated two-month bonus publicly promised by Egyptian Prime Minister Ahmed Nazif, three thousand women workers left their garment-making stations at Misr Spinning and Weaving Company in Mahalla. As they walked over to the men's spinning quarters, they chanted, "Here are the women. Where are the men?" This was the event that marked the beginning of more than seven hundred incidents of industrial action from this factory alone that culminated with the April 6 mass strike of 2008. When the men joined, they marched down to the square with ten thousand demonstrators, shouting for their rights. Several representatives attempted to reason with the workers, but the women were adamant. Four days later, the management came back with concessions, and the workers' bonuses were paid.

This was a turning point for women's labor activism. One of the leaders of the strike, Mohamed Attar recalled with awe in his voice in an interview to Al Jazeera (2012), "The women almost tore apart every representative from management who came to negotiate." One of the union leaders who were the first to stand up and march to the men's sector at Mahalla was forty-four-year-old Wedad el Demerdash. She is the mother of four, two of whom are already in college. Working at the Mills for more than twenty-eight years and being a union leader had taught Wedad a lot. Yet, as she explains on Al Jazeera's network (ibid.), she never thought of herself as a leader.

> I am a worker like everybody else, but I have this tendency to be a bit outspoken sometimes. I don't really know why or how, but if I see someone unjustly treated, I just act out of habit. I stand up. Yes, I interfere but I feel like it is my duty to ask questions, to find out who did what and who deserves what. If one of my female co-workers is harshly reprimanded by the male supervisor, I am there, asking questions. I can't help it; it is part of my nature.

It was Wedad who helped organize the first strike by her fellow workers in December 2006. The strike and its successful outcome were the impetus behind a nationwide strike on April 6, 2008. These events were the inspiration that brought together the 6th of April Facebook group, Israa Abdelfattah and Asmaa Mahfouz. The latter was the subject of a YouTube video that went viral and is considered to be one of the battle cries of the January 25 revolution. In Mahalla, where the first sparks for these ensuing events took place, Wedad el Demerdash rallied the men of the mill to join the strike, she was one who first chanted "Here are the women! Where are the men?" until the men were shamed into joining them. And the rest is history.

Wedad strongly believes in fostering solidarity among the workers. She tells the reporter she has stood by many people in her life and that it has often put her in difficult situations, but she would do it again. She even suffered the consequences of it, but that never stopped her from being the person she is. Nevertheless, she says, we need to learn to stand up for justice and break the silence. In her case, she has continued to be vocal about labor rights, especially because she feels that women are not treated equitably.

As in the case of many working women in Egypt, the changing gender roles often has little impact on gender ideology. She describes her day as a series of chores and responsibilities that continue relentlessly from 6:00 a.m. when she wakes up to the time it takes her to get her younger children ready for school and then to go to work. At the factory, she works behind the machine as a garment worker for an eight-hour shift. Though she does not complain, she points out that she actually works a two-shift day, one at work and one at home. "My husband doesn't help with anything. He sits there and asks for tea, even though it is so easy to make tea. He neither cooks nor cleans nor takes the kids to school." Then she says with a conspiratorial tone as her eyes gleam with a humor, "Men have this tendency to be a little selfish. That is the way they are."

Wedad's life and gender beliefs are certainly not much different from many women in Egypt. Yet, her husband, she recounts, became supportive of her activism when he saw that it brought positive results. He was not sure in the beginning that his wife should get "mixed up" in the strikes. But, like Wedad, he knows how hard it is to make ends meet, especially with four children. She agrees it is indeed very hard. "We couldn't afford to feed our children well. I cannot even buy meat for them."

For low-income Egyptians, the cost of buying meat protein has become quite high in the last few years. Being able to afford buying beef is an important indicator of the economic level of the family. Wedad sees herself and her family as middle class, yet they do not enjoy the things that middle families should have, she says. Many women industrial workers like her have had a taste of injustice under the privatization policies of the former Mubarak regime. Yet, it is the Mansoura-España plant's garment workers who felt the worse brunt of it. When their only source of livelihood threatened to shut down after a series of financial problems, the factory workers, 75 percent of whom are women, rallied together to come up with a plan to ensure that their late bonuses and backed-up salaries would not be lost.

By contrast to Misr Spinning and Weaving, the Mansoura-España company was a privately owned factory of only about three hundred workers. Yet Mansoura, a smaller city than Mahalla on the western branch of the Delta in Northern Egypt, witnessed a two-month sit-in workers' occupation of the plant that began almost five months after the strike in Mahalla ended. Emboldened by the positive outcome in Mahalla, the women workers at Mansoura-España refused to budge when they learned that the United Bank was liquidating the firm with little or no compensation to the workers, even though management owed them bonuses that in some cases were seven years old.

A number of the women brought their children with them during the sit-in; others took breaks to go home to check on their children and then went back to sleep on the factory floor. "You might think that this is easy for us if you do not understand our culture," said Nawal, "but for a woman like me to sleep on the floor next to strange men, that is impossible here! Yet, my family lets me because they know that I just want what has been taken from me, my livelihood." Nawal, a young, unmarried woman of twenty, recounted how her family initially refused to allow her to participate in the sit-in, but when a number of her colleagues went to her home to explain to them what they were doing, her parents budged.

Other women described how hard it was to spend hours on the hard floor of the factory and be away from their husbands and families. "But my husband had to understand. He knows we cannot feed our children if I do not get paid!" said another woman.

In the Mansoura-España Company, the younger women were paid less than twenty-three dollars a month. The joint-venture management set out to hire what they had perceived to be younger, more pliable women. Neoliberal capitalist administrations commonly apply already-entrenched patriarchal household politics to exploit the cheap labor and "docility" of their female workers (Salzinger 2003). Yet, they could not have bargained for what they got. As the days dragged on in Mansoura, the women's resolve did not waver under management harassment, police intimidation (when some of them were accused of prostitution), and the sheer lack of food and rest. Five women activists, Soad Mamdouh, Soad Salama, Sabreen Sabri, Hoda Said, and Nermin Abbas, and their male colleague Mohsen el-Shaer were fired and turned over to the local authorities (Beinin 2011).

At the end of the two-month occupation of the factory, management and government bank officials finally relented. An agreement was signed with the workers' representatives whereby they were promised the restoration of their bonuses and payment for the duration of the strike. This was yet another great stroke of good fortune for industrial workers denied their basic rights. But this was an even bigger event for women labor militants who, for two months, sustained a sit-in of such proportions under a hostile management and intimidating circumstances.

In Mahalla in July 2012, twenty thousand workers at MSWC (Misr Spinning and Weaving Company) *ghazl al mahalla* went on a strike once more to ask for a list of demands. These demands were centered on previously promised increases in company shares, retirement bonuses, and a minimum wage of fifteen hundred Egyptian pounds (approximately $187). The news traveled fast, and Twitter picked it up with a hashtag, #Egyworkers and #Mahalla. Their partial demands were met on November 12, 2012. The workers stated that September 2013 would mark yet another strike if their demands remained unmet.

In much of what followed the revolution of January 25, the role of militant factory workers and the women who mobilized them seem all but forgotten. Women industrial workers who challenged traditional gender norms and led the initial strikes work to gain a place in the newly formed unions so they can be well represented in decision-making processes. During a visit to Egypt, former American president Jimmy Carter met with Wedad el Demerdash and asked her if she was pleased with the progress after the revolution. She responded that in some instances, yes, there were some improvements and gains for members of the labor force. They can now speak freely in the unions, and they have had a few of their rights restored. Overall, however, Wedad was not so positive. Despite these small gains for Egypt's workers, not much has changed for them. They still contend with minimum pay and insignificant bonuses. What makes matters worse for the workers is that they are told that strikes are harmful to Egypt because the economy is going through a difficult time (The Elders 2012).

Wedad continues to lead in the workers' unions, and she has become somewhat of a public figure. She believes in working for the ultimate good, Egypt and the Egyptian people. Yet, her views tend to be critical of the protests in Tahrir. The time for the protests, in her opinion, has passed. For her, it is time for action.

> "All these 'revolutionaries' who called for the strike have long forgotten after the revolution about their own people and their much-needed role on the ground [in Mahalla]. Workers belong to their factories and among their fellow workers, not in Tahrir, nor in some Cairo meetings almost 100 kilometers away." She continued, "We know exactly when to start a strike, how to put it together, and when to put it on hold. But no one, not even us leaders of the workers' movement, can get workers to go on a strike without a convincing case and demands. And now is just not the time. The average people won't take our side, and neither can the economy take it. We, the middle class, are the most to get hurt by the economy when it strikes." (Etrebi and LeVine 2012)

After leading a wave of strikes for seven years, the city of Mahalla Al Kobra's textile workers' demands for wage increases were met on November 11, 2012. Although women were an integral part of this labor organizing, women's right for nondiscriminatory wage labor is yet to be granted. Women's labor activism will continue until all their rights are met. The question remains, however, whether women's labor militancy will collaborate with the women's rights groups in Egypt that are strongly challenged by patriarchal values. Class, economic issues, and the distance from urban centers will also prove a challenge. Though if women leaders like Wedad keep gaining support and respect, they can be placed on the path to government and to greater benefits for women's issues in the country.

While structural adjustment policies (SAPs) of deregulation brought a variety of challenges to women laborers and women like Om Mohamed, Naglaa, and Attiya, there were a few revolutionary women whose experiences offered a different perspective. Samya and May are two very different women whose stories I share below. One comes from the privileged upper class and the other from an upper-middle-class background. Their stories of personal success and growth through the neoliberal system are in stark contrast not just to the struggling working class but also to the factory workers and labor activists from industrial cities who learned the hard way how to fight the injustice of deregulating policies and systems.

Tapping into the Neoliberal Machine: Samya

Among the young entrepreneurial women who participated in the uprisings is one who stood out from most. Samya had just turned thirty and was at the height of her successful career in a media production company in Zamalek, an affluent neighborhood in Cairo. We decided to meet close to her office, as she mentioned that her work schedule was too busy to allow her to drive anywhere. She suggested a newly opened café that served sushi, right in front of the Gezira Club, a membership-only sports club near her workplace. She motioned me to follow her to her favorite table in the back, where we would not be interrupted, and ordered her lunch, quickly glancing at her wristwatch as she did so.

Samya talked fast and ate fast, and I had to make an effort to keep up with her thoughts, which darted all over the place. "I have ADHD. Do you know what that is?" she asked.

"Attention-deficit hyperactive disorder," I replied.

"This is a common diagnosis of children and sometimes adults who have difficulty focusing and are often hyperactive," Samya explained, mentioning that she is too hyper for most people. Her behavior is often viewed in society as unladylike. Her mother, with whom she currently lives, advises her to try to tone it down a bit because no one wants to marry a hyper girl. As I looked across from her, I found that concern hard to imagine, since Samya was an unmistakably bright and especially attractive young woman. But she assured me she had no prospects in the marital department since she broke up with her fiancé of one year. She worked too long and too hard, so all she could do after work was to have a drink, watch some TV, and fall asleep.

"First off, you should know that my father was a successful businessman until he was accused of a crime and put in jail. He is now retired and divorced from my mother. She is the office director at a multibillion-dollar corporation. So, yes, I am privileged, but I am not embarrassed or apologetic about it because it is really what you do with it that counts. I am trying to improve myself as a person and give back to my community. The sky is the limit!" she said. "Maybe I could get a scholarship in Harvard. Why not? I could run the government one day or work in the UN. I have already worked with several agencies that work to improve women's status. So, that might be where I will concentrate my efforts."

She went on, "I have a master's degree in the arts." Earlier, Samya had started work as a seventeen-year-old after her father was arrested for alleged shady business deals. The big company that employed her mother offered her a job as an office administrator. She juggled school and work and still did well with her high school exams. When she graduated, she was offered a permanent position and a "real salary" as she puts it. "It was the best time of my life! I felt empowered and confident. This was a wonderful testimony to my abilities at a young age." This offer indeed pushed Samya into the world of production and finance. She mentioned the important people she met, many of whom are celebrities like Queen Ranya of Jordan and Prince Charles. Since then, she has also worked to raise awareness of women's issues in Egypt. As a women's rights advocate, she was invited to many conferences in Europe to give talks about sexual harassment prevention and the topic of girls' education—causes in which she has invested time and energy.

Her boundless energy and quick mind were infectious, but how did she embark on all these projects while working full time and going to graduate school? Samya explains this by saying that she has a vision and determination. This is her account, mostly in English, of how her nonprofit organization to help sexual harassment victims came into being:

> I was not originally an activist, nor was I involved politically. I was just a corporate-trained employee, but something happened one day that changed all that. I went down to Tahrir on the eleventh day of the revolution. It was one of the happiest days of my life, full of a sense of adventure that shaped a lot of things for me. This was history. People were in a coma before, a collective coma. Every single aspect of Egyptian life filled me with despair. Cairo zaps your energy. People had zero dignity. Cities like New York give you energy. Generally, in Egypt no one was happy; we were getting ripped off by the state.

Just then, Samya's lunch appeared, neatly rolled sushi on a rectangular platter. Using her chopsticks, she deftly maneuvered the tiny rolls as she articulated her thoughts and, between bites—since she was in a hurry—she continued, "Tahrir was a space that was very special to me. AUC [the American University in Cairo], the German School, the epicenter of the revolution was not the suburbs. I live in Dokki. I feel that the seeds of revolt were *always there* (in me), but the seed was sown that very first day."

She described the feeling of solidarity and belonging that prevailed in the midan. Samya rarely experienced this on the streets and particularly in this very neighborhood of Cairo, where young women are often the object of catcalls and even harassment.

> People were high-fiving me on the bridge [*Kasr al Nil* Bridge] and talking to me like I was their long-lost friend. And truthfully, I felt I knew each one. As we inched into the square itself however, I suddenly found myself separated from my companions. Suddenly, I had a sinking feeling, remembering Lara Logan who was sexually assaulted here. What if the same thing happened to me? Luckily, one of my male friends snatched me from the middle of a circle of men and took me away to safety. But that memory stayed with me.

Lara Logan was brutally assaulted by a mob in February 2011, only a few weeks after the uprising toppled Hosni Mubarak's government. Her story went viral amid much controversy. She was rescued by a group of women who extricated her from the midst of the violence and away to safety.

Samya continued to describe how a few days after she had heard about Logan, she desperately wanted to join the protests, but fear held her back:

> "I was at the office by myself, knowing that Tahrir Square is full of people trying to do what I always wanted to do: change things for the better. A friend of mine was supposed to go with me, but he canceled at the last minute. There was nothing more that I wanted to do than to be in Tahrir at this moment. But here I was, fully prepared in protest dress." She explained that this consisted

of loose jeans, Converse shoes, and a long blouse. "But I was unable to go out and voice my opinion because I was afraid. I was terrified of the idea of going to voice my support of the revolution because I was a woman and liable to be harassed. My paralysis was almost physical."

As Samya kept thinking about this paralyzing fear of being in public to exercise her rights to political participation, she realized that these rights have been taken away from her by sexual harassers. "I thought, if only I had a bodyguard . . . and then, I literally sat up at the thought, grabbed my ATM card, and ran down to the bank."

She withdrew a thousand dollars. A plan was taking shape in her mind. She began tweeting: "Wanted: Individuals able to protect and intervene on behalf of women in Tahrir." Within the first day, she had a thousand followers. She bought special vests, named her NGO, and eventually began training two hundred volunteers, who started patrolling the square during protests. "It was the best money I have ever spent!" she exclaimed. "It is amazing how the project just rolled and was so successful. The women we helped save from sexual harassment were many. Their stories were often very traumatic, but what was important is that we made the square safe, so women can be present without fear." The press got wind of the story and came down to Tahrir to interview her and her crew. The story went viral. According to Samya, she was also interviewed by eight doctoral students who were interested in finding out more about her NGO.

"It is a very sexy story, but the story has moved on." Eventually, she came to the conclusion that she did not want to be identified with the NGO and that running it was not her calling. She rejected the "celebrification of activism" (her own words) by which individuals involved in activism become media stars, so she handed over the reins to one of the dedicated people who worked with her. Now she just follows their progress from afar.

Samya's sensibilities and choices, her journey in life were of particular interest, for she represented in many ways the privileged elite, yet not completely. She was more involved and aware than most and was even critical of those who "just consume and look the part." On the other hand, she was also critical of the left, and she did not approve of radical feminists. During the revolution, Samya notes that there were "a lot of upper-class Egyptian dummies with their designer handbags who picked up causes and thought they could make a difference." Clearly, she set herself apart from that crowd, because she saw herself as someone who was a serious entrepreneur, not just a consumer. Listening to her speak, it was clear that Samya was fiercely independent. To her, the individual is solely responsible for the conditions in which he or she lives. She did not have much to say about politics or how things should change. Hers was not a vision that rejected capitalist ventures exploiting the poor, nor was her problem with deregulation and the struggles of the masses. No, Samya was invested in the ideals of the neoliberal market of free entrepreneurship and free trade. However, and here too is where Samya's neoliberal background informs her understanding, she was careful to make a clear distinction between herself and other revolutionaries in Tahrir. "I am not a revolutionary, nor am I an activist. I did activism while working full time. I help people in my own way. I help people by providing opportunities for work and safe living." Her emphasis on working full time and activism being a part-time occupation is significant. Here, she clarifies what her goals are, to "help people by providing *opportunities for work and safe living*" (emphasis mine). Significantly, neoliberal systems promise these two exact essential factors for free-trading societies: opportunities and safety. David Harvey's treatise on neoliberalism is effusive on these principles, as neoliberal governments are based upon providing safety and ensuring the protection of private property and entrepreneurship.

Samya kept making the constant statement that she is *not* a revolutionary—not because she thinks revolutionaries are ineffective or blinded by their ideals, but because she sees herself as a pragmatist. She is someone who identifies what needs to be done and does it. Calling herself a revolutionary or labeling herself as this or that is therefore irrelevant to her. She does not need a revolution to tell her what to do or to motivate her to take action. This becomes clearer as she discusses feminism. "I am moved by feminism, but more of the mainstream kind. The radical militant kind where women walk around *menkushin* [with messy hair] or the leftist anticapitalist kind do not appeal to me." Her statement is quite enlightening then because Samya is not someone who will be boxed in any kind of militancy—whether feminist or leftist. Describing radical feminists as menkushin was meant as a joke, but she was aware that she was typecasting radical feminists as women with messy hair. But why this particular descriptive? Samya herself was very well coiffed with styled hair and had a careful and professional attire. It was obvious to see that she expertly conformed to corporate dress code expectations, whereas the radical women she described were the polar opposite. Even though Samya pursued feminist goals in her activism, her neoliberal values did not allow her to project them on her appearance.

Though she never actually defined herself as a capitalist or as a neoliberal subject, working for one of the largest corporations in the Middle East since she was seventeen years old must have influenced her views about the worlds of finance and politics. Neoliberalism is not simply an economic agenda but is a sociopolitical one as well. Samya grew up in a family that built itself through access to privilege and business opportunities. "Unapologetically" positioned as a wealthy upper-class young woman, Samya acquired an education and employment experience that propelled her upward. Despite these advantages brought about by social and economic capital, there were hardships and challenges.

Seeing her father lose his business and spend time in jail was not an easy thing to face as a young girl. Her resilience in facing the stigma that came with that was remarkable. She worked full time as she obtained her university degree, leaving her with no time to enjoy her college life—itself a privileged concept.

Interestingly, however, Samya sets herself apart from the "presidential milieu" that was composed before the revolution of the wealthy elite who surrounded Mubarak's family. "I am also not part of the retinue of Susan Mubarak [the former First Lady], nor am I part of the *felool* [meaning *remnants* of the old regime]." Then she added with a wry sense of humor, "Those women who roam the Marriott Hotel in the mornings for coffee, wearing their latest fashions. They're so easily read. The Egyptian stereotype of the affluent 'soccer mom.'" Her derision, of course, is not only directed at the fact that these women conform to western stereotypes of the suburban modern mother, nor because Samya sees them as of a different generation, since she herself had just turned thirty. This derision is, I am assuming, the product of Samya's neoliberal view of the world. This world in which her education, the work opportunities she has been afforded, her career achievements, and her visibility both locally and abroad underscore her individuality and work trajectory over more traditional ways of being that emphasize women's domestic and social roles in Egypt. Being trained as "a corporate employee," as she puts it, played a definitive role in Samya's story that was predictably picked up by the media. As her numerous international speaking engagements also attest to, she became quite a popular icon of the Egyptian uprising and often stood for the female face of the Arab Spring as a whole. Samya epitomized the success of the neoliberal subject.

When she eventually decided to step down and hand over the sexual harassment prevention NGO to a friend who lived in an apartment in Tahrir, she turned to her own work once more. Despite this, she continues to support any effort to improve women's lives. "I hope that Egypt will be a better place for women, for minorities, that tolerance would prevail. I hope that the government will treat its citizens correctly and that democracy will dictate the interactions between the state and its people. I wish for equality between men and women. This is a human rights issue."

"I Was Depressed from Everything That Was Happening": May

Samya's hopes are shared by millions of other Egyptian women. Women who may not describe themselves in a similar way or share her privileges in life but who nevertheless share her dedication and commitment to being successful individuals. May was an activist who used her skills as an organizer and administrator at a famous Red Sea resort owned by an international corporation to mobilize protesters and organize demonstrations. At forty years old, she is a revolutionary woman with a big heart, who is respected by many. May lived in a now-urbanized suburb of Cairo, where turn-of-the-century architectural masterpieces that had once adorned the neighborhood streets and entertained heads of state were turned into schools and banks, engulfed by high risers and endless streams of traffic. Her apartment was located on an upper story of an old Art Deco building that, like its neighboring palaces, had seen better days. May was a petite blonde woman who chain-smoked and drank Turkish coffee constantly. She was a source of numerous anecdotes from the midan and was, in her own right, a superb ethnographer.

May's memories of Tahrir during the first eighteen days of the revolt were still vivid when I met her in 2013:

> Yes, the square was socially segregated, but not completely. People formed casual groups based on their neighborhoods. Since they often marched to the midan together, the groups more or less stayed together. But, and here is the important thing, we interacted with each other. We networked and shared food and drink and gathered medical supplies for the wounded. Also, activities brought everyone together. Tahrir Cinema was one important event that created a community in the midan. It started at 7 p.m., often regularly. They showed all kinds of films but mostly those that explained the events, raised awareness of the political condition, and covered the news.

May continued to describe the unifying experiences that brought people together through shared experience: "We saw nobility among the most destitute of people. Giving. Behaviors among Egyptians we never thought possible. When you entered the midan, you were received with chants, *ahlan ahlan bil thowwar.* Welcome, welcome to the revolutionaries." What left an indelible impression on May was the feeling of belonging to something bigger than herself. The people in the square were representative of Egyptian society. There were the craftsmen, the doctors, and the millionaires. She described "*geziret al farafeer,*" where you could buy coffee or tea and even shop the stall boutiques. The garden in front of the towering *mogama'* building was occupied by "*al ghalaba,*" or the poor.

But then there was the trauma:

"When the shooting in Mohamed Mahmood [Street] began, we rushed over to the young kids who were confronting the *dakhliyaa* [Internal Security] forces, gave them liquids and face masks." May described the interactions with a few of the young kids who refused to let the upper-class women go into Mohamed Mahmood Street. "They screamed at us, 'No! No! We can't let you go there. You are the educated. We can die, *mish mohim* [not important].'" With her eyes welling up with tears at the memory, she continued, "When they fell in Mohamed Mahmood, we would go and get them or drag them by their hands. You could not believe that these could be the hands of a child" (because they were so calloused from work).

The most frightful scenes May has witnessed were at the *mashraha*, the morgue next to Qasr el Einy Street, where all the dead bodies were taken. She was taking count of the dead as part of an effort to record the casualties, since government announcements were deliberately minimizing the extent of the violence against the revolutionaries. At the mashraha, she saw for the very first time the extent of human sacrifice and suffering that can motivate young people to put their lives on the line and lose them. "The bodies that had fallen during the protests were cramped in drawers. There was not enough space to keep them properly labeled or anything. One I could see was completely charred by a fire. It was the body of an eighteen-year-old boy whose brother was there to receive it. The family had no money to give him a proper burial."

She had a lot to say about the experiences she had shared with others in the square, "We saw incredible injustice and incredible beauty. We saw a group of elderly men, *al shuyukh* go to *al dakhliya* to ask them to stop the violence. They came back beaten up and broken. We walked in the protests that were organized against the beating of women in Tahrir, *banat masr khat ahmar* [Egypt's young women are a red line]. Then there were the young teenage girls who cooked hot soup to share with the protestors at three in the morning to keep them warm. Nazli Hussein, who was arrested unfairly, a young, defenseless girl."

Clearly, May was profoundly impacted by the revolution. Her reactions to the events that took place in Tahrir Square and elsewhere were also born out of a deep concern with the conditions of injustice and lack of freedoms in the country. "Before the twenty-fifth of January, I was addicted to reading the newspapers every day. I would break down every time from what was happening in this country. Emad el Kabir, a microbus driver who was beaten and sodomized with a broomstick. His abuse was filmed and posted on YouTube to humiliate him forever. Khaled Said, the young blogger who was beaten to death beyond recognition in broad daylight! The burning of the Church of the Martyrs on January 1, 2011. The elections, when they announced Mubarak's victory with a Photoshopped picture. I was depressed from everything that was happening."

At the time, May was working in the tourism industry but had begun to think that she would like to try to start her own business. Advertising was a creative field that appeared to her less likely to be affected if Egyptian tourism were to decline due to terrorism. It was also a field that she had studied at the university, and she had friends who were willing to help her get started. After researching the idea extensively and bringing in experts who were ready to lend a hand, she realized that before she even could start her applications, she needed security clearance. May was taken aback by this. Why would an advertising company require security clearance? The more she tried to answer that question, the more she became frustrated and angry that the state should subject her creative idea to such scrutiny. The day came when she had to submit her proposal to *mabahith amn al dawla* (State Police), a towering rectangular building. "I nearly died of fright as I stood in front of the citadel-like building, with loaded guns pointed at me and barbed wire lining its roofs. It took me three hours to talk to the person in charge of my permit. As I sat waiting, I watched as groups of men with long beards and Islamic dress were being led past me to be interrogated. It was a scary experience that made you feel defenseless with no rights in your own country."

Her intimidating experience as a vulnerable citizen in the face of the security machine was pivotal in shaping May's desire to end state police repression. Contrary to what many thought about the Egyptian uprising, May believes that the revolution began to get rid of *al dakhliyya* or the Ministry of Interior. Al dakhliyya protected the corruption inside the state, and so it was the main linchpin to the dire conditions that Egyptians suffered from. May was one of ten people who sat in a meeting with Mohamed al Baradai before the uprising, "The consensus among the group was that this revolution is 'a hopeless case,' 'forget it!' 'Al Baradai is simply a diplomat. He is neither a statesman nor a politician. The man is in his seventies. He told us that this is not his story. That it is up to the young people in the country to take a position of leadership.'" May seemed very despondent when she continued. "The younger generation are not waiting for a leader. They reject the idea. They want everything by consensus, and that is just not possible. They often repeated a mantra that they have not come to solve [problems], they came to object *'ihna mish gayyin nihil ihna gayin na'tarid.'* This revolution began to oppose al dakhliyya, not Hosni Mubarak," she said.

The revolution, according to May and to many of the women I interviewed for this book, was not simply about the lack of freedoms and menacing presence of the security forces, although that was how it got its first sparks. It was also about the lack of opportunities and the feeling of injustice that comes with knowing that unless you succumbed to an unjust system that the regime was boldly establishing and safeguarding by brute force, you could not succeed.

While many women I spoke with expressed an anxiety over the future of their children if they grew up in Egypt, few spoke with May's frankness. "I am worried about the future of my children," May said. "I have to teach them how to suck up to the rich so that they can give them work when they graduate from college." In just a short sentence, she managed to reduce complex social mechanisms of class and economic difference in a growing disenfranchising economy where the bifurcation of the haves and the have-nots grows wider by the day. In such a system of inequity, where the state maintains its control through force and a paternalistic ideology that promised its people better pay and better lives that increasingly did not materialize, the children of the unwealthy not only had to struggle to acquire an education, but they also had to excel in social schmoosing, to access opportunities that were to serve the interests of the privileged.

This was the predicament of the educated, whose schooling did not prepare them for a job market that was controlled by corporations led by a few power- ful magnates. In a neoliberalizing economy, these prospects faced the younger and older generations alike with very limited entrepreneurial opportunities available for a few like Samya and perhaps May. To the majority of the Egyptian population, however, their choices became so limited that many credentialed youths remained unemployed, as youth unemployment rates in Egypt climbed to approximately 26 percent in 2015 (Al Ahram 2015). Their frustrated hopes, mistrust of the state, and disappointment in a patriarchal system that promised but could not deliver contributed to feelings of alienation and emasculation that ultimately shaped gender relations in society.

Conclusion

Largely relying on women's words, this chapter discussed the impact of state attempts at integrating neoliberal market adjustments into the daily lives of women. The rememories explored here, some moving, some traumatic, and others simply revolutionary, bring to us the diverse voices and experiences of Egyptian women engaged in revolt. No matter what the reasons that led them to the midan, their stories illustrate one thing that they have in common: that no one, no matter how privileged, is impervious to statewide political and economic practices. How women are affected, how they process these changes, and how they react and resist them is, of course, what the stories are about.

With neoliberal "reforms" underway, political repression and the lack of state support impact these women at every level. The diversity of the women themselves is an important factor in all of this and so is neoliberalism which is neither monolithic nor universal. Deregulation, for example, takes a variety of forms and is applied with varying intensity and momentum depending on the political moment in question. It is also experienced quite differently by cit- izens. Within the context of an increasingly bifurcated society in Egypt where wealth is distributed to a privileged few and the majority of the population has to contend with their economic and social marginality, women's narratives in this chapter expressed both the challenges as well as the privileges of their lives. The degree to which these experiences are the focus of the conversations mirrors the variations in socioeconomic levels and priorities. Women's bodies, livelihoods, and activism become gendered and framed through changing neoliberal and patriarchal norms in the public sphere and the growing pull of the neoliberal economic market.

Egypt's women laborers played a pivotal role in the uprising of January 25, 2011. The history of their labor movement mirrors the changes in the larger pol- itical economy of the country. The lives of women factory workers like Wedad El Demerdash and others epitomize how the neoliberalization of the Egyptian industrial sector was also gendered. Structural adjustment policies directly impacted their income, putting them at the mercy of fluctuating and fickle market changes that provide little or no employment security, health, or insurance. These are labor conditions that are designed to benefit the corporate employers, whose gains rely on the deprivation of the laborer from just pay and decent benefits. Women's labor activism was particularly impactful, acting as a precursor as well as a catalyst for the revolution. SAPs and the trend toward deregulation and privatization has fueled these laborers' activism and reconfigured the space of political participation for women in irreversible ways.

Whether Christian or Muslim, rich or poor, educated or informally educated, the women who shared the stories of their lives with me reflect the vast swaths of population in Egyptian society. They all shared the dream that animated the protests; as Zeinab put it, "Every person who went to Tahrir during those days had a beautiful dream for this country." The next chapter traces the experiences of a diverse group of women in the early days of the revolution. It takes us into the galvanizing moments for each of them and highlights the significance of these women's bodily dissent.

Women's march on International Women's Day 2013. Photograph copyright Wael T. Abed.

Women's march crossing Al Galaa Bridge into Tahrir Square. Photograph copyright Wael T. Abed.

Women's march, 2013; granddaughter of Egyptian feminist Dorreya Shafiq carrying her flag, marching into Tahrir Square. Photograph copyright Wael T. Abed.

Marching in downtown Cairo, a woman chanting and marching while carrying a flag showing Aisha Al Taymouriya. Photograph copyright Wael T. Abed.

International Women's Day march. Photograph copyright Wael T. Abed.

An organized march into Tahrir Square. Photograph copyright Wael T. Abed.

نفرتيتي

A protestor with flag of ancient Egyptian queen Nefertiti. Photograph copyright Wael T. Abed.

Women protestors were from every walk of life. Flag showing Sally Zahran, a twenty-three-year-old woman who died of internal bleeding after being clubbed by thugs in the first eighteen days of revolution. Photograph copyright Wael T. Abed.

Woman protestors chanting for the regime to fall in Tahrir Square. Photograph copyright Wael T. Abed.

Flag of Egyptian feminist Dorreya Shafiq flying juxtaposed against the statue of the most famous economist in Egyptian history, Talaat Harb. Women's march. Photograph copyright Wael T. Abed.

International Women's Day march, drumming and chanting. Photograph copyright Wael T. Abed.

Coptic Egyptian women protesting against injustice in Maspero. Photograph by Nermine Hammam.

Coptic Egyptian women in Maspero protest holding up crosses. Photograph by Nermine Hammam.

Photograph of the masses of people in Tahrir. Photograph by Nermine Hammam.

The magnitude of corporeal dissent in Tahrir Square. Photograph by Nermine Hammam.

4   The Lived Experience of Women's Struggle

Early in the morning of January 25, 2011, fifty-year-old Amal finished cooking and cleaning for her family as she does every day. And, as always, she left her home in the Basateen area on the southern outskirts of Cairo at 6:00 a.m. She would catch several bus rides from the station to reach Abbasiyya, where her government job was located. But since President Hosni Mubarak had declared January 25 a national holiday to commemorate the police force in 2009, Amal did not have to head to Abbasiya that morning. Instead, on that day, she headed to Maadi for her "other" job. "I had no particular thoughts on my mind, nor was I anticipating that anything was going to be different that day. It was a day like any other day." The teakettle boiling over her gas stove brought her abruptly back with a start from that memorable morning. She quickly grabbed the blue teakettle with a rolled-up rag and began pouring tea into our glasses. She began again, this time shaking her head and muttering under her breath, "We are very disappointed, we are very disappointed."

"I know, I know," I said instinctively, trying to be of comfort to her. But with a start, I stopped and thought, *did I really know?* What did I really know about what Amal was going through? Sitting here in Amal's kitchen in Basateen almost two years after the birth of the revolution of January 25, 2011, I was a transient, a traveler from the so-called land of excess and languidness, where I am now living and teaching. What did *I* know about Amal's feelings? What did I know about being a widowed migrant from Beni Suef, barely making ends meet in her tiny place with two children to take care of?

"I Really Did Not Mind the Man Much . . . but I Wanted Change": Amal

Amal worked as a cashier in a government office. Her office handled properties that were designated as *waqf* or endowments for public religious use such as historical mosques and *madrassas* (Islamic schools). As a head cashier, she handled large sums of money to maintain the upkeep of these buildings. She supervised the accounts and, at the end of her shift, made sure there were no deficits or irregularities. The extent of her responsibilities was not lost on Amal, who pointed out that thousands of pounds passed through her fingertips every day while she struggled to provide for her family. This is why in the evenings, Amal worked a second job. She cleaned other people's homes, washed, cooked, and took care of their children. This was her "other" job in Maadi that no one knew about—not even her closest friends. Though her second job helped pay for some essentials, it brought her shame and embarrassment because being a maid was not considered respectable work in general and certainly—according to Amal—not for someone who worked for the government as she did.

In a tone that was hesitant and embarrassed, she asked me not to mention her by her real name. She felt ashamed that as a government employee in an important job such as hers she would be also working as a maid. She chose the pseudonym Amal because it meant *hope* in Arabic. It was hope that kept her working long hours, often amounting to a three-day shift to secure the needs of her family. Her dream was to one day save enough money to buy a one-bedroom apartment in a new urban development near Cairo. She was short a couple of thousand pounds on the down payment and did not even know where those thousands would come from.

Going back to the day that was to become a historical turning point to Egyptians everywhere, Amal recalled noticing a certain tension in the air that she could not decipher. Though it was a holiday, there were many people at the bus station. Some stood in groups, talking among themselves. Others hurried across the platform to catch buses heading to Tahrir Square. She heard tidbits of earnest conversation and finally could not resist stopping a passerby. "What's going on? Why is everyone going to Tahrir?" she asked.

"They say there is a big protest there!" a young man told her. "Who knows? They might be trying to depose [President] Mubarak!"

I watched Amal's eyes widening as she relived that moment, saying emphatically, "I've lived in Cairo for eighteen years. Never did I feel so elated, so full of excitement. I didn't go to Maadi to work that day. Instead, I too took the bus to Tahrir. I didn't even stop to think that I hadn't told anybody where I was going nor that I had to call the lady whose house I was supposed to clean that day to cancel. I didn't stop to think of my family or that something could happen to me, like being arrested, for instance. All I could think of was that something big was happening and that I wanted to be part of it."

When she arrived at Midan al Tahrir, she started having misgivings. She was thinking about herself acting like a young person when she was actually *wiliyya kabira* (an old woman). She thought of the money that she could have earned. Thoughtfully, she stopped in her tracks and almost went back to the bus, but just then she caught sight of the midan. People, young people in particular, were beginning to flock to the square. Seeing the seriousness in their faces, she began to wonder if this was indeed true. That they *are* going to bring the president down?

I really did not mind the man much (speaking of former President Hosni Mubarak). I actually liked him. He did a lot of good things . . . the Sixth of October Bridge, the Fifth District [of the governorate of Cairo] and the ring road. He was good, but . . . when his grandson died, no. People in the square wanted the whole regime to fall, but I didn't. I respected him. I respect him to this day. I think they should make him a statue. But still, I wanted change. I had had enough of all the cabinet ministers, their corruption and their growing wealth while the rest of us suffered. So, I called out as loudly as I could, "*Yasqut, yasqut* Hosni Mubarak! [Down with Hosni Mubarak!]" The tears were running down my face as I yelled, but I wanted things to be different. I wanted change.

January 25, 2011 was called a "day of rage." Thousands of protestors congregated to Tahrir Square in Cairo, and all over Egypt in major urban centers such as Alexandria, Tanta, and Mansura. Aswan and Assiout also witnessed large demonstrations that expressed their dissatisfaction with the police. In Cairo, protestors marched to the headquarters of the National Democratic Party, the Foreign Ministry building, and the television building in Maspero. Confrontations between the demonstrators and the state police ensued, and three protestors were killed. Reports about police being killed as well were heard. The demonstrations continued into the week, then another week, and then a few more days. Eighteen days in all made a tremendous impact on Egypt's sociopolitical future. Over the next few days, the numbers of protestors swelled into what some reported to be millions.

Over half of those present in Tahrir, were women. Many marked their bodies with the colors of the national flag, red, black, and white, as head scarves or bands or face paint. Carrying their physical bodies as metaphors of Egypt, the presence of these women in Tahrir in the earlier days of the revolution was instrumental to its success. Protestors often remarked that having women and children in Tahrir legitimized their demands, protected them from the threat of state violence, delivering a collective message to the regime that all Egyptians—not just those who had political disagreements with it—demanded change. But about the women themselves—what were their motives? Their dreams? How do women shape the revolutionary effort, and what role do they play in galvanizing it, organizing its ranks, and most of all, sustaining it?

In their narratives about the revolution, women define themselves by their social as well as their revolutionary roles. They are the mothers, the wives, the sisters, the lovers, but they are also the revolutionaries, the activists, the artists, and the women who organized and planned sit-ins and protests, who wrote catchy chants and led demonstrations. The following chapter tells their stories in their own words as they recall the early days of the revolution. Deeply evocative and often moving recollections, their words echo the effect of the uprising as it linked together the lives of so many men and women from all over the city of Cairo. Ordinary women's lived experience of revolution is the focus of this book which makes a concerted effort to include them in the history of the Arab Uprisings. My intention was to center those who were relegated to the background of revolutionary lore rather than continue paying attention to those who became celebrities of the media or who were already prominent women in public leadership positions. Although the latter's contributions cannot be underscored enough, their stories are already familiar and documented elsewhere. What concerned me were the women who are seldom heard—they had my research priority. Bringing their accounts into discussions of revolution was also necessary to illustrate the involvement of women at every level in the uprisings in Egypt. This was of pivotal importance. For it is only when all of the perspectives are brought together that we can begin to see the rich tapestry of women's embodied revolutionary action.

In recounting their experiences and daily practices, revolutionary women evoke multiple registers that animate the process of recollection. Rememory as a process of revisiting experience awakens and engages the material dimension of their bodies. To these women engaged in revolt, participating in political action is a bodily practice that cannot be separated from the set of registers that shape their revolutionary subjectivity. Their rememories animate the emotional and physical energies that activated their corporeal power, bodily surfaces, collective voice, and performance of revolutionary action as they became catalysts of civil disobedience.

"You Seem to Be a Madam. Why Would You Do This?": Yasmin

Among those who were determined to join the protests in the midan on the twenty-fifth was twenty-five-year-old Yasmin, who lives in one of Cairo's cosmopolitan neighborhoods. An island in the middle of the Nile River that is connected to the mainland by several bridges, Zamalek has epitomized the upper middle class, the highly educated, and the more affluent communities among the Caireen population. Home to several class markers such as its international schools, hip cafes, the Cairo Opera House, and the Gezira Sporting Club—a remnant of British colonialism, where cricket is still played and members only are admitted—Zamalek is a generator of class capital like no other suburb in Cairo. Yet, it was also one of the most activist neighborhoods in all of Cairo during the uprisings. Its inhabitants organized daily marches to Tahrir. They held meetings to raise awareness, recruited each other, and bought and organized supplies and food for the demonstrators. Yasmin knew all this as she sat across from me behind a large metal desk in her office located in Zamalek's central shopping area.

"Look," she said to me, "I wanted to know what was going on!" To Yasmin, Mubarak's corrupt regime, the videos exposing police brutality, and Galal Amin's books all contributed to her belief that change had to happen. Galal

Amin was a prominent Egyptian economist and political analyst who wrote a popular series of books that were translated into English entitled *Whatever Happened to the Egyptians?* (2001) and *Whatever Else Happened to the Egyptians* (2004). The latter was expanded and updated to include the revolution in 2014. Amin argued in his first book of this series that economic liberalization had some unintended consequences that were not handled well by the government (2001).

The lack of attention to the poor and the growing gap between the wealthy few and the rest of the population were a few of the factors Amin examines in his work. Though some social change appeared to him to be positive, such as the improvements in women's status, he did not deal with how the changing socioeconomic conditions affect women's access to resources, for example. In his second- and third-latest updated version of *Whatever Else Happened to the Egyptians* (2014), Amin went on to analyze further state blunders amid the economic challenges that had detrimental effects on society and consequently led to the revolution of 2011. Yasmin explained how these three books had compelled her to head to Tahrir Square to answer the call for protest on Facebook.

"At the time, I had no friends who had any activist leanings. My mother and grandmother did the usual charity work but nothing political. Even my fiancé told me what has now become an unforgettable statement, that 'there is no revolution with an appointment!'" Yasmin laughs out loud at how her fiancé's words were so ill-placed, since this revolution was exactly that—a revolution with an appointment, which was set for January 25.

Calls to meet in Tahrir Square (as well as the closest squares or streets) on that Tuesday went viral on both Twitter and Facebook. On YouTube, the April 6th movement co-organizer Asmaa Mahfouz's deeply moving vlog, posted one week before the revolution, imploring all the young men and women who were watching to meet her in Tahrir, also went viral. She instantly became the face of the revolution, a young, veiled Egyptian woman whose views could not be described as politically sophisticated but more humanistically oriented. "Four Egyptians set themselves on fire to protest the humiliation and hunger and poverty and the degradation they lived with for 30 years. Four Egyptians have set themselves on fire thinking maybe we could have a revolution like Tunisia, maybe we could have freedom, justice, honor, and human dignity. And the human being in it [this country] is a real human being not living like an animal." She closed her statement with the following words: "Come down with us and demand your rights, my rights, your family's rights. I am going down on January 25th and will say no to corruption and no to this regime."

Yasmin was one of the thousands of protestors who answered that call. Unable to convince any of her friends or family to accompany her, she finally found a friend of a friend who agreed to take a taxi with her to Tahrir Square.

Normally, the trip from Yasmin's home in Zamalek would have taken ten minutes in all, but on this day, it was excruciatingly slow going. Anxious not to waste any time, Yasmin and her friend paid the taxi driver got off in front of the Cairo Opera House and headed toward Tahrir on foot.

"I was stunned by the enormity of the numbers of bodies pushing toward the Qasr el Nil Bridge towards the midan. I looked around me, and everyone looked like us. Normal, well-dressed people—not thugs or punks like what was being reported on the news. *Al amn al markazi* [Central Security Forces or CSF] armed with batons were pushing people, but there was no real violence." Estimated to be 450,000 men strong, the CSF is a paramilitary group, which is tasked by the state to deal with major threats such as riots, disasters, and antigovernment action.

It was no cakewalk across the bridge to Tahrir, and Yasmin was afraid she was not going to make it. The chanting helped make the short but very slow one-mile walk more tolerable. It also had an incredible effect on Yasmin, who found herself repeating uncontrollably the calls for, *'ish, hurriya, 'adala igtim'aiyya* (bread, freedom, and human dignity or social justice).

> How can I describe how my body felt? Honestly it should have been aching in pain as I walked slowly, putting one foot in front of the other across the bridge for what seemed to be hours, but it didn't. I felt elated like my body was buzzing. Being so close in a crowd to other bodies can be a bit awkward but you don't think about that at all. You are part of the human tide and you go where the tide takes you. It was the adrenaline! The chanting, the thrill of the moment when you sense that the floodgates are open and you, as well as everyone else can fly. Plus, there is also the threat of danger, not knowing what will happen to you whether the police will start shooting or whatever.

As soon as they had crossed, the authorities closed off Tahrir Square, and she and her friend were trapped in between. The CSF cordoned off the square so no one could get in or out. She was on her phone immediately, calling her fiancé. After several unanswered calls, Yasmin nearly gave up attempting to connect with him. About two hours passed before she heard her cell phone ring and it was her fiancé who, despite his earlier doubts, he had made it to Tahrir after all. "He came after me!" Yasmin recalled. "He wasn't going to leave me by myself. We decided on a meeting point, and I stayed put with the same group of people I crossed the bridge with, until he showed up. Our phones kept cutting off, but we finally managed to find each other, and I never felt so elated as that moment. We were both chanting and calling for the government to step down. It was the first day of our revolution, and neither one of us was going to give it up."

Listening to Yasmin as she unbottled her feelings about those days in the midan drew me into the circle of her rememories. She was, at that moment, reliving those days and nights of uprising, the emotions clearly visible on her face as her eyes brightened and her face got slightly flushed. Her voice began to rise and acquired a higher pitch. The events came flooding in. She kept talking, unchecked, giving life to the story.

In the days that followed, they decided on a designated meeting point in the square, the traffic light into Tahrir from the Qasr el Nil Bridge. Their friends began meeting there as well during the protests, either to join each other early in the morning or late at night when they were ready to leave the square and head home. It was safe in Tahrir in those first eighteen days, safer than anyplace she had ever experienced. "You could leave your purse or your backpack, and no one would touch it," said Yasmin.

Many days later, she was to experience the joy of being shoulder to shoulder with her loved one but also the intense worry and fear about their safety.

> The twenty-eighth was the worst day of beatings witnessed in the midan. This time, I came in [to Tahrir] through Galaa Bridge, but they (the security police) beat us with batons. Until 1 a.m., I had no idea where Omar was. But I spotted him from a distance limping towards me with a gash on the side of his head, blood pouring down onto his left ear. I thought he was shot and ran towards him with a towel, but he was beaten by *baltagiyaa* [government thugs who were often tasked with beating protestors and inciting chaos] when he was "frontlining" with others.

The term "frontlining" has found its way into the Arabic lexicon and was used by several other women who described these events in similar ways. The term means that they were in the front lines, combating government forces with rocks or Molotov cocktails. Yasmin continued:

> All I could think of was, I could have lost him that day like many others had lost their husbands and brothers, so I was so relieved. We were inseparable after that. I was at the frontlines with him too and threw rocks and Molotov bottles at those who were shooting us [officers with the internal police] mercilessly. I am not afraid to say this. I had a whole box of them with me [Molotov cocktails]. I had smuggled them into the square with two other friends. It had to be done. But I was terrified.
>
> People thought that those who were in the frontlines were *suya'* [punks]. But there I was, in my western clothes and dirty blonde hair. So of course, they [undercover police] stopped me and asked me all kinds of questions. "Why are you here? Are you a journalist? You seem to be a madam [meaning a respectable woman]. Why would you do this?" It was obvious that my presence disturbed them. They just did not know what to do with me. Every time I was caught or arrested, they let me go after a few minutes. I realized after this happened several times that they could read class privilege by looking at me. That my social class protected me from police brutality. That my presence among the demonstrators even protected others. They avoided coming near me. Class worked in interesting ways in Tahrir.

The realization that class markers could be read on her body took Yasmin by surprise. Being part of the demonstrations, out on the streets among the masses put her in touch with her internalized privilege. She came to the conclusion that security forces not only noted her class but also avoided hurting her as a result. Class and class privilege continue to be essential markers of difference in Egypt. Society is primarily organized around socioeconomic class, which intersects with gender and race, as discussed in previous chapters. Having a lighter complexion also signaled Yasmin's Ottoman roots—a fact that most times associated her with the elite class, even though she herself was not wealthy. Political participation, then, appeared to have been selectively allowed—at least in the first eighteen days—depending on corporeal indicators of class privilege.

Yasmin and several other revolutionary women who were of middle- or upper-class backgrounds were quick to notice the fact that they were—for the most part—immune from state brutality. It occured to them that they could use this to their advantage to help smuggle others in and out of the square or even to protect those who did not partake in this class immunity from being arrested or violently treated. Negotiating state violence with corporeal markers, the women of the midan demonstrated their nuanced understanding of social boundaries and the privilige of certain bodies over others. They recognized that at least in the first few days of revolution their gender, age, and class afforded them some safety from brutal violence. This safety however, was short-lived, as the next few chapters will show. Even then, however, Yasmin's privileged social status did not always come to her rescue. Were it not for the young street children who fought with their lives in the uprisings, she would have been sexually assaulted during the demonstrations.

When she joined the demonstrations against Ahmed Shafik's appointment as prime minister by Hosni Mubarak on the twenty-ninth, internal security forces fired real live bullets at them. Undeterred, they kept advancing. The so-called "battle of the camel" happened right before Yasmin's eyes, as men riding horses and donkeys (a few were on camelback) stormed the square, slashing protestors with long weapons, leaving eleven dead and six hundred injured (Fathi 2012). She was in the square, tending to the wounded in the field hospital. In December 2011, the Egyptian Institute or the *mogama' al 'ilmi* as it is known in Arabic, that is considered part of Egypt's cultural heritage and home to about two hundred thousand valuable manuscripts, was torched by fire. The demonstrators were accused of starting the fire, but Yasmin's account (as do other accounts) points to how the demonstrators who saved the precious collection.

> I was in Tahrir that day when I heard that the *mogama'* was on fire. It was dark and there was water everywhere. Who would have thought that the building was burned down? I had no idea. I saw the fire trucks next to the building and several members of the army there as well. When I looked closer I saw the revolutionaries putting out the fire by themselves. I used my mobile to call a few

influential women I got to know from Tahrir. They, in turn, sent specialists to the site who picked up the salvageable books and manuscripts, and it was the young men from the demonstrations who were handing over the documents.

But later that day, Yasmin was unfortunately thrown into a situation over which she had no control. She came very close to being the victim of sexual assault. "We women were told not to go by ourselves outside the circle of the group of people we were with. I noticed a group of small street children trying to salvage the remains of books that were on the floor, so I walked over to them unaware that I was being followed. All of a sudden felt someone behind me and these men on either side of me. The street children saved my life. They saw me, and knew what was about to happen, so they ran, and formed a circle around me that pushed me back to where I had come from."

The chilling events leading to assaults on women in the midan began as Yasmin describes in her quote. A woman is drawn to a scene away from her companions and as she moves, men intent on violence against women follow, isolate and then circle the victim. Fortunately for Yasmin, a group of street children who had repeatedly witnessed these horrific events taking place in Tahrir Square recognized what was happening to her and running faster than the men formed a cordon around her to protect her from harm.

Yasmin continued to protest and agitate for equality and justice even after the Muslim Brotherhood's candidate won the elections, Mohamed Morsi, became president in 2012. Many of her friends quit political action after that, but not Yasmin.

The Brotherhood betrayed us in Mohamed Mahmood [known as the "Cabinet Clashes" of December 16, 2011]. The consequences were terrible. The tear gas was unbearable, and seventeen people were killed and many were injured. So when Morsi was in the Itihadiyya Palace, I wanted to help the protests there by setting up a field hospital. We took our supplies and navigated the crowds approaching the palace. I was terrified, as the beating of the protesters was intensified by the security forces. Not knowing where to go, we hid inside a small store and turned off the lights. We crouched down so they couldn't see us—all the while watching as one army tank after another began pulling up. But we knew they would soon find us, so one by one we ran towards the entrance of a nearby apartment building, and the tenants took us in, locking the building gate behind us. It was a long time before we were able to sneak out unnoticed and morning when we got back to our homes.

During the events of Mohamed Mahmood, Yasmin was working in the field hospital. This was the day protestors were shot in the bloodiest battle with the Ministry of the Interior Forces, and she had to deal with a traumatic experience involving her fiancé. As she administered disinfectants and bandaged wounds, she spotted him being carried by two men who were coming toward her. "They called out that Omar was hurt. I panicked when I saw that he was unconscious.

I knew I could not call an ambulance because we discovered what they did. They took the patients straight to *amn al dawla*. Instead, we revived him at the field hospital and did what we could to get him better. But we could not leave the midan till much later when things quieted down. He had a broken leg and a head injury when he fell. It was awful."

"No! And We Will Die Here. Do Not Call Me Again": Dalia

Like Yasmin, many protestors showed up to the midan with their loved ones or ended up meeting them there. The stories are many; some are unfortunately tragic. Brothers who headed there together only to end up being separated by death, friends standing shoulder to shoulder with each other only to turn around in and in the blink of an eye to find one of them unmoving on the Tahrir floor with a bullet to the head. The poignant recollections of parents who were in the square those first days of the revolution when they realized that their lives were on the line and that sudden death or injury could come from any direction and that they may never see their children again were particularly moving. Those same parents described their feelings about having their young teenage children sleeping on the floor somewhere in Tahrir and not knowing where they were and what unexpected fate could befall them all. What would compel people to put themselves in such situations time and again? What endurance do these circumstances require of someone? And what impact do these experiences have on oneself?

I asked these questions of Dalia, a member of the Muslim Sisters (the women's branch of the Muslim Brotherhood), who was one of those parents. We got together at a café in Mohandisseen, a busy commercial neighborhood across the Nile from Zamalek. With us were two other women who were MB supporters but who had yet become full-fledged members of the organization. All three had been active in Tahrir during the protests. We had first met earlier that year, in July 2013, after Mohamed Morsi was deposed by the military and placed under arrest. Since then, Dalia and her family had left the country; she was now on a brief visit to Cairo, and so we joined her for a cup of coffee.

Things had shifted dramatically in the country since our first meeting. A total of eleven hundred people, supporters of deposed president Mohamed Morsi, were killed during police and military raids (Human Rights Watch 2014). After the ultimatum issued by the military to an encampment in Rab'a was up, police and military forces surrounded and then opened fire on those who remained on August 14, 2013. There were five other confrontations with Morsi supporters, and many more were injured. The Muslim Brotherhood was subsequently banned as a group in September, with most of the group's leadership placed under arrest.

Dalia, whose husband was well known in the MB, had to flee the country for fear of meeting with a similar fate. Their entire family was granted refuge in a nearby Arab country. Recalling the revolution and her family's involvement, she described the first eighteen days in Tahrir Square, revealing how, as a mother, she experienced these first weeks of uprising.

> The beginning was January 25 for my family. My son read about the plans for demonstrations on Facebook and was at first worried that we would decide to participate. I found out that the Muslim Brotherhood had announced to its members that participation is individual. So if we were to participate, it would have to be on a personal level, independent of the organization. I had also learned that my sister-in-law, who is married to a leader in the Muslim Brotherhood, was arrested at Cilantro Café as she and her daughters were preparing their signs for the next-day protests. The secret police then promptly released then somewhere in the desert. This was meant as a warning. Because of this random misuse of police authority involving someone very close to us, and of course because of the brutal murder of Khaled Said and others, everyone in my family agreed to go down to protest police injustice.

Dalia and her husband with their two children joined her sister-in-law and her daughters in the demonstrations on January 25 (Police Day, renamed as the Day of Rage). To them, like many others, their participation in the demonstration was not intended to bring Mubarak down but to object to police brutality. Like Amal, Yasmin, and others who witnessed those first eighteen days in Tahrir, Dalia described the intensity of police violence against the protestors on Friday, the twenty-eighth of January, only days after the protests had begun. Cell phone reception was shut down, and the military was deployed to the squares and main areas, but they remained neutral.

> The twenty-eighth was when the real beating of the protestors started. The police beat the protestors in the area of Ramses and continued to do so for some time till sunset. There were many injuries. About the same time, they said the CSF [Central Security Forces] fell and the military will take over. I was in Mohandisseen at the time, and my husband was in Saudi Arabia. When I called him, he said he was coming home right away. In the meantime, I went to donate blood at the hospital. At the hospital I met with an important public person who had supported us in the March 9 movement. I found out from him that the military will side with Mubarak and that they will force us to leave the midan. It was on the thirtieth [of January] that we decided to stay at a friend's apartment in Tahrir. We ended up staying for three days. Her living room floor became our bed. We were about ten women "sisters" with our daughters as well as my sister-in-law and her two daughters. We didn't see our men during this time, and I had no idea where my husband and son were. Just that they were in Tahrir Square in the sit-in.

Dalia mentioned the March 9 group that was founded in 2004. This was a movement that called for the autonomy of Egyptian university campuses from state security and ideological control. A number of the members of this movement participated actively in the January 25 revolution. These individuals include Laila Soueif (whose son Alaa Abdel Fatah remains in prison for breaking protest laws), Mohamed Abdel Ghaffar, and Hany Elhosseiny (Geer 2013). From the beginning of Dalia's account, there was an underlying theme that distinguished her experience from that of other women revolutionaries. As a prominent Muslim Sister, Dalia had access to information and political support networks not available to other women. The members of the MB followed certain protocols. They received directives through preorganized phone trees, and they were able to communicate with each other and know which areas were safe and which were not. It was these networks that helped Dalia feel connected in the midan during the protests, even though there were times that filled her with horror when mobiles were down and she could not reach her husband and son.

Later that day, however, it became clear that despite the warning about the army getting ready to evacuate the square, no one was going to budge. There was a Tahrir vote to remain in the square no matter what. But let us turn to another scene that is unfolding with another woman who does not know yet that she will be one of the most active revolutionaries of the midan. We will return to Dalia momentarily.

"What Will You Choose to Do in the Face of Adversity?": Malak

While all these events were unfolding in Tahrir Square in downtown Cairo on the twenty-eighth, in the suburb of Medinet Nasr (Nasr City), several miles east of the city, twenty-seven-year-old Malak was drinking her morning coffee and contemplating her plans for the day. Like many single Egyptian men and women, she was still living in her parents' home, commuting to her job in Dokki, where she worked for a well-recognized American grant-funding organization. It being Friday and the beginning of the weekend in Egypt, she decided to get a haircut in one of the salons nearby in Misr al Gedida (meaning New Cairo in Arabic) or Heliopolis, the older suburb from which Medinet Nasr grew. Misr al Gedida was built at the turn of the twentieth century by a Belgian developer named Baron Empain. It housed a number of the area's most sumptuous elite palaces in its early days. After the 1952 revolution, the area became the center of military operations in Egypt, with both the army and air force headquarters located there. Then-president Hosni Mubarak hailed from this neighborhood, but as president his residence was a substantial edifice. Malak, however, lived in a middle-class neighborhood somewhat apart from the more affluent established Heliopolis.

Around 1:00 p.m., as Malak maneuvered her tiny car through Heliopolis traffic in midan al sa'a, she noticed a woman walking by herself, carrying a sign. Ironically, the sign said "No to protests!" Malak parked her car and observed the scene as groups of people began to appear from the side streets along the square, carrying similar signs and supporting President Mubarak. Having no prior knowledge of protests, and no personal history of being in demonstrations, Malak was very intrigued. She drove her car across a Heliopolis bridge so she could watch the numbers of people rapidly congregating below. Afterward, she went home with her head swimming, determined to find out more. Upon arriving at home, however, she was shocked to find the following scene. "My father was sprawled in an awkward angle on the floor. He was crying in agony from a broken hip. My mother, pacing and wringing her hands, was urging me to take him to the hospital. She would pick up my sister from school and meet us there. I didn't even have a chance to tell them about what I saw. We sped across the streets to Cleopatra Hospital."

A few hours later, with her father now resting in a room at the hospital, her mother and sister arrived, looking pale and seeming visibly shaken. "People were shot, and there was a curfew. We stayed together in the hospital that night not daring to go out into the streets." With these difficult family circumstances taking her attention away from the protests, how Malak ended up demonstrating in the midan is a story that picks up a few days later.

But first back to Dalia two days later in Tahrir square, the night of the thirtieth of January, a Sunday. It was a night of all-out rebellion as thousands of protestors insisted on staying put in the square. Dalia, who had remained with her family in Tahrir, recalls how the Muslim Brotherhood men asked their wives to prepare drinking water and to collect as many rocks as they could find and to have them ready. She notes, "Our participation in this way was a major transformation in the way the Brotherhood operates." As women members know as "Sisters," their roles focused on mobilization and galvanizing the group but seldom being involved in actual disobedience. This shift could have been because members of the MB were acting on their own, rather than taking orders from the Supreme Guide, but it signaled a change in how the organization was to operate in the uprisings as a whole.

With the police absent, as per the government's orders, the military took over the streets, establishing checkpoints and stationing armored vehicles at major intersections. The army did indeed deploy in large numbers all over Cairo and major cities in Egypt, just as Dalia had been told. Unlike what her anonymous official told her, they did not side with Mubarak. Neighborhood vigilantes began to organize as reports were spreading fast about thugs breaking in, hijacking cars, and kidnapping people. The new suburbs away from the center of Cairo were particularly vulnerable, as neither the army nor the absent police were in a position to travel these distances to answer calls for help. It was among these suburban residents that forty-seven-year-old mother and restaurateur Yara found her family caught in a vise that night when she heard gunfire and explosions outside the suburban compound (gated community) where she lived in the Sixth of October city.

"I Realized How Isolated I Was": Yara

When Yara heard about the call for protests on the twenty-fifth, it was not from Facebook. Having finished dinner in a downtown café with a group of artists the night before, they were on their way out when a young man came in, distributing flyers to remind people of the protests next day. Yara remembers feeling mildly anxious and confused. She recalls that she knew nothing at that point but some brief tidbits here and there about the April 6th youth movement, so it made her uncomfortable to be faced with this information and not to know what was happening. Beginning with the night of the thirtieth, however, she was to be wrenched into the thick of things, and quite unexpectedly too.

Late that night, Yara heard the guards yelling incomprehensibly in the dark. This was followed by loud thuds on the door. Her husband rushed to see what the commotion was about. It appeared that a group of men had climbed over the wall of their residential community and had broken into an unknown number of houses. He grabbed his gun and ran out with the guards, who were carrying their rifles in pursuit of "the thugs." The next few hours went by like a slow-motion nightmare for Yara as she sat clutching her children to her and trying not to shake from fear. Rumors were spreading that day among the gated community's residents about the police withdrawing from their stations. So, this break-in, she concluded in her mind, must have been a result of that. As they sat waiting in the dark, not knowing what was to become of them, she thought about her husband, who was out there with the others. What if he was shot? Did he even know how to use a gun? What if the shooters came into their home and threatened them at gunpoint? What would she do? Yara had no idea what her reaction would be. In all her life, she had never even contemplated a moment like this.

Early that day, in response to the rumor about the police discharging its forces, the men in the neighborhood, like many other men in Cairo, formed groups of vigilantes. They pooled their resources and somehow were able to obtain guns and ammunition; she did not know how. Sounds of doors slamming and running feet were all part of this "attack," as she later put it to me in forced lightheartedness. Then it was suddenly quiet, and all she could hear were muffled voices. In the dark outside, the men formed lines of defense. They armed themselves with torches, guns, kitchen knives, and even wooden sticks, taking turns to guard the compound after it was established that whoever was attempting this break-in had indeed left. They never got to the bottom of this, and the intruders were never caught, but to Yara, it was enough of a wake-up call to make her join the protests in Tahrir Square. "I realized how isolated I was! We all live in a bubble behind our walls, thinking that they can protect us. I found out that night what a fantasy that was. The only way we can be protected and protect my children is to live in a free and transparent state where we can identify what the real dangers are and who is creating these scary scenarios."

It is not surprising that Yara reached this conclusion. In the chaos that spread across Cairo and close to her in Giza, many Egyptians sensed that they were being forced to make a choice. It was either the corrupt regime or the thugs or the terrorists or whatever nightmare the regime could think of. This feeling of having their arms twisted drove even more people, like Yara, tired of the old manipulation, to Tahrir. A week into the demonstrations, these newcomers could see the seriousness of the political situation in the country. A few of their stories will be discussed below, but first we return to Dalia, who has spent an entire week camping on her friend's apartment floor. Her husband and her son had been sleeping on the floor of the square itself since the first day of demonstrations.

This particular day, February 2, later called the "Battle of the Camel," began strangely, she recounted. Earlier in the day, she heard bullets being shot from the rooftops of buildings. Several confrontations took place between protestors and youth groups from outside the square. These would flare up and then die down. Then marches supporting Mubarak entered the square from various points, culminating with eruptions in violence. This was all unsettling to Dalia because it increased her anxiety about her family. As if those events were not enough to rattle her nerves, her cell phone kept ringing with calls from members of her extended family chiding her and blaming her for being part of the Muslim Brotherhood organization. They warned her of the dangers that could befall her and her children. The finger-wagging and the warnings of dire things that would befall her were not new to Dalia; her family had always disapproved of her Islamist activism (not that they understood it), but this time it was different. Hers was a military family with several uncles as well as her own father in important positions in the army. They could therefore not accept the fact that she was in Tahrir Square in a standoff with Egypt's defense forces, so they pursued her relentlessly, hoping she would listen and take her family back home to Nasr City. When Mubarak offered superficial platitudes to the protestors, her younger brother, who is a military cadet, tried to convince her to give up the fight by telling her, "Enough, my sister, enough. Can't you see that the man has told you things will get better?"

To this, Dalia retorted, "No! And we will die here. Do not call me again!"

At some point during the day, she began to be aware that army tanks had surrounded them in the *midan* and that neither her two children nor her husband were anywhere to be seen. The phone calls from her extended family, instead of convincing her to leave, only strengthened her resolve because Dalia had arrived at an important realization: "My children were both in the *midan*. The idea that children and husbands were all there in danger *fi sabil allah* [for the sake of God] *salimna amrina* [we surrendered our fate to Him], that made our situation more tolerable. And nothing, not my uncles' and aunts' calls nor the rumors circling that the army will strike, and not the F-16 planes that kept passing over our heads described by CNN as 'stretching their muscles' could shake my belief in what we were doing."

Hearing Dalia describe her activism in the *midan* as *fi sabil allah* deserves a pause here. From all the accounts we have heard thus far, none had described their sacrifices for the uprising as an act of faith or for the sake of God. As a

Muslim Sister, Dalia evoked God and religion as integral parts of her political action and that complimented—and not contradicted revolutionary efforts. Framing her motivations in religious terms reinforced her family's decision to join the protests, despite the Muslim Brotherhood's explicit directives against participating. When we first started talking, Dalia had mentioned two issues that drove them to the midan: police brutality and the fact that family members were especially targeted by police injustice. Yet, these pragmatic and personal motivations did not counter her conviction that their activism was *fi sabil allah*. Her statement further highlights the ways Muslims navigate political and religious motivations—not as dichotomous desires but as fully integrated and fluid conceptions.

Muslim televangelists and preachers became highly vocal in the debates around which Egyptians were split. While the majority of the public was supportive of the uprising, there were still many who opposed it. Citing the dangers of instability and the fear that Egypt would become yet another conflicted zone in the region, the opposing camp had access to the media, and its members were important figures in the public. On the other hand, the revolutionaries were a diverse group of multiple affiliations and visions that were not always well represented in the media. There were all kinds of *fatwas* [religious decrees] making claims about the uprising—some causing much damage. Amr Khaled, Khaled al Guindi, and Moez Masood (who enjoyed great popularity and influence among pious Muslim young people) were often in disagreement regarding the revolution. Their rise to fame had relied in the past on a rejection of the old Azhar University sheikhs. The latter were viewed as being out of touch with the daily needs of young people and therefore ineffective and too abstract to be of any help in dealing with twenty-first-century problems. The new preachers, on the other hand, were considered brave and outspoken before the revolution had forced them to take sides, often not the ones they had seemingly been courting when they first started their careers. Various forces that were against the revolution, such as the regime itself, with its media and administrative apparatus, its supporters known as *felool*, as well as the repressive police and the military were heavily engaged in delegitimizing the revolution by any means necessary. During these early developments, Islam too was invoked to declare the protests "unreligious." So, as young people were facing the barrels of army tanks and guns, Muslim preacher Khaled al Guindy, for instance, declared the protests to be anti-Islamic and prohibited any public disobedience of either Mubarak or his later successor, Al Sisi.

On the other hand, Moez Masood protested against the military in 2011. At the time of this sit-in, Masood inspired Dalia because he was in Tahrir supporting the demonstrators. Later on, however, when the Brotherhood assumed office, he publicly opposed them, labeling them as a "wrongful religion" (Ahmed 2014). But at that point in time, Dalia saw him as a hero. "Masood was calling for revolution;

he galvanized a lot of youth to fight the despotic ruler. This really affected me personally. Despite this, my own brother would tell me on the phone bring me a fatwa [a religious ruling in Islam] from Qaradawy." Although often controversial regarding issues of gender, political allegiance, and religious diversity, Yusuf al Qaradawi is a prominent Egyptian theologian and Islamic authority. He enjoys great popularity among the masses, with his television show attracting as many as sixty million viewers.

Despite these debates and the pressures from her parents and relatives, Dalia's resolve was firm. To her, their activism was the most valued in the eyes of God, since it involved speaking back to power. "*Bas ihna kunna nasrukh fi wagh sultan ga'ir,*" (But we were screaming in the face of an unfair sultan (Mubarak, in this case)). As she explained her point, she leaned over across the table, looking earnestly at me to ensure that I understood her well. She was projecting all the hurt and anger she was feeling at the lack of support shown by her own brother and her parents, but also the larger debates trying to discredit the sacrifices they made in the midan for what they believed of importance: justice, freedom, and of course, the need to live a safe and secure life. There were all goals that eluded her at this particular moment, since her MB husband had become a fugitive after the events of 2013. Paraphrasing Prophet Mohamed's hadith that the most exalted struggle is a just word to an unjust sultan, she concluded by saying, "And that is the most favored martyrdom."

> Honestly, I am fifty-two years old, brought up by my family and the Muslim Brotherhood. I believe in the example set by the Brotherhood that one is devoted to worship God and that the road is not easy. There will be hardship and harm. I read about *al sahaba* [the companions of the prophet Muhammad] and about the Brotherhood. I never imagined, though, that I would be in their situation one day. But this was the reality, and it was a frightening and difficult reality. When I found that my husband and my children were in the midan with me, this knowledge strengthened me. We walk together and we die together. Why should it be us who will escape death? The revolution, from the beginning, was a test of values and principles. What will we do during adversity? Are we going to sacrifice our lives and stand our ground, or will we run and only think of ourselves? Those were the difficult questions.

Martyrdom, death, and sacrifices for freedom were on Dalia's mind as she reflected back on her days in the midan. The feelings were still relevant to her today as she contemplated a life away from home. It did not escape me that remembering these events was more difficult to her than most. Dalia's rememory was akin to a repeated experience that reconstitutes her body and her resistance. The inseparability of rememory and the body causes pain and trauma to be relived, making these conversations all the more precious and important to document.

During the days of revolt however, the questions on Dalia's mind were probably on many people's minds as well. How much are they really willing to give up so that the revolution can live? Their money? Effort? Time? Even their lives? Was everyone there in the midan willing to give these up? There is no way of knowing that, but for young, secular Malak who, during the first days of revolution, was tangled up in her own family crisis, her job, and her life in Heliopolis, these questions were soon going to plague her. Since the day she witnessed the lone woman in the square carrying a sign and later watching the marches from her vantage point on the bridge, she could not stop thinking about what was going on in the midan.

The answers to some of those questions came from an unlikely ally, her cousin, Sami, a retired officer in the army who came to visit her recovering father in the hospital. Having a reputation as the family radical, Malak's cousin did not disappoint. She bombarded him with questions. He seemed to know quite a bit about the protests because he had been part of the demonstrations since the twenty-fifth. His long military career only served to disillusion him, and he took an opposite turn politically from the conservative politics of the army. "Sami really opened my eyes," she told me. "The next day, I decided to go to Tahrir to see for myself before the nighttime curfew."

In Tahrir, Malak wandered around the square with a new discovery:

> For the first time in my life, I saw people apologize profusely if they accidently bumped into you. I saw people smiling, excited, motivated. I saw a women's march cut through the midan, chanting revolutionary slogans. I joined them, started chanting with them, but I was too shy to continue, so I left the march and kept wandering around the midan. I ran into people I knew, friends and colleagues. Later my sister joined me with a group of her friends. We stayed in Tahrir and left a little after dark.

In the next few days, finding herself getting more and more involved, Malak brought food and drink to help those who were occupying the square in tents. She brought medical supplies to the field hospitals. She came to know people, other activists and revolutionaries. Gradually, she found herself coming out of her shell, bonding and connecting with others in the midan which was a new experience for her.

As it was to millions of people, the day Mubarak stepped down was to Malak cause for celebration. Many of my interviewees mention the extraordinary moment when they heard the statement read by Omar Soliman (former head of intelligence who had been recently appointed vice president to Hosni Mubarak) the night of February 11, "In the name of God the merciful, the compassionate, citizens, during these very difficult circumstances Egypt is going through, President Hosni Mubarak has decided to step down from the office of president of the republic and has charged the high council of the armed forces to administer the affairs of the country. May God help everybody" (*New York Times* 2011).

This day—the last of the first eighteen days of revolt, however, ushered in the beginning of a troubled revolution that weathered quite profound moments but was now about to face a more drawn-out and complicated process of regaining equilibrium. For all the protestors involved and particularly the women mentioned in this book, they chose to face whatever may come and "stand their ground," a choice Dalia had made many days before in Tahrir Square. For all of them, the choice was not only a difficult one to make but one that tested everything they stood for.

Perhaps more immediately, Malak was to experience this moment much earlier than others because she suddenly became aware that the square was no longer safe. It was no longer that space where people seemed apologetic at the slightest impingement of another's space—in fact, she witnessed a woman being savagely harassed right in front of her eyes the day Mubarak stepped down. Soliman's last words, "May God help everybody," still echoed in her ears, indeed, she thought to herself as she ran for help—the prayer sounding more like a veiled threat. The sexual harassment she witnessed that day, it seemed to her, was organized and planned. She took pictures and wrote about what she saw and posted it online, on Twitter and Facebook. Malak had discovered her vocation.

The next few weeks were busy and difficult but filled with a sense of commitment that brought a new energy into her life. Between her job, taking care of her father, and bringing supplies to Tahrir, Malak's plate was pretty much full. In March she stumbled upon the Twitter feed of a human-rights lawyer calling for volunteers. Lamya (whose name, like the others in this book, has been changed to protect her anonymity) had become the designated defender of those who were arrested in the protests. She posted a message on Twitter calling for volunteers to bring food supplies to the main Qasr El Nil entrance to Tahrir for the hundreds of people who were imprisoned since the demonstrations started. Malak began thinking about volunteering more formally now. She contacted Lamya and started meeting her in the midan to discuss how she could be of help, when a tragic event had a life-changing impact on her.

The death of twenty-three-year-old activist Mohamed Mohsen on the twenty-third of July left an indelible mark on Malak's life. Mohsen was part of a peaceful three-thousand-strong march that proceeded out of Tahrir Square heading toward Nasr City to protest military rule. A group of pro-army thugs ambushed them. The attack continued for two hours in full view of military guards, who did not intervene even when rocks and firebombs were thrown at the march from the roofs of nearby buildings. One of the attackers crushed Mohsen's skull with a large rock that left him bleeding heavily. He was taken to five hospitals and was refused treatment in each one, till he was finally accepted at El Nasr Hospital. He died a few days later from the prolonged untreated injuries. When the news reached them, Malak and Lamya, the human rights lawyer, were in a tent in Tahrir with other activists. The news left them feeling shocked, but it was Lamya who broke the stunned silence and turned to Malak and said, "So, are you going to do something about this?"

Only months ago, Malak would have perhaps walked away from this painful situation and chosen instead to throw herself into her work and her family life. But, like Dalia, who put it succinctly in the first days of the revolution, Malak asked herself, what will you choose to do in the face of adversity? The answer came a few days later:

> We continued to witness the violence that was perpetrated by the military police. There was the blue bra incident, where a girl was badly assaulted by a group of soldiers. As she was running away from them, they pulled her cloak and exposed her nakedness and kept stomping on her. A friend I know from Tahrir, Moataz, tried to pull her away, but the poor guy was badly beaten by their batons, and when one soldier broke off his stick from the sheer force of the blows over the boy's body, he took off his helmet and kept hitting Moataz in his head with it. Then there was the Maspero massacre of a Coptic Christian march. I was there moments before the march had arrived. The soldiers started shooting immediately, and one by one the protestors fell. A rain of bullets hit them in their bellies, their backs, and their groins. I remember this all in slow motion as I stood out in the open, in the middle of it all. My friend pulled me into safety. He yelled at me, "What are you doing? Are you crazy?" I was in a daze, shaking my head, and just not in touch with myself at all from the shock of seeing so many dead and wounded. Then I remembered why we were there! We had medical supplies in case there were assaults, so we set up a field hospital right in front of the Ramses Hilton Hotel. We disinfected wounds, tried to stop others from bleeding, sprayed yeast mixed with water on people who were sprayed with tear gas. The overwhelming feeling subsided, and there I was utterly focused and efficient. I even surprised myself! That night I decided to hand in my resignation to free myself up for the revolution.

Free to pursue revolutionary activism full time (with the exception of nursing her father), Malak joined a movement called *misr al hora*, meaning *Free Egypt* and began working on building political alliances between groups. She was in the middle of organizing a meeting that was to coordinate party efforts when she found herself pulled into the subject of sexual harassment and the gang rapes that were taking place more and more frequently now. Eventually, she brought herself into the middle of a feminist collective organizing to protect women from harassment in demonstrations. She attended the meetings of an established anti-sexual-harassment organization, and from there, she volunteered to work in the field and became part of an on-ground task force for the prevention of mob assaults.

Nothing could have prepared Malak for the kind of trauma that was inflicted on women who were victims of mob assault in the protests. Not even her master of arts degree in gender studies equipped her to deal with the sheer brutality of sexual violence committed against these victims. The weapons used, the horrible narratives that legitimated these attacks, and the way that women's bodies were appropriated by these attacks with such impunity were particularly difficult for her to stomach.

> "There was no security, no psychological support or even medical care for the women victims of these attacks. The media fetishized these incidences, and some media outlets claimed that these were 'normal,' given the large scale of the protests. But these attacks began happening twice and three times a day! They were not 'isolated' incidences. The first eighteen days of the revolution were completely different. After Mubarak stepped down, a dark force was unleashed from the gates of hell," said Malak.

The new organization that Malak joined to protect survivors of sexual assault dealt with five hundred cases of sexual assault between June 2012 and June 2014. The voracity of the cases and the senseless violence were quite disturbing, as she went on to describe some of the cases she dealt with directly. "There was a woman who was inside a car. Can you imagine? Inside a car! They wanted to break the car windows and ended up carrying the car with the woman inside. The thirtieth of June anti-Morsi protests saw a spike in gang rapes. Forty-six in all. I dealt with five or six by myself. It was painful. They tried to prepare us, but we were not expecting what we saw that day."

> A wave of fifty to sixty men, who seemed so tightly woven together you could not pry them apart, carried away one of those young women. We tried to stop her, but she was in the clutches of death. Every time we caught up with them, they moved her. And with every movement, someone raped her. She was raped with their hands, their bodies, and even though penis-to-vagina rape was not common in these instances, there were worse fates. This woman's vagina was penetrated with a knife. We finally got her to safety behind the gates of a building. They were big wrought-iron gates that nearly collapsed from the sheer weight of that mob.

According to Malak, the rapists were eighteen to thirty-five years old. She noted that they wore jeans and T-shirts; none of them wore the traditional dress or galabiyya. This was consistent with data collected from other mob-rape incidents in Egypt. Despite the large number involved in the attack on this woman, only seven of the perpetrators were arrested for their crimes. They were tried a year later, and five of them were found guilty and sentenced to life in prison; the other two were given twenty years in prison.

Human rights issues in Egypt received much attention during the uprisings and more importantly in the postuprising period. The Supreme Council of Armed Forces, which seized control of the country after Hosni Mubarak was deposed, was implicated in various human rights infractions such as torture, censorship, the shooting and tear gassing of protestors, administering virginity tests to women, as in the case of Samira Ibrahim, and trying civilians in military courts while keeping them in custody for long stretches of time with no formal sentencing. Malak, like many human rights activists, began by devoting part of her time to supporting political prisoners. She visited them, brought them food and supplies, and ensured that they had legal representation. Over the last few years, she became indispensable to one of the country's most renowned human rights lawyers, who considers her to be to be her right hand.

At the end of our long conversation, a sudden wave of sadness crossed Malak's face. When I asked her why, she replied with a laugh, "I am not completely sad! This is because as much as there is corruption and darkness, there are people out there like my colleagues and like Lamya who bring goodness into the world. My work with the political prisoners is now taking some priority over my work against sexual harassment which I have not abandoned, because if we do not stop the injustice, everyone is going to suffer. Violence against women, I learned, is an extension of social violence. They are inseparable."

She is driven, to a large extent, by an unlikely sentiment: "Guilt! Guilt gets me going, honestly. I was definitely ambivalent. This kind of work changed who I am. Secondly, I am still inspired by the revolution, and I am not giving up! I avoid the term *activist* because it makes me squirm. I feel I am undeserving of it. The general atmosphere is dark. I saw the inside of those prisons, where innocent people are left for months with no rights. And there are others who paid a much higher price. Once you know something about the dark underbelly, it makes life more difficult, but you can't go back."

Pivotal moments in people's lives, such as the ones Malak describes when "you can't go back," seem to emerge as a central theme that runs through the stories we have heard so far. These are the moments when these women of the midan asked themselves the crucial question echoed in many of these stories, what will you choose to do in the face of adversity? Though they may be radically different women—and additionally disparately located geographically on the map of urban Cairo, they nevertheless arrived at these crucial moments in their experiences. They had to confront their inner fears and make a choice. To all, these choices took them in the direction of revolutionary activism.

There are, however, others who had made up their minds about where they need to be in life, long before the Egyptian uprising. Those who had perhaps realized earlier in their lives that they are indeed the ones who stood their ground. A number of those women—now in the later years of their lives—were also mobilized by the revolution. Their worlds too intersected with everyone else's in Tahrir and in other squares in Egypt. These women also have a story to tell.

"I Ask of You No Fee, Therefore, Save Loving Kindness among Kinsfolk": Hoda

In her modest family apartment in Garden City, only a few blocks from Tahrir Square, Hoda, a recently widowed, retired lawyer in her sixties, recalls these first few days of the uprising: "I used to go every day. I'd leave my home carrying my folding chair, walking slowly on foot until I eventually arrived there. I'd go sit with people. All kinds of people, young people and old people. . . . From going almost every day, they soon started making a pathway for me in the crowd so I could pass through the throngs towards my known spot in the square."

Hoda did not learn about the protests on January 25 from Facebook or Twitter; she had no time to learn these things, she said. She found out about the protests from her nephew. "He came over one day with my sister and told me that there were protests in Tahrir and that he and my sister were going to participate. I said *me too. Take me with you!*" She was not new to political activism. Hoda was a member of the lawyers' syndicate that had been left-leaning at one point and is still quite politically vocal in the country. Though she had long since retired from law, she views herself as someone who never retired from political life.

Since our conversation was evoking many memories, Hoda beckoned me to the kitchen and offered to make me tea or coffee. She advised me to choose coffee, since she had just bought a special Turkish blend from the coffee store, made especially with cardamom for her. Her 1950s kitchen still functioned, with its decades-old appliances, looking beaten-up and crusty with use but nevertheless faithfully producing and preserving countless meals for the family. Hoda stood behind the stove, as she had probably stood every day in the last forty years. She carefully stirred the finely ground Turkish coffee into the old brass *kanaka* (Turkish coffeemaker pot) while she delved into the details of her life. She was an avid cook, she said, unlike her mother who, back in the day, "had an array of servants." Hoda's meals were always flavorful and familiar because they were lovingly prepared by her own hands, she added. Working as a lawyer, she and her husband were called to court at all kinds of hours. They did not follow any specific schedule that she could remember. When children came, the couple just made things work somehow by pitching in together. There was no magic formula, no secret process; things just fell into place every day as it came. Hoda and Ibrahim had two daughters, twins who are radically different, just like Hoda and her sister.

"My sister Nivine, my twin, is a member of the Muslim Brotherhood. I am not on good terms with her. She has a problem in her brain!" Hoda smiled, indicating that this was not really true, but she nevertheless continued on this theme for a while. "She brought her son with her into the Brotherhood. He has been a member for years now. Those two are deeply committed. There was a time when she wore the niqab [veil covering the face] and black robes and gloves. Her son has a long beard to his waist and wears the traditional skullcap and galabiyya. When we went to Tahrir Square together, I knew beyond a doubt that they were still active in that organization."

Although twin sisters Hoda and Nivine chose different paths at some point in their lives, their story is not unique. Like Dalia and her family, Hoda and Nivine's lives illustrate how constructs of the religious/secular divide play out among members of the same family. What makes this particularly interesting is the fact that they were twin sisters raised in the same environment and with the same family. Hoda was saying that despite the fact that she went to the midan with her sister, she had some suspicions about what Nivine was really doing in the protests. While they stood in the square among the thousands of protestors, Nivine's son slipped away, and Hoda did not really know where he went, but she watched Nivine's face as it became more and more constrained. Recalling this now, Hoda paused and seemed lost in thought. It was a difficult moment, I could tell, a moment when a sister began feeling mistrustful of her own twin.

"She was afraid. She was afraid for her son . . . that something would happen to him and kept staring at the roofs of the buildings. Nivine must have known that the snipers would be there, hiding on the rooftops. She kept saying how they would 'get us' from there. You know?" She looked at me now almost for confirmation. I realized what Hoda meant, that snipers would shoot them from the rooftops. But instead of what is commonly believed, that the secret police and even uniformed police caught on tape with shotguns clearly visible in their hands, Hoda believed a different scenario, that she was now about to tell me. "I am certain that it was the Muslim Brotherhood who were the ones who shot protestors from the rooftops of those buildings in Tahrir. Nivine knew this was going to happen then. Her son must have gone up to the roof to make plans. *They* did it!"

Apparently, Hoda's suspicions were unfounded, as eyewitness accounts reported that the two snipers who were caught red-handed shooting at protestors on January 30, 2011 were not members of the MB but were most likely security forces. While there is still much disagreement about this contested fact, rumors that claimed members of the Muslim Brotherhood were inciting mayhem and mysteriously plotting against the revolution were circulating widely. It was easy to understand why Hoda was implicating the MB with such certainty, despite her lack of evidence. The history of mistrust between the sisters played right into larger dynamics in society, where Islamists are pitted against the rest of the population to rationalize the use of violence in the fight against terrorism. These dynamics, unfortunately, find their way into the closet of relationships among families and siblings. Many Egyptian families shared similar experiences when one or two members in an otherwise moderately religious family joined an Islamist organization. These experiences split families and created deep rifts that never healed.

The lives of these two twin sisters, in many ways, epitomized Egyptian society and how it was beginning to unravel after the election of former president Mohamed Morsi, his imprisonment, and the Islamist protests that followed, where hundreds were killed and injured. Hoda and Nivine were both born to a traditional rural family. Their father, a well-known lawyer in Cairo, came from an old landowning family. Their mother, a distant relative to the former royal family, sheltered, westernized, but upper class, brought an alternative style to his rural sensibilities. She was a kind-hearted but passive individual who was not in her element at home with an overbearing and somewhat remote patriarch and two modern daughters.

"We basically did whatever we wanted," Hoda said. "My mother was a lovely but delicate woman, fair with blonde hair and blue eyes after her Circassian roots, but she was no match for my sister and I, who increasingly became wild and willful and made her cry all the time." In college, the twins took very different paths, Hoda joined the Left, while Nivine joined the Religious Right, and so it all began. As Nivine began covering her hair in traditional Islamic style, Hoda wore miniskirts and sleeveless tops. She eventually married a socialist classmate, while Nivine married a young member of the Muslim Brotherhood. As the sisters drifted apart, their mother was caught in the middle and to her dying day tried to no avail to bring her daughters closer together again.

Writing about the lives of the two, Hoda who took a secular left turn while Nivine took a pious Islamist route, the contours of a dichotomy that is all too familiar begins to emerge. Yet, as I sat sipping my fragrant Turkish coffee from its delicate china cup across the room from Hoda, it became clearly apparent that the twins did not represent a binary at all. My hostess wore a traditional hijab that was neatly tucked around her face and was, in fact, at that very moment reciting a verse from the Quran.

"*Qul laa as'alukum 'alaihi ajran illal mawaddata fil qurbaa.*" The verse was from *surat al shurah* (42), and it meant the following: "I ask of you no fee therefore, save loving kindness among kinsfolk." Hoda was referring to how the Quran calls for kindness among kinsfolk, indicating that all she really aspires to is kindness between herself and her sister, according to Muslim teaching, regardless of the differences between them.

Over the years, and in addition to her passion for socialist politics, Hoda was interested in pursuing her faith. She had explored various religious interpretations of Islam and had also attended religious classes. It was several years before she realized that most of the classes she attended were designed for basic thinkers and that they did not provide the answers she was looking for. Then, finally, she stumbled upon a Muslim preacher whose teaching strongly appealed to her. He emphasized a critical approach to understanding the faith and encouraged her to think for herself. He did not try to prevent her from being an independent thinker, as others have done. Her learning experience progressed more deeply into his teaching, and she became his mentee. Eventually, she started preaching to other women, but after a while she found out that preaching was not for her.

Hoda's views were the result of years of thinking, reading, and discussion. She summarized these views to me. "Politics emerge from people's agendas. Their reward is a worldly one. Politics change and are fluid but religion [Islam] is solid, it is unchanging. Religion's reward is in the afterlife." Thus, Hoda clearly defines a divide between politics and religion that would fit quite nicely with modern secular thought. She continued her reasoning. "Take for instance adultery. Any accusation of adultery in Islamic law requires four eyewitnesses which can never really be obtained. You see, God made the proof of adultery almost impossible because adultery affects and harms everyone. These are clear and just teachings; however, I cannot rule with religion. No! Because there is no negotiation with religion, a ruler cannot give a religious ruling and then change it. Islam cannot be desecrated this way. People have to conduct their daily business and be ruled by laws that respond to their needs. Islam cannot rule people because it is too sacred."

Then Hoda turned to the subject of veiling, explaining her own interpretation of the tradition and revealing a thoughtful, well-researched point of view. She explained how Quranic teachings recognize that there are several levels to piety and therefore there are varying expectations for each. "The verse in the Quran that addresses veiling, mentions it is recommended for *al mo'minat* [Muslim women believers], not *al muslimat* [Muslim women]. This means that there are degrees. Hence, it is not a requirement for *all* women, as some would want it. We used to wear minis (short skirts) and walk around with sleeveless dresses, and we were in a society that found that acceptable. In conclusion, we must look around and judge the moment."

Our conversation took us back to the Muslim Brotherhood, although I had a sense that we had never left that discussion. "Who said that the Muslim Brotherhood ever worked on social reform?" she asked me with indignation when I mentioned the social projects supported by the MB. "They were not involved in development at all," she continued. "These are all propagandistic things so that people will look at the *ikhwan* [Brotherhood] and think they are doing well for the country. They never did reform society, simply because they did not want to do the government's job for it. No, they provided no real services; they merely created the poor's dependency on their charity." This made Hoda's position toward the Muslim Brotherhood crystal clear. Although she saw herself as a pious and learned Muslim, she was vehemently opposed to any mixing of religion with politics. Her dislike of the MB seemed to go beyond an investment in the privatization of religion. It was a sentiment driven by mistrust in the Brotherhood's motives, which she believed were motivated by a hunger for power and control.

Whereas religion had no place in politics for Hoda, it was certainly the inspiration for her own personal choices and practices. It was because she considered herself a devout Muslim that she placed emphasis on nurturing family relations. When their mother passed away in November 2010, Hoda made an overture toward her sister that was well received. The two decided to try to mend fences. Hoda continued to live in their parents' smaller apartment, which replaced their old, sprawling one when things became rough financially, while taking care of their ailing mother in the last few years of her life. The family estate in rural Egypt that had dwindled over the years went on to the other twin. Eventually, they fell into a routine in which they called to ask after each other's children and husbands and attended major social events like weddings, funerals, and childbirths. But despite the social niceties, they never went back to the closeness they enjoyed in their early childhood. Their views seemed to them too divergent to make that possible. The uprising in Tahrir Square was the first time they had gone out together as sisters for a long, long time.

"I Was at Home in Tahrir for the First Time in My Life": Magda

Tahrir Square was indeed a space that brought very diverse people together. Almost everyone I talked with about the revolution discussed animatedly the bonding that took place in the midan and the energy that catalyzed the various kinds of people who became united as *eid wahda* (one hand)—a slogan that was echoed again and again in the midan. Whether being one hand referred to the people and the military or the Muslim sheikh (clergyman) and the Coptic priest or the Quran and the Bible, being one hand gave the revolutionaries hope that they could not be beaten.

One powerful force among the diverse revolutionary community were the artists of Egypt who, with their creative ability to articulate social sentiment, produced powerful revolutionary messages that kept the demonstrations going, even when it seemed almost impossible to do so. Whether through musical performances, mural paintings, or street theater, art in all of its diverse forms was a revolutionary medium in Tahrir Square. It expressed the ethics and sentiments of the protests on one hand, and galvanized and memorialized the protests on the other. The role of the arts and the artists in Tahrir cannot be underscored enough.

Among the women artists I got to know in the making of this book was Magda, a performing artist with a long legacy in the theater. Her contribution to the revolution is one that merits particular attention for its sensitive rendering of the Tahrir experience that remains so evocative in the minds of people who shared its moments. "I am the daughter of a poet, but on a more human level, I am a performing artist," she said with a laugh. "What do I begin to tell you about myself? My parents were really from very different backgrounds. I suppose they were in for somewhat of a shock, the mix between the leftist and the humanist. Even though he was a leftist, my father was often criticized for not having a 'loud' enough voice [not being critical enough of the regime]. We lived all over the world. Growing up as a third-culture kid, I learned that people were diverse, that acceptance between people was possible, and that religions, whether Muslim, Christian, or Buddhist, merge together fluidly. Though our family is Muslim, we celebrated all those holidays, and our dining table welcomed the people who shared their lives with us as we traveled to faraway locations."

This perfect picture of cultural and religious harmony soon unraveled when they returned to Egypt where, as an only child and the daughter of a famous dad at that, Magda began to feel ostracized. "I guess I had always felt like a misfit. It was hard at first to try and fit in, but I found my niche in college with theater people like myself, many of whom felt the same way I did." After graduating from college, Magda went on to graduate school, and she received a master's degree in drama arts. "I continued living in a bubble. My old friends from college, I guess would now be considered *felool* [supporters of the old Mubarak regime]. Yet, despite how my life was wrenched in the opposite direction in the last few years [referring to the revolution], I still feel like a misfit. I take comfort in that. I choose to be a 'street cat.'"

In the years before Mubarak stepped down, Magda was part of a politically active artist crowd. She is therefore not new to corporeal dissent, but it was not always the case. In fact, before the uprising, when her friends engaged in protests and were beaten by the police and dragged to prison, Magda was content just to observe. She occasionally went to the places where her friends were demonstrating, only to make sure they were all right, but did not engage, preferring to be on the margins, just as she had always been placed. "I used to tell them it was not worth it to get beaten so badly." As a performing artist who engages her body on stage, she was comfortable enough following theatrical choreographies, but this did not translate, at first, into actually using her body to protest.

On a hot summer night, when Magda was feeling especially dissatisfied with the status quo, "I felt downtrodden. I was discontent and rebellious. I saw the people in the metro looking miserable, harassment everywhere, and mediocre people becoming more and more prominent in society." She decided on the spur of the moment to go to a demonstration with her friends. This time, she was not simply observing. Deeply dissatisfied with the conditions in her country, she found herself being swept into the tide of protest. Although she is a petite woman, she surprised herself by getting into the thick of things. Right when things were getting intense in the protest, she turned around to find herself face to face with the secret police. She was surrounded. She felt the blows to her back, her stomach, and even her breasts. Yelling and at the same time raising her arms to deflect the punches put her at a disadvantage. She was pulled by her arms, dragged and thrown into an unmarked truck. Humiliated by the secret police, she was then thrown in jail. They called her father to come get her, and she felt even more humiliated. The memory of it still haunts her.

They called her name and then shoved her toward the office where her father sat across the desk from the officer. Her clothes were torn and dirty, her face streaked with tears, and her hair disheveled. She lowered her head, unwilling to meet her father's eyes. How ashamed she felt in front of her father who, at an elderly age, had to get out of bed in the middle of the night to go pick up his daughter from jail. A man who was not politically inclined and who preferred not to engage with the regime, it put him in a difficult position as an apolitical poet. They never discussed it again, but Magda knew it distressed him. When he died a few months later, she blamed herself.

To deal with the profound loss of her father, she threw herself into all kinds of sports. Focusing on remaking her body, Magda sought the solace she needed, "It was as if I wanted to murder this body by making it disappear through rigorous swimming, boxing, and aerobics." As she sat remembering all this, she hugged herself. Magda explained that the tough treatment she subjected her body to was also partly empowering. Months into this tough bodily regimen, she emerged stronger and more muscular than before. Part punishment to herself for breaking her abstinence from protest rule and part arming her body with strength against being physically beaten, she did not let herself be defeated by her experience. As her bodily confidence grew, so did her political awareness. She became absorbed by stories of the "underdog," as she put it. "The burning of the Coptic All Saint's Cathedral on January 1, the death of Khaled Said, the tape of the microbus, Emad Al Kabir being raped by the police—all pointed to one perpetrator: the state."

And, like millions of concerned citizens like her, Magda read the call for revolution on Facebook. Everyone, it seemed, was going to be in the midan on the twenty-fifth of January. "I said yes when my artist friends said they will go too. Everyone was saying this was an *intifada* [uprising]—even a revolution." But even then, after all that happened with the death of her father, her beating by the secret police, and the numerous causes she had gotten so interested in, there was a part of Magda that was still reluctant to commit completely to demonstrating outright. "I said to myself, ok Magda, I will just go for a while, and then maybe I can grab a coffee with some of my friends."

By 3:00 p.m. on Tuesday, January 25, 2011, Magda was sitting in the metro by herself, headed toward Tahrir. When she got out of the metro, she went look-ing for her friends, who were consumed by news that Habib Al Adly (the then minister of interior) will disperse the protestors. "So, just as I had anticipated, my friends and I decided to leave and get some coffee somewhere."

For the next few days, Magda was on and off in the midan. The next day, the protestors started a *"kar we far"* tactic against the security police (this entailed running, throwing rocks in the direction of the police, and then retreating). One of the officers looked up and recognized her from her television acting. "He yelled at me, 'You! Get to your home, now!' They grabbed me and took me aside. I started to cry uncontrollably." When she finally got home, she went to sleep, trying to shut out the turmoil of what she had just experienced, but the world did not seem like it wanted to let her. The next day, newspapers mentioned her by name as one of the "delusional" demonstrators. On the twenty-eighth of January, she headed out once again toward the midan, only this time she could not cross Qasr el Nil Bridge. Stuck for hours, she headed back feeling despondent.

Everything changed on the thirtieth of January, when she joined her theater group in Tahrir Square. They stayed on a bit longer, discussing what was to become of the protests and whether this indeed would be a revolution. Just then, a friend who was in touch with the assistant minister of interior urged them to leave, warning that "they" (security forces) will attack the midan. They grabbed what they could from their belongings, alarmed by this news from a reliable source, and spent the night nearby in a friend's apartment. During the night, as they sat huddled on the floor, they could hear the gunfire coming from the square and the sounds of tanks moving in on the protestors. She could no longer bear the sounds. What if they killed the women and children who were camped in the square? What about those nice people who gave her tea when she was shivering from the cold? She became consumed by worry. So, at dawn, Magda—without waking up her friends—picked up her shoes and, tiptoeing out of the apartment, went down the street to Tahrir Square.

She continued to show up at the midan almost every single day until the military dispersed the camps in December of that year. This is how Magda describes her feelings when she changed from a spectator to a marginal protestor to a person completely dedicated to political work:

> It was purely a selfish need. I had no chants or slogans. I did not suddenly become "political." I have always been political; I just didn't know it. It came out as a shout at that break of dawn in Tahrir. I found a voice for everything I had been feeling and thinking. This is where I needed to be. I was at home in Tahrir for the first time in my life.

Magda describes the range of emotions generated by that early-morning experience in Tahrir Square as a kaleidoscope of color—a beautiful metaphor that encapsulated the spectrum of feelings and impulses felt right before a person takes a leap. Throwing herself into activist work, she explored various venues of activism and different ways she could be of help. The field hospital seemed to be a good place to start, so she decided to volunteer her time there. Initially, she felt uncomfortable to find out that the hospital was run by the Muslim Brotherhood. Because of her prior impressions about the MB's reputation of being particularly conservative in their gender ideology, Magda, with her background in acting and drama, anticipated trouble. "To my surprise, they accepted me as an equal. They never looked down on me." Her first task was to compile a list of the people who were injured. She found herself running from one end of the square to the other, taking notes and documenting the injuries. She kept a detailed ledger with information listing the injuries she had witnessed during the day. When she went home after a long day's work, memories of what she saw stayed with her, leaving her deeply shaken, but she accepted her burden with no complaints.

Magda described a particular phenomenon that emerged in Tahrir Square during the revolution. She seemed to be defining herself in opposition to what many called "*geziret al farafir.*" "Actors and intellectuals I know used to hang out in geziret al farafir. They'd pull up a chair and sit in the sun with their friends, sipping their [café] lattes from Beano's [a chain of western-style coffee shops in Cairo]. Then they'd go home to write on their Facebook pages and claim to be patriotic. There was a clear class distinction in Tahrir. But I didn't want to be part of that. I went down to Tahrir because my own survival depended on it."

As interesting as this phenomenon was, where people created hierarchies and levels depending on their level of involvement in political action in the square, I was more interested in that moment to understand why Magda saw her activism as a way to survive. In Magda's case, just like it was for Malak, Yasmine, and many others joining the struggle in Tahrir, there was rekindling of a dimension of themselves buried underneath layers of a lulled existence, while living in general apathy and disinterest. To a privileged few, like Magda herself, entitlement went unquestioned, enhanced by a segregated social structure that, even when it threw her in other directions, continued to isolate her intellectually and physically from others. Selim Shahine (2011) captures this in his discussion about the decades of depoliticizing Egyptians under the yoke of long regimes that were only interested in prolonging their time in office at the expense of popular "voice." In Magda's case, the transformative impact of the uprising in Tahrir Square takes an existential turn—one that reached cathartic dimensions only one night after intense involvement in the events of Mohamed Mahmood and the clashes that took place at the Cabinet. "They [the military police] hit the field hospitals! The number of casualties that resulted could not be counted. I think I had kind of a nervous breakdown. I sat in the metro station on the floor at night, just crying and waiting for the trains to run again so I could go home."

Her instincts told her to go home and hide from the horrible reality she had witnessed that day in the midan. She waited for the metro station lights to turn on so she could escape the horrors of what she had just experienced. She recalled the images of the young and old people dying in front of her, and the realization that these were people who were simply trying to effect change, gunned down by the army that was supposed to protect them, was too overwhelming for words. Magda sat in silence in front of me, her eyes transfixed on the floor and I could sense she was in the grip of a wave of strong emotions. A moment later, she looked up at me and said with a slight smile, "But I did not go home that morning. That is not where I went."

This was Magda's decisive moment, the moment Dalia and Malak had described to me before, when one had to make a decision, the fork in the road, to fight or flee. This was the point of no return, as Malak had remarked. Magda chose not to go home. Instead, she left the metro station and walked past Tahrir Square and into the Qasr al Dubara field hospital.

"I knocked at the door and went inside. I just asked to volunteer." This was the largest of all the field hospitals, set up in a church to treat those injured in the protests. A woman, a doctor who ran the field hospital around the clock, welcomed Magda. It was the beginning of a three-year commitment to work with the wounded and the human casualties of civil disobedience. From that moment on, she continued her political activism; traveling to Mansoura and Port Said after the *ultras* (fans of Al Ahly soccer team) came under a brutal attack following a match with a rival team. Magda recounted what happened from what she had gleaned from the survivors. On February 1, 2012 the ultras were trapped in Al Masry team's stadium in Port Said as exit gates were padlocked shut, preventing them from escape. The lights in the stadium were dimmed just as the fans of the rival team, who had smuggled knives and machetes into the stadium, set upon the ultras. More than seventy people died, and three hundred others were injured. The magnitude of what happened hit all the revolutionaries hard. In the ensuing confusion, few were able to make sense of the violence, but it was clear that this was not about soccer alone. Many alleged that the remnants of the regime were behind this horrific attack. The Ahly ultras' ability to mobilize and organize marches and protests played a pivotal role during the uprising of the year before. Eyewitness accounts claimed that civilian-dressed policemen also participated in the attack. Magda was deeply shaken by the extent of the casualties she witnessed in Port Said. She continued to protest the lack of policing that led to its deadly conclusion.

Despite the death and destruction that she had witnessed during that last year, it was not until the protests in Abbasiya that she came face to face with the specter of death. "I saw death and looked it in the eye in Abbasiya," she said with eyes fixated as if on a distant unfolding scene as she relived that horror. It was hard not to be moved by her recollection. Though we sat talking in a ridiculously noisy café, her rememory was so powerful that the next few moments seemed as if they were spent with her in Abbasiya amid the bustle of protest, the loud bursts of gunfire, and the sounds of pounding feet as the protestors took flight in a stampede, once they realized that they were ambushed again by unknown thugs.

Tensions brewing a few days earlier culminated in the violence in Abbasiya that took the lives of eleven Egyptians and injured almost fifty more on Wednesday May 2, 2012. The unofficial count of the field hospital attending physicians placed the dead at twenty and those injured at sixty (Mourad 2012). Protestors from various political groups had gathered in front of the Ministry of Defense to oppose SCAF's handling of the presidential elections. The objections were specifically directed at Article 28 and the disqualification of several candidates based on what they believed were far-fetched allegations (ibid.). The newly minted Article 28 stipulated that the "committee of experts" who were in a powerful position to influence the outcome of rewriting the constitution would include six judges out of ten experts. This stipulation in particular was rejected by many of the progressive revolutionaries, who were aware that Egyptian judges are known for their conservative views and therefore could derail the process (Al-Ali 2013).

On the other hand, Salafi groups in support of their candidate, Hazem Abu Ismail, who was disqualified from the upcoming presidential election slated for May 23, also called for the sit-in. As more disaffected protestors joined them, the peaceful sit-in began to shift, and tensions began to mount. State media reports represented the protestors as anti-military Islamists and claimed that the protestors were preparing to storm the Ministry of Defense. Locals from the immediate neighborhood openly blamed the protestors for prolonging the tensions between SCAF and their communities, while others were outright furious, throwing insults and accusations. In turn, the protestors reportedly felt that the Abbasiya residents were disloyal to the revolution and accused them of selling out to the media and to SCAF (ibid.).

In the early hours of the day on Wednesday, armed but unidentified men took the protestors by surprise, brandishing their weapons. The men stormed into the crowds, shooting their shotguns and throwing tear gas bombs, causing such violence that the mayhem is bound to remain in people's memories for many years to come. Magda is among those who will never forget the scenes of the dead and the injured being trampled by the stampede of hundreds. She herself was among the 350 protestors who were arrested that day. One of her friends, Atef El Gohary, was killed by the thugs who had infiltrated the area. As she was dragged to jail, kicking and screaming, she thought she saw a glimpse of him. She was later accused of conspiring against the regime of Mohamed Morsi. Once again, when the officer found out who she was, they let her go. A legal case against her, however, continues to run its course in the courts.

Instead of terrorizing her and undermining her revolutionary spirit, these turbulent experiences became milestones to her. They strengthened her resolve to fight social inequality and to call for justice. In the summer of 2013, news reached her that Delga, a village in Minya, became yet another Upper Egyptian village to face sectarian violence. Groups of Muslim Brotherhood supporters had apparently seized weapons and ammunition and cast out what small police force existed in the village. They claimed that Copts were among those who plotted for the removal of former president Mohamed Morsi and forced them to pay tribute. A church was attacked, and a Christian barber's shop was ransacked. As the violence continued for weeks, it caused the displacement of many Coptic families. Magda put together a caravan of medical and food supplies for these families. She worked around the clock to coordinate with the Red Cross, the local security administration, and a good number of donors, when one day she received unexpected visitors.

Two men stood outside her apartment door dressed in casual clothing but looking to her now-trained eye like *mukhbirin* (undercover police inspectors). They wanted her down at the station for questioning about the village of Delga. "I am a peaceful person, and I do not want to step on anyone's toes. There is a law that enables civic organizations to help during social crisis, and this was all I was doing. I was told that I could not go with the caravan myself, that they could not guarantee my safety." The officer sitting behind his desk advised her to coordinate with the Red Cross. Having been given no choice, Magda handed over the supplies to them and, at the time of my conversation with her, she was still waiting to hear if the supplies had reached the villagers.

Having dedicated her life in the last five years to pursue new possibilities for Egypt through her field activism, Magda seemed unsure about the future the last time I met with her, right before the presidential elections that were to bring Abdel Fatah Al Sisi to the presidency. "In order to continue our struggle, we need to be very shrewd. My friends used to call for the military to fall, but I disagreed and told them not to say this, because people were not ready. But this time, I am a bit afraid, I do not have much hope. My fear is that this could be another form of 'stability.' I would not be able to stand that. There was a high cost that people paid. Not just the high cost of an eye or a limb, those who lost their lives, but also the cost of what each one of us paid personally. There is no society that is without injustice, but this cannot go on. People who dream of a better life have no place here. They will die depressed."

Conclusion

For many, the revolution of January 25, 2011 caught them by surprise; others anticipated the protests but did not expect its magnitude, and few predicted its coming. When the people rose in revolt in Tahrir Square and the streets and centers of major cities in Egypt, it was as one hand. Egyptians from every walk of life, religions, genders, classes, races, and ethnicities—came together. But they did not all come together at the same time. Some were there the first eighteen days, others joined a few days after the twenty-fifth, and there were those who came to revolution even weeks and months after the first sparks ignited. Just as their timing differed, and the dreams and aspirations they had were varied, the revolutionaries themselves also came from diverse backgrounds. Seeing how incredible this diversity was clarifies the galvanizing effect of this event. When millions of people reach across these divides to bond together over their dreams for their country, it makes for a transformative moment in history—one that will never be forgotten.

The collective memory of a nation is often written on the body, as Paul Connerton argues in his book, *How Societies Remember* (1989). Through action, the corporeal is intextuated with the meanings and memories linked to these actions, thereby producing an archive of the lived experiences of a people in the body. The corporeal archive of revolution is accessed through the rememories of the experiences women revolutionaries shared with me in this chapter and in the rest of this book. As they remember their days of revolt, they access this archive stored in the material dimension of the corporeal. Rememories, in turn, are performances that (re)intextuate the body with resistance and thus are counterhegemonic. These lived experiences act to disrupt, reorganize, and restructure the hegemonic modes of knowledge production of the history and politics of the years between 2011 and 2015.

The varying perspectives of the revolutionary women who share their stories here illuminate the multiple layers that constitute the experience of the Egyptian revolution of 2011.

Amal worked as a cashier in a government office but also secretly worked as a maid to make payments on a new apartment. Her experience of the midan contrasts with twenty-five-year-old Yasmin frontlining with her fiancé. Still, there is the emerging revolutionary in twenty-seven-year-old Malak, drinking her morning coffee on the twenty-fifth of January, oblivious to what was happening in the midan, but who ultimately quit her lucrative job to free herself up for revolutionary action. Yara lived in a gated community until chaos knocked at her door, motivating her to take control and to engage in revolt. Then, there were those women whose political action fluidly intersected with their religious beliefs, posing no problematic binary or contractions for them. From a Muslim Sister to a former leftist lawyer, engaging in social change also meant being pious Muslims. An artist, Magda, who viewed and experienced her body only as an instrument of performance and athletic discipline, discovers how much more power can be accessed and deployed in the corporeal for revolutionary action. Her lived experience as she becomes aware of this potential was also part of this chapter. Looking back to these days of revolt beyond the first eighteen days provides a broader perspective and contributes to our knowledge of revolutionary milestones and of the joys and traumas of revolution through women's eyewitness accounts. These reconstruct the narrative of revolution that centers women as authors of their own lived experiences.

Centering women revolutionaries within the complexity of the events of the uprising is significant for how the revolution will continue to be remembered as a historical event. But more important, acknowledging their lived experiences and reflecting on their nuanced multiplicity clearly captures the impact of the revolution of January 25. The lived experience of women's struggle lends perspectives that are revealing of the relationship between gendered bodies and the political process but also of relationships to the country, to family, to each other, and to political action that are deeply personal as well as social and cultural. The next chapter problematizes the gendered body at the midst of the forces vying for control in the midan, to clarify the centrality of the corporeal in revolt and the need for a theorization of the ways bodies are intextuated by power but also how the corporeal intervenes in restructuring the political and social landscape.

5 Bodies That Protest

A FEMALE PROTESTOR in Tahrir held a sign with the following slogan: "The revolution will not pass *through* the bodies of women. The revolution will pass *with* the bodies of women. No to sexual terrorism." In just a few words, this protestor captured the gender politics of an entire revolution. While women's bodies are enshrined in nationalist ideology as iconic subjects of the state's protection, they inversely legitimate the state as a governing power. This treatment of women's bodies as surfaces to rationalize power systems is referred to as "sexual terrorism" in this protestor's sign. The statement implicates not just the state and its supporting mechanisms and parties but also Islamist groups and liberals—to name a few who competed over representing women's bodies. It also refers to sexual harassment and reported assaults on women. During the revolution, narratives about gendered corporeality reflected the multilayered confluence of these competing political powers. As the sign asserted, however, women articulated a counter discourse that reimagined the female body in public spaces and revisualized the gaze. Deploying their bodies in ways that were both deliberately as well as strategically orchestrated, these efforts were to have diverse and varying outcomes.

Spanning the period between the beginning of the revolution to the year after the end of Mohamed Morsi's presidency, the following chapter focuses on gendered bodies and the fluid processes by which they constitute and are constituted by the forces of Islamism, militarism, protest, and sexuality in the context of the revolution. I explore four vignettes that highlight how these forces employ policies, legal codes, and public discourse to regulate dissenting bodies. I then analyze the significance of these processes of regulation and dissent, in an examination of the theoretical literature to conclude. The first vignette describes the court case of Samira Ibrahim against the military apparatus's virginity tests; the second vignette presents the circumstances surrounding the brutal attack on a female protestor dubbed "the girl in the blue bra." Aliaa Al Mahdy's "nude activism" follows, and finally the case of the "Virgin Trials" or *banat sab'a el sobh* (the girls of 7 a.m.), where young women affiliated with the Muslim Brotherhood were tried for alleged crimes against the state in Alexandria. A corporeal analysis of the Virgin Trials offers an alternative reading of the Muslim Brotherhood's gender politics and strategic ways of negotiating the repressive politics of the state. The four cases point to the centrality of female corporeality amid the political transformations taking place during and after the revolution of 2011 as new contentions rise to the surface of the public debate.

Gendered corporeality in the Middle Eastern setting is a layered and complex subject that is often overlooked theoretically. The topic is also fraught with land mines, since feminists often intentionally avoid the topic of "the body," for fear of contributing to the reduction of the gendered subject to its material dimensions. Yet, the corporeality of dissent cannot be ignored when discussing revolt, on one hand as a material factor where bodies physically push boundaries and on another because the politics of the body, the discursive forms of gendering the body, and the larger social and cultural "bodyscapes" deserve more than a passing glance. Examining the gendered body in the Middle Eastern context as a dissenting force rather than as a victim of female genital cutting, honor killings, or interpretations of veiling and segregation provides for an alternative reading of corporeality in this part of the world. The previous chapters looked into the corporeal archive and its relationship to rememory; here I turn to the specific forces that the body in the Egyptian context contends with. My intention is to critically evaluate the various cultural, social, and political dynamics with which we come to understand the gendered corporeal other.

Virginity Tests and Women's Virtue

"In God's name this is not fair. There is only injustice in our country now. This case has turned into a theatrical play!" exclaimed twenty-five-year-old Samira Ibrahim as she rushed out of the courtroom where the officer accused of defiling her body with a virginity test during the uprising of January 25, 2011 was acquitted (Human Rights Watch 2011). The court hearing took place in November of the same year, when former president Mubarak had stepped down and SCAF (Supreme Council of Armed Forces) assumed office, presumably to keep the peace and prepare the country for reelections. Samira Ibrahim, who was among seven women subjected to virginity tests, had filed a formal complaint with the military prosecutor.

Ibrahim was born in 1986 in Sohag, Upper Egypt, where she attended college. She comes from a political family, where her father and uncle both faced persecution as a result of their membership in Islamist groups. In a video interview with Tahrir Diaries, an organization working to record the events surrounding the 2011 military use of violence on peaceful protestors (Tahrir Diaries 2011), Samira recounted the events of her arrest. On the day of January 25, 2011, she was on her way to Cairo University when she stopped at Tahrir Square to join the protest advertised on Facebook. Although the square was nearly empty when she got there, many soon started to arrive until almost a million people had joined her. Samira spent that night in Tahrir with the other protestors, dodging the police while they called for Mubarak to step down as president. When the morning came, Samira was arrested by the armed security forces and taken to Al Gabal al Ahmar (where the Central Security Forces' headquarters are located).

After she was released a day later, she returned to Tahrir again. She was arrested a second time, but this time one of the officers in charge of her arrest claimed that she was arrested in a house of prostitution.

Samira described the abuse and violence she experienced as a result of her participation in the protests. "They spat at us, threw water on our bodies and electrocuted us, kicked us in our faces with their shoes. They wanted us to regret ever having participated in the protests" (ibid.).

In custody, Samira Ibrahim's body became an instrument of inflicting shame and humiliation. Her humiliation was so utterly painful that she repeatedly prayed she would die. As she recollected these hours, she was unable to stop herself from weeping, her voice trembling with emotion. First, she was taken to a room (as were the other six young women who were detained) where she was told to undress so the prison warden, a woman, could conduct a search. This body search was to take place in front of a big window and a door that led to a hallway, where numbers of soldiers and officers could clearly see into the room. Samira described the laughter and the invasive stares at her nakedness, as if "they were having a party with me (my nakedness)." When all their bodies were strip-searched, all the girls were made to sit on the ground and to group themselves by whether they were married women or *anisat* (young unmarried women or virgins). Samira joined the *anisat* when her name was called once more so she could take a virginity test. An officer dressed in uniform waited to conduct the test. When she would not comply, she was electrocuted again. Eventually, she did submit to the exam, which was an extremely painful experience. The humiliating effect of this invasion of her body, coupled with the fact that she had to lie naked once more on a bed in a corridor in front of the cell in full view of the passing soldiers and officers was enough to make her wish her life would end.

Ibrahim filed a report and took the officer who conducted the virginity test to court. Her case brought much attention to the plight of women protestors who are arrested and subjected to the assaulting test and exposed the role that SCAF had played in the physical and psychological abuse conducted against the activists in Tahrir. SCAF issued denials but then admitted to the tests, claiming that "We didn't want them to say we had sexually assaulted or raped them, so we wanted to prove that they weren't virgins in the first place," according to an unnamed SCAF general (Fleishman 2011). "The girls who were detained were not like your daughter or mine. These were girls who had camped out in tents with male protesters in Tahrir Square, and we found in the tents Molotov cocktails and [drugs]" (ibid.). Impugning the virtue of young women revolutionaries became a collective endeavor in which the military, the media, and pro-Mubarak supporters took part. This made it difficult and equally painful for women to continue their political work.

Ibrahim emerged sobbing from the court proceedings that acquitted the army doctor who conducted these tests, but she was to win the civil court case only a month later. Virginity tests are now outlawed in Egypt as a result of Samira

Ibrahim's civil suit—a major victory that came at an immense cost to her. Being the only woman out of the seven who were subjected to this invasive assault, Ibrahim's life and privacy were once again violated by the court proceedings and the public attention she was subjected to. As one television broadcaster put it, "She was raped all over again every time someone mentioned her name."

In 2012, Samira Ibrahim was at the center of yet another ordeal involving a different kind of purity test—this time on an international level. Earlier in 2012, she was chosen by *Time* magazine to be one of the World's 100 Most Influential People (2012). Hollywood star and Oscar-winning actress Charlize Theron, who is also a UN messenger for peace and avid activist fighting violence against women, wrote of Ibrahim, "It takes a strong person to stand up for what is right in the face of ostracism and public scrutiny. Samira represents the model of how to stand up to fear, and the impact she has made reaches far beyond Egypt." In 2013, Samira Ibrahim was slated to receive the International Courage Award from the US State Department. When anti-Semitic and anti-American tweets were ascribed to her however, and Ibrahim refused to apologize, the award was withdrawn (Egypt Independent 2013).

Interestingly, this last controversy is not altogether different from the first one that Ibrahim found herself at the center of. Protest and public action brought an unsuspecting twenty-five-year-old Upper Egyptian woman to the center of media attention, with which Ibrahim was neither familiar nor prepared to confront. Just as the virginity tests sought to determine the status of her hymen as an indicator of her purity and therefore value in a patriarchal society, the award that she was vetted for required that she hold views that are internationally acceptable and neutral towards the United States and Israel. Samira's trials and tribulations epitomize the intense scrutiny that women protestors were subjected to during the revolution, revealing the challenges of political work under conditions of intense visibility and multiple levels of scrutiny.

The stigma and public shaming that Samira Ibrahim was subjected to more than once during the ensuing years after the revolution are witnessed once more in another case that caused much-heated public date, the case of the woman in the blue bra.

Struck Down, a Woman in a Blue Bra

Her identity remains a mystery—the young woman in the blue bra who lay on the ground of Tahrir Square after being viciously beaten and stomped on by military personnel. That this brutal display of state violence took place at the very epicenter of Egypt's recent revolution was not lost on the protestors and supporters of the revolution. The brutal event that drew much attention from human rights organizations, local and international media, occurred only a few months after the events of January 25, 2011 toppled the regime of former president Hosni Mubarak. The millions of protestors who occupied Tahrir Square had dispersed, except for small numbers of protestors who continued to occupy the square who demanded that SCAF step down and allow a civilian transitional government to carry out elections. SCAF came down on the peaceful encampment with violent force. Soldiers destroyed the activists' tents, chased them into the narrow streets around Tahrir Square, and those whose ill fate placed them in their way were viciously attacked and arrested. The "woman in the blue bra" was known to distribute water to the occupiers of the square and to tend to the wounded. One activist who met her on several occasions described her in a personal communication as follows: "She was kind and thoughtful. I saw her several times around Tahrir. Her generosity was strongly felt by all of us. But she kept to herself; she was not part of the "occupy" (the demonstrators who chose to remain in the *midan*) who spent the night here."

On December 17, this woman was fleeing the square, hoping to escape the wave of SCAF forces descending on it. She tripped and fell as the soldiers rapidly closed in on her. Footage of the incident show how a young man turned around, saw her on the ground, and reached out to pull her to her feet when the soldiers gained upon them. The man was viciously beaten with batons while soldiers kicked her in the stomach and stomped on her with their heavy boots. As one of them was attempting to pull her by the corner of her black *abaya*—a cloak-like garment covering her body, it came undone and exposed her pale and vulnerable body against the dark asphalt of the Tahrir floor. She was wearing a blue bra. Cameras clicked as she received blow after blow from the soldiers, who seemed bent on breaking her limp, pale body. As they kicked her stomach and stomped on her chest, there was no sign of a struggle from her as she remained limp on the ground. She seemed to be unconscious. When the brutal scene ended, one of the soldiers returned and with the edge of her cloak covered her exposed body.

The case of the "girl in the blue bra," as she was later called in the media, is emblematic of how women's bodies are rendered vulnerable, debilitated, feminized, objectified, and sexualized. While public discourse was woven around this body to strategically legitimate the state's use of brute force, women's groups adopted the image of the gendered, pale, young body of the fallen protestor as an iconic metaphor representing the inviolability of all Egyptian women's bodies.

The release of the photos of the "blue-bra girl" contrasted dramatically with SCAF's repeated denials of the use of violence against the Egyptian people. Finding themselves cornered and unable to contest the reality of the pictures, SCAF's spokesmen promised to have them investigated. As inadequate as this response was, the campaign that followed this was not. Television programs broadcast debates mirroring a split in public opinion; one side opposed violence against protestors and noted that the soldiers targeted women (and men who were attempting to shield them from the violence), while those siding with the military's actions came up with complex conspiracies to rationalize the incident and accuse the victim. State media efforts to influence the public debate in favor of the latter group worked relentlessly, making it clear that the post-Mubarak military-led state still operated per the guidelines of the former regime's agenda.

Gendering Deviance

In the face of growing scrutiny and to discredit the continuing protests in Tahrir, SCAF drew upon classic patriarchal social norms and values to establish a common cultural platform with the Egyptian people, revolving around public morality. The military's version of the events during which the assault on the young woman took place was reported to the media by Major General Adel Emara. "The armed forces," he said in a prepared statement, "do not use violence systematically. We exercise a level of self-restraint that others envy. We do not do that out of weakness but out of concern for national interests." (El Hennawy 2011). In his disavowal of the protestors, he described them as drug addicts, street children, and thugs. The same message that was used to smear Samira Ibrahim was repeated in the case of the blue bra. Major Emara was careful to assure the public that the "girls" who were out in Tahrir were not "like yours or mine" (ibid.). His intended meaning being that they were not "the children of good people." Emara claimed that "these girls" were seen in compromising positions with the young men in the square and dismissed them as immoral and sexually promiscuous.

Soon after Emara made these statements, state media unleashed a defamation campaign to underscore the depravity and immorality of those participating in the protests. A few of the satellite channels that opposed the revolution also joined the cacophony of voices by openly impugning the fallen young woman in Tahrir Square. "She was wearing a bikini and not a bra!" exclaimed one commentator. "Why, my dear, were you wearing your bikini to Tahrir? Did you think you were going for a swim?" he continued his satire.

One anchorman posed a question to the blue-bra girl: "Truthfully, what were you thinking wearing that abaya with nothing underneath it? And an abaya with snaps? Come on. Couldn't you find one with buttons?"

TV cameras took to the streets, collecting corroborative opinions; one veiled woman commented, "I don't believe this girl was veiled. You do not dress that way if you were veiled. She is a fake!"

Another one quipped, "She is not one of us."

An entire corpus of programs was dedicated to blaming the victim and creating as much suspicion and conspiracy theories around her as possible, to deflect from the beatings and killings that took place that day.

These allegations against the uprising were not uncontested, however. On December 20, an epic women's protest, "Egypt's daughters are a red line," spread from one end of the capital, Cairo, to the other. Carrying signs painted in the colors of the Egyptian flag, but with a blue bra replacing the golden hawk, women protestors claimed national signifiers as a space for feminist resistance. Other signs transformed the unconscious, limp body of the fallen young woman into that of a springing Ninja fighter, leaping into the air to deal a blow to the face of the soldier who brutalized her. The visual reversal of the young woman's body from vulnerability to superhuman strength inverted the state's defilement of the female body and gave rise to the symbols of resistance in its place. Women activists reversed the stigma and shame of the vulnerable and bare woman's body and turned the state's metaphors of control into battle cries of dissent.

In addition to directly opposing the injustices of the Supreme Council of Armed Forces, other women chose to negotiate the legal and disciplinary modes of control by holding themselves up to the highest possible standards set by the law and by patriarchal, cultural, and religious values. Instead of opposing patriarchal expectations, these women capitalized on the metaphorical and iconic positioning of women. They deliberately marked their feminine bodies to counter the anti revolutionary rhetoric of the military and state media. Scholarship on gender in the Middle East has dealt with the conceptual gendering of the nation as a woman or as a mother of the nation (Badran 1995; Baron 2005; Kandiyoti 1991), explaining how the depiction of women as primarily "mothers" of the nation corresponds to the metaphor of the nation as a patriarchal family. Mothers and wives, in this metaphor, are expected to uphold the values of this family by preserving tradition and sustaining patriarchal bonds. Most important, women are to epitomize notions of purity and honor. This ensures that the patriarchal system, which revolves around ideas of prestige and honor/shame, is mirrored both in the nation and in the family. Female purity is therefore essential to the nation.

Women themselves, however, are not unfamiliar with these semiotics of gender as they chose to challenge their imposed boundaries from within these norms. They strategically used notions of purity, piety, and dedication to the family to affirm the legitimacy of their public presence. Numbers of women came to Tahrir with their children and their husbands. The presence of women and children was clearly essential for emphasizing the patriarchal validity of the protestors against the head of the nation, who was perceived as a tyrant or as a father who relinquished his fatherly obligations.

Over a period of time, women affirmed their public political voice and thwarted the claims of military leadership that the protestors were disloyal outliers, impious and immoral. They used their corporeal power to do so. Some deployed their bodies as canvases to proclaim their loyalty to the nation by painting their faces in red, white, and black—the colors of the Egyptian flag. Others wore the flag as a garment or a headband or carried it in their hands while some participated in pious and religious activities such as praying and religious chanting. During Friday prayers, hundreds of Muslim men and women prayed side by side; sometimes women prayed in the front, which is not customary. In addition to directly protesting and resisting, revolutionary women also embodied the virtues of loyal citizenry, pious subjects and mothers of the nation.

An institution, which plays a lasting role in gendering human bodies through discipline and violence, the military state apparatus played a rather fluid role as a marker of masculinity and morality and as a repressive force in society in the wake of the Egyptian revolution of 2011. Various scholars have pointed out how militarism generally constructs aggression as a masculine ideal and naturalizes violence against the normative creation of a dehumanized enemy "other" (Enloe 2000; Peach 1993; Shalhoub-Kevorkian 2009). Other studies have shown how the growing phenomenon of military violence has generally influenced a growing trend of global violence against women (Marshall 2005). In events that took place after the public demonstration of violence against women and men who were protesting in Egypt, the construction of masculinity, the naturalization of violence, and the demonization of the enemy were strategies that SCAF employed to legitimate its authority in the face of growing public dissent.

The stigmatization of dissent in the wake of the Egyptian revolution became an exercise in state violence aimed at sociopolitical control and the reaffirmation of the state's hegemonic power over the public sphere. This state-led campaign managed this by defiling revolutionary women's honor and painting them as "immoral" and "loose"—women who are not entitled to social respect, while the men who demonstrated against state corruption and injustice were, in turn, denigrated and publicly labeled as homosexuals. Constructed in this parody as the guardians of the women protestors, men's masculinity and honor, as defined by patriarchal norms, became suspect and were publicly stripped of their privileges as men. The revolutionaries were thus dismissed as "unmanly," and the credibility of the entire uprising was framed by SCAF as a charade played by social outcasts.

The Body as Spectacle: Nude Feminism

Born in 1991 to a middle-class Egyptian family, Aliaa Magda Al Mahdy describes her family life to a reporter from the French women's magazine *Elle* as follows: "My father is an engineer who was previously an army officer, and my mother is an accountant. Since I was a small child, I have been in a war with them. My father did not think I would get an education; he thought that I would be illiterate and find a husband to cook for. To them the devil entered my life at 15 years old when for the first time I went on the Internet" (Trétiack 2013). Aliaa believes that she is no longer of value to her parents because she lost her virginity to her boyfriend while getting nothing in return. Her body exposed to the world on the Internet further debases this body to them. Her mother has called her a "whore," she tells the magazine.

In an infamous black-and-white photograph she took herself, Aliaa wears nothing but a pair of red slippers and a red rose tucked behind one ear. Naked and vulnerable, she posed defiantly in front of her self-timed camera. She posted her picture online a few days after January 25, 2011. It went viral. On her blog, she added these words: "Put on trial the artists' models who posed nude for art schools until the early 70s, hide the art books and destroy the nude statues of antiquity, then undress and stand before a mirror and burn your bodies that you despise to forever rid yourselves of your sexual hang ups before you direct your humiliation and chauvinism and dare to try to deny me my freedom of expression" (El Mahdy 2011). Amid the uproar that ensued, two questions seemed to occupy many demonstrators: "Why now? Why this?"

While the bulk of the initial comments of the public condemned her naked photos as inappropriate and an affront to Egyptian and Muslim ethics and traditions, a few curious souls reached out to Aliaa, gently repeating the questions, "Why now? Why this?" Her answer was always the same. "When the woman is taking off her clothes, it is a way of revolution. When she took off her clothes, it was not for men, it was to protest oppression," Aliaa commented to Al Arabiya (Ajbaili 2012). Rather than surrender her body to be consumed by the male gaze, to be a symbol of masculine honor and patriarchal standards of femininity, she reclaims the freedom of her corporeal form by severing the ties that bind it to its cultural matrix. By being naked, Aliaa simply claims that she is free.

Claiming her body to expose hypocrisy and male chauvinism, El Mahdy chose a most unusual mode of rebellion, which is now known as "nude feminism." She joined the radical nude feminist group FEMEN, a Ukrainian-based feminist group that employs public nudity to voice their objections to the objectification of women. They began their activism in 2008 to protest the rise in sex trade in their country and from their adopted international causes, particularly what they deemed the oppression of women by Islam and Islamism. They have called for a "Topless Jihad Day," for instance, in solidarity with Amina Tyler, a Tunisian woman whose naked photographs incited a call for an Islamic punishment of death by stoning.

Joining forces with FEMEN, Aliaa embarked on a campaign to publicly oppose Islamism and the application of Sharia Law (Islamic law) as a constitution. This latter objective was the subject of a nude photo shoot and public protest with two FEMEN activists, which they titled, "The Apocalypse of Muhammad" (Salem 2012). In black lettering painted across her chest, Aliaa proclaimed to the world, that Sharia is not a constitution. With radical deliberateness, Aliaa drapes the Egyptian flag on her shoulders and in some pictures even raises it up behind her as she protested naked in front of the Egyptian embassy in Stockholm. She posed nude in other photo-ops, wearing an ancient Egyptian wig, complete with black pharaonic-style eye makeup. Another photo posted in 2014 on Facebook shows Aliaa menstruating on an ISIS flag, while another woman wearing black veils, seated facing away from the camera, is seen defecating on the same flag. This photo objected to the extremist policies of the group but was eventually removed by Facebook, and her account was shut down. Nevertheless, the picture went viral. "I was reproached, but at all the rallies in Egypt, the protesters brandished the national flag. It was said that I was insulting the Qur'an, but my body insults nothing and nobody, it is a body, that is all. It should please them, in Egypt, men think precisely that a woman is only a body!"

Though Aliaa refuses to be defined by her body, she still appropriates national markers such as the flag, but only in an effort to push her political agenda of gender equality and the recognition that women are not merely objects. By rejecting the hold religion, patriarchy, and nationalism have on defining her body, she asserts that it is only *her* right to claim her own body, regardless of the male gaze and regardless of traditions and nationalism. This is where Aliaa's message becomes problematic, and indeed the FEMEN campaign altogether. In taking on "nude activism," they are simply reversing the dominant discourses that they perceive to be limiting to women, without tackling the larger problem, which is why the gendered body is at the center of this debate at all. By uncovering, they reject covering, associating it with backward traditions and misogyny, in so doing, they appropriate the choice of millions of women who find empowerment in covering. Yet, covering or uncovering the body is a moot point when the real issue is women's right to exercise their agency in whichever way they choose. For Aliaa personally, given her own history and feelings of being repressed sexually by her environment, nudity appeals to her as a form of resistance against the gaze. As an activist, her choice is not the only choice, and her nudity is not liberating to other women. It is therefore not surprising that Muslim women around the world rose in unison to oppose the FEMEN campaign. A counter-FEMEN campaign called "Muslim Women Against FEMEN" on Facebook has called the nude activists Islamophobic and imperialist. "Feminism comes in many forms," came the response. "You bare all, I cover up." Another noted, "Nudity does not liberate me! AND I DO NOT need saving." #MuslimPride # FEMEN.

Aliaa had to leave Egypt when she was assaulted in Tahrir Square and received hate mail and death threats. She has since sought political asylum in Sweden, where she was given a passport and granted a full scholarship to attend university. Though she states that she is lonely and that she misses her cat, she regrets nothing. "Of course, I too have dreams. I would like my country to change in all aspects," she says. "But, at this moment, my real dream would be to live in Stockholm! I'm not sure I'll go back to Cairo one day. In my childhood, everyone wanted to leave Egypt, not me, and finally I left. I miss my cat. I'm a little confused. I am told that I shocked everyone but the most shocked is me. Since I left, I have received testimonies from women and men who tell me what they are experiencing. I receive messages of support from women who do not dare to express themselves in public. But also threats of death. Sometimes I'm depressed, I feel like no one understands me. At times, I think of the past, the places I used to go when I was little" (Trétiack 2013).

Aliaa provides a counterstrategy to how revolutionaries are officially and legally (according to the new protest laws) criminalized in Egypt today. Ironically, by taking off her clothes, she divests her body of its social and political markings as transgressive, impious, immoral, and even irrational. While the authoritarian government shores up its fragile legitimacy by applying brute force over the chaos of revolution, the corporeal becomes a space of contention over domination. In contrast to Aliaa's nakedness and affirmation of corporeal liberation, the case of the Muslim Brotherhood young female cadets presents itself as the other side of that coin. Young, pious, covered, and "virginal," these women represent the epitome of the patriarchal female ideal. Yet, when these bodies protest, they too are subjected to processes of defamation and are constructed as deviants. In their case however, the Muslim Brotherhood organization comes to the rescue.

"The Virgin Trials"

Fourteen Egyptian women members of the Muslim Brotherhood organization stood behind bars in an Alexandrian court in November 2013. They prepared to stand trial for allegedly inciting violence in Alexandria in the preceding month. They were young. Seven of them were only fifteen and seventeen years old. The girls were uniformly dressed in white, with white veils covering their hair. Youth, purity, and innocence were accentuated by the anxious scrubbed faces peering from behind the bars. Their age, gender, and dress prompted newspaper reports to call them "virginal." In fact, in no time at all, the trial and its subsequent proceedings were dubbed "The Virgin Trials."

Looking straight at the cameras, smiling, and turning to talk and giggle with their friends, these young girls seemed like any other regular teen their age. Except they were not. These young women swathed in white standing trial in an Alexandrian court was not perceived as other teens their age. They were accused by the state of being members of a terrorist organization, blocking roads in the city, and inciting violence against the government during the protests of October 31. Eleven members of the Muslim Sisters were also arrested and tried with the younger group.

In photographs and news footage of the young women, two discourses emerged in direct opposition to each other—a binary of two realities competing for people's hearts and minds. On one hand, the power of the collective image of fourteen young women dressed in white, representing everything that is pure and pious, while on the other, allegations of violence, mayhem, and insidious sabotage. This was perceived as a travesty of justice that epitomized the state of unrest and instability in Egypt following the end of the MB government in Egypt after former president Morsi was deposed.

White is worn for *haj* or pilgrimage to Mecca and is also the color of the *kafan* or funerary shroud followers of Islam are buried in. White is also a symbol of purity and of purification, which has connotations related to the young age of the detainees, many of whom were minors. Despite the message of innocence conveyed by their dress however, the young girls were entangled in larger discourses of corporeal politics. The Virgin Trials epitomized how vying political projects in Egypt today are played out over women's bodies. The competition over women's bodily comportment is not new in the Arab region, as liberation movements, postcolonialist nation-states, and Islamist groups have traditionally engaged in a perpetual symbolic war to define it (Baron 2005; Hale 1996; Kandiyoti 1991; Lazreg 1994; and others). Modernity, Islamist piety, modesty, authenticity, and purity have always been the purview as well as the restraint to women's bodies in the Arab world. This is even more poignant in postrevolutionary Egypt, where women's bodies have increasingly become the site of struggles for power and hegemony over public discourse. What do the bodies of these youthful, pure, and pious "virgins" tell us today? What statements do they make about piety, femininity, and authenticity? And what are the implications of these statements on the political scene in Egypt at the time?

After the ouster of President Mohamed Morsi in July 2013, contentious debates over who is right and who is wrong in Egypt pointed to a growing fact, a trend if you will, which can be described as the emergence of increasingly uniform notions of selfhood that strengthen their consistency within divisive and distinct group dynamics. Witnessing how forms of ideology are inculcated and disseminated in Egypt, how they are aimed at honing consistent, uniform, and homogenous selves begs the query into the ways women's bodies are placed on display, utilized, and often deployed in public to further political aims and hegemonize public discourse. Piety, authenticity, and femininity are factors that play an important role in establishing group boundaries. The case of the Virgin Trials points to how consistency and uniformity are communicated through women's bodies to a Muslim majority public in Egypt to counter state hegemony and challenge its domination over the public sphere. Alternatively, the criminalization and demonization of these bodies characterizes the state's response to militant Islamism. In the wake of the massacre of Muslim Brotherhood followers at the *Rab'a* protest camp by police, the state resorted to its usual rhetoric to undermine protests and vilify its opponents. The unity of the Muslim Brotherhood message of piety and innocence thus became a graphic battle cry in the discursive struggle over bodies, public space, and political dominance.

One of the young women who was protesting on October 31 and who was arrested and tried in November with the rest of the young "virgins" was Ola Ezzat. Her story can perhaps provide some insight into how women's bodies are often socially deployed to underscore traditional notions of femininity that demarcate political boundaries.

A Portrait of a Virgin

Ola Ezzat was eighteen years old and a medical student at Ein Shams University at the time of her arrest. Her family still lives in Alexandria where she was born. Ola comes from a family of Muslim Brotherhood devotees. She grew up in a home in the neighborhood of Sidi Bishr, where many leading figures of the Muslim Brotherhood were often read and discussed. Although Ola's arrest in October 2013 was a traumatic event for her and her family, she is bound and determined to continue protesting. Her parents are understanding when it comes to Ola's activism, since to them, being part of the Muslim Brotherhood is akin to being part of a large family. Their eldest son and Ola's brother participated in the Rab3a sit-in, and various other family members have been to prison over the years or are still there now. It is a way of life for the Ezzats, one that mirrors their beliefs and somehow enables them to see hope for the future they envision for all Muslims. A strong and unified Islamic *"umma"* or global Islam *al 'alamiyya al islamiyya*, where Islamic culture and traditions can bring back justice for everyone.

Ola belongs to the *"zahrat,"* which refers to the plural of flower, a clearly feminized descriptive that refers to the beauty and freshness of a socially perceived natural symbol of femininity. On the other hand, and rather predictably, young men are called *"ashbal,"* which is the plural of a cub. It is a gendered metaphor of strength in the making and a future as the ruler of the jungle, the lion who presides over nature and protects his herd. The young recruits are trained and prepared for full membership later on in life by being placed in these smaller groupings. Ola Ezzat recalls the events that led to the protests that put her in jail, quite differently from what the picture police reports have described. She insists that she never blocked the roads or incited violence, as she was accused of doing. "We were simply protesting. That is my right." And what were they protesting? Ola and her fellow zahrat came out with the supervisor of the group to protest the deposing of former president Mohamed Morsi. Much to her surprise, they were all arrested.

While Ola and her fellow zahrat were put in jail, the state and its judiciary prepared to make a case against them. They were described as dangerous women who incited violence and destroyed public property. Police claimed they attacked the security forces and damaged the glass windows of several shops. The state's accusations ran in contradiction to the corporeal statement made by the young women in their white virginal garments. The girls' youth and innocence held no sway over the court whose judges criminalized them. The social and political affiliations of the young cadets, as members of the Muslim Sisters framed them as guilty.

A Plea for Purity

The court's initial harsh ruling of eleven years in prison for the adults and juvenile detention for the teens made headlines. Ola and her friends' pictures were plastered all over the news and social media. The youthful faces of the young detainees sent strong messages to the public, while the white garments emphasized their purity and piety as well as their liminal status. Here were these young women or "virgins," as some put it, who despite their innocence and piety were still unable to escape the wrath of the system. Muslim Brotherhood campaigns to free the young zahrat occupied social media for several days. The campaigns pointed to the innocence of the young women and their pious purity and made a strong bid for their freedom. Their plight became the occupation of the general public, who were outraged at the arrests. So successful were these media campaigns that both liberal and secularist groups who opposed the Muslim Brotherhood sympathized with the young women and objected to the severity of the sentence.

The detention of the young women was, in fact, part of a widespread series of arrests of supporters of former deposed president Morsi, which amounted to two thousand arrests (Human Rights Watch). Despite the serious allegations and the eleven-year sentence for a few of the MB women, the courts reversed the verdict only two weeks later, after considering their lawyers' appeal. Within days, however, the government proposed the "no protest law" which prohibited individuals from protesting without permits. It was clear that the court's initial approach was not conducive to public stability, but clearly the Virgin Trials were enough pretext to push forward the much-hated protest law.

The dynamics of political conflict and the struggle over the definition of women's bodies exemplified in the Virgin Trials emerges from a long history of the Muslim Brotherhood as an eighty-year-old organization that has been often persecuted and marginalized by the state in society. Although by no means a binary opposition, these two forces, the Islamists and the Egyptian state, are stacked on either side of a political debate that serves to create a deep and unequivocal rift in a country often plagued by larger issues such as poverty and lack of basic human services. The Muslim Brotherhood helped define the character as well as the political orientation of the Egyptian street for decades. So where does the MB place women? And what role, if any, does the organization play in this discursive corporeal struggle over articulating the meanings produced by female bodies?

Gendered Corporeality and the Muslim Brotherhood

In the past few years since the Egyptian Uprising of 2011, much attention has been directed at the Muslim Brotherhood association that emerged as a major contender for power in Egyptian politics. Despite its sweeping victories in the presidential, parliamentary, and several national elections, however, the Muslim Brotherhood's "Freedom and Justice Party" was unable to match its success in popularity with success in administration. Regardless of the so-called role of the "deep state," which posed a major impediment for the elected MB regime, the group, estimated to include five hundred to six hundred thousand registered members (with an equal number of supporters and funders; women are 25 to 30 percent of the MB membership) struggled to implement its promised agenda and was soon toppled by a popularly supported coup. Analyses and speculation about the hierarchal and somewhat conservative organization were a few of the reasons popular among observers for the "failure" of the Brotherhood and their former president Mohamed Morsi. Yet, the plethora of books, articles, and journalistic reports paid no attention to what the Muslim Brotherhood actually did well. And this marks a sad omission, for the MB have demonstrated time and time again that if they have failed in almost everything, they have demonstrated an extraordinary ability to organize and mobilize in the blink of an eye. Their record-keeping, painstaking communication systems, and careful accounting of each and every member of their group has gone largely ignored. The recruitment, training, and organization of the Muslim Brotherhood intentionally create uniformity and homogeneity among its members (el Kherbawy 2013). It is this consistency that presents a public persona that epitomizes the doctrine of the group and serves to mobilize, galvanize, and deploy large numbers of its members despite internal conflicts and external challenges.

State institutions, such as schools, the military, and hospitals, shape subjectivities through inculcating systems of discipline and obedience. Specific ideologies among the MB's organizational structure inculcate particular forms of subjectivity as well. These forms of subjectivity, although paralleling state organizations in their ability to indoctrinate and mobilize, challenge state authority and work to trouble state hegemony. Gender dynamics and gender ideology within the organization best illustrate how these processes of subject formation underlie matrices of organization.

Scholarly work on gender in the Middle East and Muslim-majority countries has demonstrated how power systems undergird organizations and state systems. I will draw upon this work as I examine the memoires of Intisar Abdel Moneim, whose book *Hikayatī ma' al-Ikhwān: Mudhakirāt Ukht Sābiqa* (*My Story with the Muslim Brotherhood: The Memoirs of a Former Sister*) came out in print during the early days of the revolution of 2011. Perhaps this account can help shed some light on the internal organization and gender ideology of the Muslim Brotherhood.

Gender Ideology in the Muslim Brotherhood: An Evolving Picture

The Muslim Brotherhood was established in 1928 by Hassan Al Banna. The organization enjoyed great appeal among the disenfranchised in society, many of whom, isolated from discourses informed by westernization or experiencing marginalization from a capitalist market economy or exclusion from social transformations, increasingly sought solace in a grassroots movement calling for an Islamic state in Egypt. The MB's history of countercolonialism against the British also embellished their credentials as a resistance movement. In contrast to the perceived corruption of the upper class, morality was stressed and Islamist values and authenticity were reinforced. Their teachings maintained that the patriarchal system is the ideal system for the Muslim family, where gender differences are clearly delineated and men have authority over women. In 1933, the Muslim Sisters group was established, whose leadership was soon entrusted to Zeinab Al-Ghazali, the daughter of a cotton merchant from a well-to-do conservative family. With a reputation of being a "soldier of God" among Islamist women and men, Al-Ghazali had a solid following. Her career focused on establishing the framework for women's activism in the Islamist movement in Egypt. She is said to have regrouped the Brotherhood after government imprisonment had fragmented their ranks.

Women's role as mothers and tutors to the future generations is central to the Muslim Brotherhood discourse. To founding women like Al-Ghazali, there is no women's issue in Islam. She finds that Islam views women and men in a unified sense, with clearly defined roles for each. To her, while women are the "indirect builders," the building is entrusted to men. Al-Ghazali attributes the debate over women's issues and rights to be caused by the disruptive forces of the West, which she describes as a conspiracy. The West, she claims, robbed women of their right to have children. According to her, western women "became a distortion and a commodity available for the lust of the wolves" (Al-Ghazali 1982). This kind of critique of western women continues to be employed in Islamist discussions about women's roles in society. Islamic women's chastity is seen as the desired opposite of a demeaning western freedom for women. The first one is a shift toward the latter part of her career from singularly perceiving women as mothers and wives to seeing women as individuals with the freedom to choose what suits them, whether it be a career outside the home or a career inside it. The second is the fact that Al-Ghazali may not have followed what she preached, since she herself divorced her husband when she found that he impeded her Islamic mission.

Among the Muslim Brotherhood organization in Egypt, the numbers of women have climbed since Zeinab Al-Ghazali (one of the key women figures in the early days of the organization) represented the female branch of the group in the 1950s and '60s. At present, women constitute 25 to 30 percent of the Muslim Brotherhood organization, but despite their efforts to raise levels of representation, they have yet to gain the right to vote within the group. Despite this glaring limitation, however, women affiliated to the MB have run for parliament as independents and as members of the MB's Freedom and Justice Party. In the year 2000, Jehan Al Halafawi ran as an MB candidate, as had Makarem Al Deiri in 2005. In 2010, the MB boasted twelve candidates who were women. One popular FJP female candidate, Dr. Susan Zaghloul, has met with considerable success in parliament and in the Shura Council and is quite active in trade unions and scientific circles, yet she advocates a rather conservative agenda for women. Like Al-Ghazali several decades before her, Zaghloul claims that women's rights are a nonissue, maintaining that it is men who are the ultimate support for women. Her views emphasize the complementarity of the sexes, in that each gender retains its identifying elements to create cohesion in society, as opposed to absolute equality, where genders have competed with each other to the detriment of the family members.

Although Muslim activist women engage politically and participate in mobilizing, representing, and endorsing their Islamist organizations, they do not do well in male-led organizations. Overall, women often play a rather prescribed role, carrying out the MB's gender agenda to enable the Islamization of the public according to the vision of the Islamist political parties. Despite what appears to be a disappointing picture, however, the persistent presence of women in several of these parties, beginning with the Freedom and Justice Party in Egypt, is already shifting the balance of power in the larger organizations by pushing for a more autonomous space for women in their fold and more awareness of women's rights.

The Muslim Sisters: One Woman's Experience

Like the young zahra, Ola Ezzat, Intisar Abdel Moneim was born in Alexandria to a middle-class Egyptian family. In her memoirs *Hikayatī ma' al-Ikhwān: Mudhakirāt Ukht Sābiqa* (*My Stories with the Muslim Brotherhood: The Memoirs of a Former Sister*), Intisar recounts her story as a former Muslim Sister or *okht*. Although she begins the book by stating that hers is an individual experience and may not be the experience of all women who join the organization of the Muslim Sisters, her book relayed a woman's candid insider perspective of the organizational and ideological structures of the group. She recounts how her father had always given her opportunities that pushed her to challenge gender boundaries as she was growing up. Fondly, she remembers how he taught her how to use a fishing rod, and later how to fish in the sea, though this was traditionally a boy's hobby. Although Abdel Moneim's upbringing did not exactly break gender molds, it provided her with a basic ability to understand gender differences and to be aware of the subtleties of gender oppression. In her memoirs, Abdel Moneim maintains that women in the Muslim Brotherhood organization are not afforded opportunities to realize their potential and are in fact often expected to obey and to carry out orders. Women, she writes, often play a perfunctory role dictated by a conservative gender agenda to enable the Islamization of the public according to the vision of the Islamist political parties. Within this restrictive framework, however, the few opportunities to assume leadership roles were only the purview of a select few whose kinship relations to male MB leaders and venerated heroes placed them in a position of trust.

However, the gender conservatism that Abdel Moneim became aware of in the Muslim Brotherhood organization was not an unchanging ideology. She explains that, to the Brotherhood, women's bodies act as public statements and are often deployed to reflect changes in strategy and political deliberations. For instance, she describes how in the elections of 2005, when the Mubarak regime allowed groups such as the MB to run as independents, the organization grasped at the chance to mainstream their image. This meant that there would be unprecedented changes in women's dress, women's public image, and women's political participation in the Brotherhood. Here Abdel Moneim details the processes that the leaders of the group put in place to ensure that both their members as well as the public begin to see, accept, and envision the Muslim Brotherhood as a politically friendly group with modern, progressive leanings. "And when it was time to be open and to prepare for a new political maneuver, it became necessary to find *sanad shar3i* [a legitimating source from the *shari3a* or Islamic law] . . . conservative ideas changed just like the clothes to suit the awaited media campaign" (2011, 40). Top-down orders from MB leaders directed the women of the organization to remove the *khimar* or face cover. Women were now encouraged to shop at famous fashion stores and to dispense with the semi-uniform look of the *isdal*, which refers to the topcoat popular among women in the MB. In their public meetings, the Brotherhood began to invite women to attend. A few were chosen to sit side by side with the male leaders, and several MB wives were handpicked to run for parliament.

According to Abdel Moneim, rethinking women's dress and their public appearance depended on the political moment. The Muslim Brotherhood employed female corporeality as a strategy to mark a progressive period or a conservative one. As long as it was needed to establish an image of progressive politics, women's faces remained uncovered, and their bodies sported fashionable attire, while during times of political repression, when the Muslim Brotherhood came under attack, conservative measures took place, and women's bodies were placed once again under the long isdal.

It is during such repressive times that the Brotherhood began to see the necessity for homogeneity and uniformity. After the army deposed former president Mohamed Morsi, who had risen in their ranks, the Brotherhood was subjected to a series of repressive and often brutally violent measures. The Freedom and Justice Party (the party of the Muslim Brotherhood) was disbanded, and its leader held under house arrest, pending his trial. This action led followers of the MB to occupy the square in front of the Rab3a al 3adawia mosque in Nasr City, where thousands of their supporters protested for six weeks. After warnings to disperse, police raided the camps in July 2013, killing hundreds of the remaining protestors. A number of MB followers who were protesting at Al Nahda Palace were killed by the security forces. These deaths, as well the imprisonment of thousands of its members, placed the Muslim Brotherhood in a state of crisis. More attempts to regroup, to sustain group cohesion, and to ensure a consistent and uniform image were presented to the public. More than ever before, there was a need to present a unified but somber front to the public. A return to an emphasis on homogeneity in the group and uniform ways of dress, which imposes an understated corporeality, became essential once more. These were the messages communicated to the public through the Virgin Trials, where the innocence of the young zahrat was threatened by state injustice. The effect was to humanize the MB as a group and succeed in galvanizing the public's opinion behind them again, if only momentarily.

Women's corporeality in this context embodies both the boundaries of the group as well its inclusiveness. But as it communicates discourses of authenticity and righteousness to the public, it is not a blank or passive slate. As we have witnessed in many of the accounts, women deploy their bodies in various ways, be it resistance, privilege, nationalism, or piety. Bodies negotiate spaces as well— political space or actual physical space. In the Virgin Trials, bodily comportment signifies a great deal about the credibility of the Muslim Brotherhood; as they invite public empathy, they simultaneously shape public opinion through reinforcing patriarchal gender norms and reinstating their authority over the limits and demarcations of public behavior. The MB's access to some measure of public power can be read in Intisar Abdel Moneim's own words as she described in her memoirs her thoughts about the Muslim Sisters from her college campus. "I had no idea how to be like them and I thought that wearing the khimar that they wore would make me a 'sister.' I hoped to be like them, a 'sister' if only to avoid their derisive glances which ostracized me because of the way I dressed" (37).

Women's dress and bodily comportment deliver specific messages about group boundaries and political climate and mark the public space as a space of Islamization (or secularization) through social notions of authenticity, piety, and femininity. Why, might we ask, are these factors important for political dominance? The answer is quite simply because historically in Egypt, the pact between a secular style of government and the Islamist trend has usually revolved around an exchange. This is the exchange of the public space of politics for secularism, in return for the space of the private sphere for Islamization (Hatem 1994). Yet, as the events of the revolution of 2011 have propelled the Muslim Brotherhood onto the public sphere of politics, their long sojourn shaping the private sphere have paid off. The social welfare activities, as well as the activism of the group itself in mobilizing the masses around the idea of an "authentic Islam," exemplified by the slogan *al Islam howa al hal* ("Islam is the solution") succeeded in the first presidential elections after the revolution and led to the victory of the MB candidate Mohamed Morsi.

On the other hand, the state's response to the growing hold of the Muslim Brotherhood on public morality and religiosity was to counter the message of innocence and victimization with its opposite, to criminalize and demonize the virginal bodies of the teenage girls behind bars in the trials of Alexandria. Regardless of which bodies dissent, those who oppose the nation are criminalized, denigrated, and gendered as deviant. The continued use of violence against supporters of the MB, however, led public opinion to question the logic of accusing the group with terrorism when army forces were massacring Muslims. The MB's consistent public message of piety and innocence was instrumental in affirming the public's outrage, despite the loss of the group's popularity.

As the previous histories for the struggle for independence, nationalism, and revolution in Algeria, Iran, Egypt, and Kuwait have demonstrated, women's bodies relayed similar assertions of authenticity and innocence. In fact, an important change in MB attitudes toward women took place in response to the coup that ousted their president. Brotherhood leadership began relying almost exclusively on women and children to organize and lead protests. Groups such as "Women Against the Coup" as well as "Girls Ultras Azhari" became instrumental in leading public protests against state violence and the removal of Mohamed Morsi from the presidency. Once again, the female body is dressed and staged to serve the purposes of two bastions of male hegemonic patriarchy in Egypt, the renewed militarized state and the Muslim Brotherhood.

As these young and virginal female bodies seamlessly shift from one category to another—the girl, the virgin, the pious subject—to the sexually promiscuous, the guilty, and finally the terrorist, social meaning and the body are collapsed into a fluid medium of discursive production through which struggles over power find expression. Once more, women's bodies become visible markers of authenticity, piety, and justice. Their feminine corporeality establishes loyalties and demarcates sociopolitical boundaries. Thus, notions of authenticity, piety, group boundaries, the exclusiveness provided by the gender ideology of the

Muslim Brotherhood group—all crystalized in the image of the young girls clad in white, standing behind bars on that cold November day in 2013.

A Corporeal Analysis: How Women's Bodies Speak Today

What conclusions can we glean from these four cases that can help shed some light on the role women's bodies play in revolution? An important theme that emerges from the stories of Samira, "the girl in the blue bra," and Aliaa is how women's bodies are spaces of contestation on which battles over authenticity, cultural dominance, and political control are fought. While these "feminine" bodies are disciplined and regulated through discourses of patriarchy, Islamism, and secular modern masculinity, they are also sites of dissent and revolution. These bodies, as explored in the vignettes described above, offer novel forms of corporeal practices that, as they appropriate systemic forms of discipline and regulation, also reconstitute them into new and personal ways of expressing counter discursive means of resistance.

Examining the key literature that problematizes how women's bodies are viewed in society and their engagement in protest may enable a discussion of these cases and clarify how they might alter the balance that Mary Douglas describes as essential to the way the physical and the social come together in the body: "rituals enact the form of social relations and in giving these relations visible expression they enable people to know their own society. The rituals work upon the body politic through the symbolic meaning of the physical body" (Douglas 2000, 129). In what follows, I discuss how women's bodies in Egypt are employed as visible markers of sociopolitical values and norms, just as they are simultaneously deployed to counter these normative symbols themselves.

Feminist literature on the body is extensive, from problematizing the gendered body's construction in society, discourse, and performance (Butler 2004; Fausto-Sterling 2000; Martin 1991; Hubbard 1987; Lorber 1991) to the systems of discipline and enforced boundaries on the body, its objectification and disempowerment, and the subtle ways the gendered body resists and pushes against oppressive forces (Bartky 1997, 2003, Bordo 1993; Brooks 2006; Hall 2000). Few studies, however, have theoretically problematized the gendered body in Muslim-majority countries in the Middle East and the Arab and North African regions (Barlas 2009; Kanaanah 2002; Kandiyoti 1991; Mahmood 2004). Barlas discusses how Muslim women's bodies are inscribed by the western gaze. The homogenization and eroticization of bodies that resist western (and male) objectification by covering is the focus of her work. She therefore pays intimate attention to the politics of veiling in Muslim-majority countries and argues that veiling is not simply an inscriber of identity and female virtue but can also be considered a form of protest and rebellion against hegemonic oppressive forces in society.

While the female Muslim body is constructed by the politics of the veil in Barlas's work, Kanaanah explores how the female reproductive body becomes an instrument of resistance to Israeli occupation and genocide in Palestine. In appropriating the tropes of biological sex, however, these Palestinian women reverse the naturalization of their bodies to deploy the body as a form of resistance to death and destruction by increasing, procreating, and inhabiting their land. In some similar aspect of this, Deniz Kandiyoti coins the term "negotiating with patriarchy" as a useful concept for feminists to think about women who learn how to maximize their gain under limiting and oppressive situations. By fulfilling their patriarchal obligations, women in patriarchal societies, argues Kandiyoti, are able to benefit from systems that initially seemed to marginalize them. In a theoretical critique of western feminism's understanding of agency as contingent on liberatory subjects, Saba Mahmood argues that women in a mosque movement in Egypt embody piety and discipline through repetitive enactments of religious practices. In so doing, Mahmood argues, these women submit rather than resist structures of patriarchy that generally contradict notions of western agency, yet among the Muslim community, this can be seen as a form of alternative agency. Her work encourages a reconsideration of agential embodiment in Muslim societies.

One of the central tropes of recent feminist theory that problematizes the social construction of the gendered body views the body as an effect of discourse rather than as a prediscursive material being. In so arguing, these scholars of the body emphasize the fluidity of the corporeal form and its temporality, as opposed to earlier feminist views that treated the body as the fixed and permanent register of sex and gender. Judith Butler notes that studies should be concerned with the constructiveness of the body at the expense of its materiality. This is because she finds this approach to be limiting to our understanding of the body. Instead, one needs to properly situate the body in relations to its "performativity" to appreciate the processes that that make it possible. One that does not deprive those analyzed from the possibility of action,

> The controversy over the meaning of construction appears to founder on the conventional philosophical polarity between free will and determinism . . . Within those terms, "the body" appears as a passive medium on which cultural meanings are inscribed or as the instrument through which an appropriative and interpretive will determines a cultural meaning for itself. In either case, the body is figured as a mere instrument or medium for which a set of cultural meanings is only externally related. But "the body" is itself a construction, as are the myriad "bodies" that constitute the domain of gendered subjects. Bodies cannot be said to have a signifiable existence prior to the mark of gender; the question then emerges: To what extent does the body come into being in and through the mark(s) of gender? How do we reconceive the body no longer as a passive medium or instrument awaiting the enlivening capacity of a distinctly immaterial will? (Butler 1990, 8)

Albeit with some reservations regarding the specific body that Butler fore-grounds, Susan Bordo (1993) attempts to answer that last question. Bordo dem-onstrates how gendered bodies subjected to extreme forms of social expectations about the aesthetics of the body and its regulation engage in psychosocial forms of resistance like hysteria, agoraphobia, and anorexia. Bordo argues that wom-en's bodies are often vehicles of resistance that reinscribe the very principles of social control being resisted. "Nonetheless, anorexia, hysteria, and agoraphobia may provide a paradigm of one way in which potential resistance is not merely undercut but utilized in the maintenance and reproduction of existing power relations" (168). In so doing, as bodies appropriate the forms of dominance that oppress them, they normalize the logic of male-centric gender ideologies, even as they seek to overcome them. "To reshape one's body into a male body is not to put on male power and privilege. To feel autonomous and free while harnessing body and soul to an obsessive body practice is to serve, not transform, a social order that limits female possibilities" (179). In this regard one can argue that to transform a social order is to reconstitute the body in terms that lie outside the hegemonic forms of bodily comportment. Reenvisioning, therefore, new spaces or alternative bodily comportments and novel deployments of discourse that sur-round the body might, according to Bordo's stipulation, begin to make a fissure in what is otherwise an impermeable system of power that undergirds society.

Women's bodies act as conduits of subject production. They relay important messages about authenticity, piety, and justice. They create loyalties and instill norms and demarcate social, political, and religious boundaries. The physical and the social bodies, as Mary Douglas states, are in dialogue with each other. Meanings are relayed through the expressive ability of the body to convey them. She maintains, "The social body constrains the way the physical body is per-ceived. The physical experience of the body, always mystified by the social cat-egories through which it is known, sustains a particular view of society. There is a continual exchange of meanings between the two kinds of bodily experience, so that each reinforces the categories of the other. As a result of this interaction, the body itself is a highly restricted medium of expression. The forms it adopts in movement and repose express social pressures in manifold ways." In similar ways, women's bodies navigate this tension between the physical and the social, producing meaning in the process while simultaneously being produced. I would offer that this duality Mary Douglas refers to in her quote is fluid rather than reified. The social and the physical are collapsed into one by the powers they negotiate. The meanings bodies produce are a continuum that respond, negoti-ate, and produce discourse.

Moving beyond seeing the gendered body as simply one that is subjugated to complicate its potential to fluidly reconstitute itself, consequently shifting dis-cursive power structures, Daphne Brooks's *Bodies in Dissent*'s (2006) treatment of resistance can provide an example of how bodies may step outside social constraints to forge resistance against oppressive forces. Her research is based on African American entertainers and performers in the early years of the twentieth century whose "bodily insurgency" presented new forms of resistance. These actors, singers, and activists, Brooks shows, reconstituted their bodies in ways that "defamiliarized" hegemonic notions of blackness in transatlantic populations. Their performances, she argues, created a powerful counterdiscourse to dominant narratives of race relations.

"The figures in this book experiment with ways of 'doing' their bodies differently in public spaces . . . Dense and spectacular, the opaque performance of marginalized cultural figures calls attention to the skill of the performer, who through gesture and speech as well as material props and visual technologies, is able to confound and disrupt conventional constructions of the racialized and gendered body . . . they demonstrate the insurgent power of imaging cultural identity in grand and polyvalent terms which might outsize the narrow representational terms bestowed upon them," (Brooks 2006, 8). Hence, Brooks inverses the point raised by Mary Douglas (2000), which states that bodies perform rituals that reaffirm acquired knowledge by seeing how bodies also have the power to disrupt that knowledge. This disruption is performed by insurgent bodies that reconstitute the space of meaning and discourse in society.

Similarly, in Egypt, during the ongoing uprising of 2011, women's protesting bodies articulated this discourse of dissent. Their bodies performed new meanings and reinscribed new understandings of what a woman's body in a public space can do and say. The very presence of nonmale bodies reconstituted the patriarchal logic of public space in the midan. As dissenting bodies, they pushed the boundaries of the state, the military, liberal and Islamist groups. Women's corporeal dissent during the uprising unsettled the old dynamics, characterizing these conflicting forces by gendering the political debate, drawing attention to women's struggle, representation and contributions.

The heated debate caused by Aliaa's "naked activism," which began in 2011, starkly illustrated the tensions growing quickly on the ground in Egypt today among Islamists, liberal secularists, and western freedom pundits. Similarly, the scene of the woman in the blue bra lying unconscious under the heavy boots of army personnel caused an uproar among many supporters of human rights. The women's march which they called, "Egypt's daughters are a red line," reflected the power of the corporeal to shift discourse in the symbol of the woman as a ninja warrior, leaping into the air and kicking back her attackers on one of the banners carried in the march. Instead of a frail, pale, naked body of a girl in the blue bra, the painted caricature depicted her as a muscular figure dressed in fighting clothes, with her face still covered and a fierce look in her eyes as she struck the face of the soldier who struck her. In the illustration, she was still wearing her blue bra.

Graffiti slogans under the symbol of a blue bra vindicated her, calling her "*sit al banat*," a term reserved for the best among all young women. Despite her anonymity, she clearly occupied the hearts and minds of people in the revolution. Yet, as strong as the support of the young woman in the blue bra was, the response of state-run media was louder. Airing programs around the clock that denigrated her and raised questions about her character and virtue, state media presenters ran a counter campaign, which was meant to support the leadership of SCAF and undermine the revolutionaries. The campaign mirrored what Holliday and Hassard (2001) describe as the construction of unruly subjects that require control. In contrast, however, was the symbolic transformation of the victim's inert body into that of a leaping ninja which, similar to black performing bodies in Brooks's study (2006) who "did" their bodies differently, acted as a counterdiscursive narrative directly undermining hegemonic discourse and reworking the female body into a strategy of dissent.

Samira Ibrahim's lawsuit against the military doctor who violated her body with a virginity test was also supported by a large constituency in society. Yet, when Samira lost the initial battle, it seemed as if only a handful of public figures spoke in support of her. Within a legal system dominated by male judges and officials, it seemed predictable that hegemonic gender ideology would prevail. Samira's private life, family name, and patriarchal loyalties were compromised. One reporter commented that Samira Ibrahim's name was forever linked to virginity tests. Despite the initial outcome of the first trial that acquitted the army doctor who conducted the virginity test however, Samira won a civil case on December 27, 2011 that prohibited the army from carrying out the tests.

Seen to deride religion and tarnish Egypt's image in the world, Aliaa received numerous death threats and at least one complaint to the attorney general to strip her of her citizenship. The first groups to denounce Aliaa's photos, however, were the liberals who, sensitive to the growing participation of Islamist groups in the revolution, opposed what they saw as blatant disregard for Egypt's culture and tradition. Feminist groups in particular were emphatic about distancing themselves from Aliaa, lest their demands for gender equality at such a critical time be compromised by her act of nudist feminism. In reality, however, Aliaa Al Mahdy's photographs directly challenged the patriarchal system that employed women's bodies as the locus of piety, chastity, and honor. It is essential not to discount her efforts to confront this oppressive structure in the starkest way possible, yet her attempts at challenging the growing misogyny in Egypt employed the very same discourses of gender ideology but in reverse. Uncovering or covering validates patriarchy's hegemony over sexualizing the body. Ironically, Aliaa, rather than escape the terms of corporeal politics, became mired in its discourse. Many Egyptian women I talked with also pointed out that Aliaa reduced the complexity of women's struggle to the superficial issue of dress/undress at a time when feminist activists were walking a tightrope to change the gender climate.

Her associations with FEMEN, a group that imposed a western brand of feminism indiscriminately over various cultures and societies around the world, also made matters worse for Aliaa. Their particular naïve and simplistic emphasis on veiling and its removal as a form of liberation was particularly ridiculed by Arab women who rose to oppose these high-handed assumptions regarding their culture and traditions. Hundreds of these women led protests that were anti-FEMEN and put together a Facebook page dedicated to their views on liberation and rejection of what they perceive is FEMEN's meddling into their affairs (Muslim Women Against FEMEN 2013).

Conclusion

While feminine bodies were encouraged and in fact embraced in the early days of the January 25 revolution, these bodies grew more controversial as the revolution progressed. More and more women were harassed, some brutally assaulted, and others arrested or beaten or their bodies violated by virginity testing under callous and deliberately humiliating, invasive processes. Why this shift in the perception of the female body? Perhaps it is best to ask, what does this shift tell us about how gendered bodies are represented in masculine spaces?

As Brook (1999) points out, the masculine gaze controls the boundaries demarcating the space of the public. Nonmasculine bodies are admitted into this space according to a set of rules and regulations that are never static or absolute. In fact, discourses that shape and frame gendered bodies are as fluid as the bodies they construct. The long history of feminist activism in Egypt attests to the central role women's bodies have occupied in the pursuit of freedom, independence, and nation-state building. Yet, despite a history that is well recognized for its accomplishments, these female bodies remain predominantly constituted from within power processes that determine the terms and outcomes of political participation. This analysis of women's bodies in the Arab Spring still concedes to Butler's question, "How do we reconceive the body no longer as a passive medium or instrument awaiting the enlivening capacity of a distinctly immaterial will?" (1998). Women's bodies transformed the terms of gender ideology as the women's march against state violence reconstituted the body of the girl in the blue bra as a warrior. Alternatively, women's corporeal resistance has also reinscribed the terms of their subordination. Women who seek to transgress the limits placed on their bodies, like Aliaa or Samira, do so bravely enough, yet often end up either outside of the discourse or worse, as reinscribing the notion of the grotesque and the uncivilized on their bodies.

In performance, therefore, there is always the potential for disruption. Public performance in particular holds much potential for transformation for women who are otherwise construed as belonging to the private sphere and who, more often than not, are perceived as disruptive and unruly. Once in the public sphere, women's bodies are regulated and disciplined by the "male gaze," which ensures that the masculinity of the public domain remains protected from the potential of chaos introduced by nonmasculine transgressive bodies. As a spectacle, these nonconformist bodies are disciplined by means of the public domain: "the conditions of entrance are often marked by prescriptive dress and body regulations intended to preserve what is known as the "professional" standard of workspaces, when in fact, these spaces are simply gendered masculine and are unwelcoming to women. The power of these regulations, both in the workplace settings and other public arenas, is understood even by very young women" (Brook 1999, 113). The practice of veiling in Muslim societies, for instance, is one such comportment perceived as a religious requirement for women to enter the public sphere in acceptable ways. Women who do not fulfill these requirements are not only harassed, but after the initial phase of the January uprising, even those who wear the veil were often assaulted. There were several recorded cases of rape by male mobs, thus signaling to all Egyptian women that their bodies are no longer allowed in the space of political deliberation.

Perhaps the contrast between what is described by Foucault as the disciplined and regulated body and Bakhtin's grotesque body linked to unruliness and lack of control can capture the discourses that frame the corporeal actions of bodies in protest in Egypt today. The construction of the other, the revolutionary protestor as the antithesis of the rational modern progressive and civilized subject, disciplined and obedient, these bodies respond favorably to a strong and dominant government that seeks to impose order on chaos. On the other hand, the body that is transgressive, out of control, and associated with lack of rationality and lack of civilization becomes increasingly alienated, stigmatized, and denigrated.

Within this binary construct of human subjects that depicts the disciplined versus the undisciplined body lies a key strategy to the control of populations and especially the nonmasculine body, according to Holiday and Hassard (2001) "This is a double process: first the body of particular subjects is coded in need of (physical) control, second this coded body is reflected back upon the subject's mind, as in need of (psychological) control. This process is at the heart of imperialist and patriarchal imperatives that sought to keep unruly subjects in their place. It is central to modernist cultural thought and has justified its repressive practices" (10). This system of control is first and foremost applied to women's bodies in the cases recounted in this chapter. Their stories merit historical scrutiny to get at the contextual background of how, where, and when these women's bodies are constituted, and how they become dissenting, grotesque and unruly bodies.

6 The Specter of Gender Violence

Kᴴᴀᴅɪɢᴀ Eʟ Hᴇɴɴᴀᴡʏ, or "Mama Khadiga," as she became known to the protestors of the midan, recounted in an interview, "We are a family in the midan, and as a family, there must be a mother and a father. And I am proud to be the mother [of the protestors]." On December 17, 2011, during the events known as the Cabinet Clashes, where confrontations between the protestors in Tahrir and the security forces became violent, Mama Khadiga was brutally beaten by the police. Footage taken of the incident shows an older woman carrying a package, suddenly surrounded by soldiers who shove her aggressively, pulling her viciously by her hair and arms.

> I was bringing food to the protestors so they could have something to eat. All of a sudden, the police ambushed us. They came out like cockroaches—a huge number. They started arresting people. Of the people they arrested, they took me. While I was being taken, the soldiers beat me up and broke my arm. They hurled insults at us so I said to one of the soldiers, "Shame on you. I am as old as your mother," at which point the soldier became hysterical hitting me and slapping me on the face. (Saad 2012)

An older maternal figure during the revolution, Khadiga El Hennawy's violent treatment by the police was especially brutal. Watching her on the screen during an interview, it is difficult to miss the motherly affection she exudes. She calls everyone *ibny* (my son) or *binty* (daughter), as if she has loved and nurtured them all of their lives, and, like many older Egyptians, she refers to death and *jannat al firdos* (Elysian fields) frequently, but specifically as a place where she will one day meet the martyred youth of the revolution. Khadiga embodies Egyptian maternal values, and her speech is gentle as she says, "I am the mother of the revolutionaries, the soldiers, and the officers. And even to the ones who are not well brought up—those I know how to bring up (to discipline them)," with a slight smile (ibid.).

Clearly, Khadiga is one who is comfortable in her role as an Egyptian matriarch. And yet, when she chides the soldier who mistreats her in the manner befitting her place of respect in a classical patriarchal society by saying to him, "I am as old as your mother," the soldier loses all restraint—viciously striking her. In her words, "he became hysterical" and slapped her so hard across her face that she lost sight in her eye for several days. How might we understand this brutal scene, with its social undertones that defy the patriarchal tenets understood and respected by most Egyptians? An older woman like Khadiga would ordinarily be protected from violence—even honored, yet here she is in a situation where she pleads with a soldier who is tasked with keeping order and stability to consider her age and her maternal standing—"as your mother," she implores. Instead, these very words cause even more brutality.

In the midst of the violent clashes between the protestors and the police in Tahrir Square, this particular exchange between the matriarch of the midan and the security policeman could not have exceeded a few minutes. Yet the incident graphically illustrates how the subtleties of power structures—at once brutal and nuanced—reverberated in the choreographies of violence in Tahrir Square. It was a fleeting encounter where the fully armored, face-shielded soldier with his bulletproof vest emblematized the state's repressive force against the elderly civilian woman, as she unsuccessfully tries to escape his unyielding grasp. Even as she hunches her body to shield herself against the soldier's anticipated blows, he is seemingly blind to her age and frailty as his arm descends to strike again. She is not his mother, just as he is not her son. As their social worlds collide, neither of them is aware of how their roles were already set, already imagined and prescribed.

The dynamics that were set in motion by the disruptive presence of women in Midan al Tahrir reconstituted the normative frames of social and political control in Egyptian society, often with violent consequences. While the previous chapter largely dealt with how women's bodies negotiated the complexity of forces seeking to repress women's political participation, in what follows, I focus more squarely on the violent encounter. I analyze the relationship between gendered corporeal dissent and the structures of power during the revolution by reflecting on the ways gendered revolutionary bodies are imbricated in the politics of death.

Normative gender categories that write women's roles in society shift in response to discourses of power that serve the status quo. Even in seemingly staunch classic patriarchal systems where gender dichotomies order and organize people's understanding of the world, gender is still fluid and changing. To Khadija, who described the social structure of the midan as a heteronormative nuclear family, "We are a family in the midan, and as a family there must be a mother and a father," she is shocked when the soldier is seemingly unaware of her corporeal markers as a woman who is old enough to be his mother.

Motherhood is contested in the case of Khadiga, who invokes its status with a soldier carrying out his commanders' orders to brutalize protestors—women and men. In fact, in a number of cases documented elsewhere in this book, the deliberate targeting of women poses as a serious possibility. Recalling the famous statement made by Major Emara, "They are not like your daughters or mine," it was as if he declared women protestors as those who have fallen out of social respectability. In so doing, the military smeared all women engaged in civil disobedience as women of no virtue or respectability. Women's bodies were targeted as an ideological Achilles' heel of the protestors in Tahrir by the military junta aiming to wrest control from the revolutionaries who occupied the square. By undermining the authenticity, patriotism, and honor of the protestors—especially women protestors, military discourse aggressively reframed them as misguided, impious, and even criminal drug addicts who were sexually promiscuous. Portraying women in this light in opposition to the core qualities of Arab Egyptian heroism informed by patriarchal values (namely masculinity, honor, honesty, and virility) was a deliberately cultivated strategy to emasculate the male protesters noted as the leaders of the protests, therefore discrediting the uprising altogether. For a woman such as Khadiga El Hennawy to compare herself to a soldier's own mother was extremely insulting to him.

The state continued to clamp down even more viciously on gendered bodies rendering a number of them stateless, as the case of Hind Nafea, others imprisoned or killed like Shaimaa Al Sabbagh. Such violence makes visible the security state's selective politics of disposability that deems who is to live and who is to die. When describing South Africa under apartheid, Achille Mbembe's take on sovereignty is, "sovereignty means the capacity to define who matters and who does not, who is disposable and who is not" (2003: 21). Although class and socioeconomic privilege may appear to explain the state's selective politics of disposability, as in how some revolutionary women came to realize that their class markers are "read" by security police, therefore affording them safety from violence, it is, in fact, the randomness of state violence, as discussed previously, that represents what Giorgio Agamben refers to as "sovereign exception" (1998). The implementation of the politics of death is the exclusive "right" of the sovereign as well as the determinant of sovereignty. Khaled Said's horribly disfigured face after he was viciously beaten to death by secret police in plain view of the public bears testimony to the sovereign power that normalizes such acts as its "exceptional" right in the fight against "terror" (or whatever the state of exception may be). Even as it denies responsibility and may punish the perpetrators, popular opinion implicitly recognizes the state as responsible.

The normalization of this implicit right of the sovereign to inflict pain or render humans lifeless inculcates subjectivities of worthlessness relegating those already vulnerable to conditions of "bare life," as Agamben puts it (ibid.). In chapter 3, May recounted how the young street children refused to let her and her companions advance toward Mohamed Mahmood Street off of Tahrir Square, where tear gas and gunshots rained on the protestors. She recalled what they said to her: "No! No! We can't let you go there. You are the educated. We can die, *mish mohim* [not important]." To hear a young child of eleven or twelve years old vehemently argue that their lives are "unimportant" shook May, who wept as she remembered how, when she held the hands of the children who fell during the clashes, they were so calloused that she could not imagine how they belonged to such young children. The National Center for Social and Criminological Research in Egypt puts the numbers of children in Egypt living on the streets, otherwise known as "street children," at three million (NCSC 2011). The sheer magnitude of that number of children who receive little or no state support save for the centers established to help street children cope with their dire conditions is staggering. The conditions of their lives on the street are even more so when considering that the trafficking, the abuse and labor exploitation, as well as the precariousness of living young and defenseless in the Cairene metropolis, constitute conditions of "bare life," where lives are deemed disposable by sovereign exception.

The construction of the other, the revolutionary protestor as transgressive, irrational, antipatriotic and disposable, is the linchpin of governmentality. For authoritarianism to rise anew, to impose order on chaos, the body that is transgressive, out of control, and associated with lack, is increasingly alienated, stigmatized, and reduced to conditions of bare life. As a spectacle, women's nonconformist bodies are disciplined in the public domain by means of its androcentric standards of comportment and exclusionary politics. Yet, there are many who continue to dare to transgress and whose gender fluidly negotiates the regulations imposed on their bodies and the state's politics of death. I turn now to the woman called "the Lion of the Midan."

The Lion of the Midan

The woman called "the Lion of the Midan" by those who knew her in Tahrir Square repeatedly stood in the face of state violence. The lion evokes a metaphor of virile masculinity, illustrating the kind of courage and bravery culturally reserved for males. The cover of a local magazine published a photograph of Naglaa (her real name) standing in profile, wagging her finger in the face of an army general against a backdrop of protests in Tahrir Square. Her engagement with revolution begins with this story. (Her background story was covered in chapter 3.)

"My mother took me back to Alexandria, where we are originally from, for a few days to keep me from joining the protests on the twenty-fifth. She made up a family event that we needed to attend, but it soon became clear that there was no event. So, I insisted on going back home [in the Sixth of October City, roughly twenty-eight miles from downtown Cairo]. But the next day, the twenty-ninth of January, my mother announced she was going to accompany me to work, to make sure I would not go anywhere. But after four hours of futile attempts at working, I took my mother home, and she allowed me to leave her after making me promise not to go to Tahrir Square, but this is exactly where I went, of course."

She continued, "I was totally unprepared for the midan. All alone and in high heels, no food or shelter, I was walking around in a daze. Staring at people, talking to strangers who did not seem to be strangers at all. I completely embraced it. I spent that night on the floor in the square. On the thirtieth of January, the Muslim Brothers began to show up among the protestors in Tahrir; there were women from the Muslim Brotherhood there too. When the police force withdrew from the streets, many people started to go down (to Tahrir). Anger at Mubarak's speeches made many people join us, but we were all afraid, because we had heard that they were kidnapping protestors. Then the day of *mawq3at al gamal* [the Day of the Camel] happened. Monday and Tuesday there was lots of violence as well. But, despite the horrific deaths, the army standing towards the museum at the end of the square were in *samn we 3asal ma3a al baltagiyaa* [literally, they were in a honeymoon with the thugs]. Right in front of me, and I am a witness, we would capture the thugs responsible for the mayhem and killings and deliver them to the army officers. A few minutes later, we would watch as they released them from the back entrance, allowing them to come back into Tahrir again. The 'Day of the Camel,' I saw with my own two eyes as the army opened the gates and let those goons on camelback in. It was 2 p.m. in the afternoon."

Naglaa pauses, letting this little fact sink in. The army let the goons in? *Why?* I asked. "You will see," she said. "That day, I was beaten viciously, repeatedly. I could not move from the pain. I was taken to the Omar Makram mosque to recover, but there was no rest for me. After I went back to the square, I felt too weak to do anything, so I went home."

The next day, Naglaa tells me, she went to the radio and television building with a group of protestors; they were trying to figure out where the political trend was going. Sure enough, she says, the army soldiers had a completely different attitude toward people. They were smiling, giving out cold water bottles to the thirsty throngs. "I turned and said to my friends, 'Mubarak will step down.' And we rushed back to Tahrir in time to hear his resignation speech." Naglaa's face lit up as she remembered those moments. "I was jumping from joy; tears were running down my face. We succeeded! We got rid of Mubarak. But to be honest, as much as there was joy, there was also fear. The position of the army was unclear. Some people said 'don't anybody move from the midan,' although I had to go home myself. How could I not, when I had to check on my children and my mother?"

Her whole mood changed then at this recollection, and she seemed to visibly slow down. The excitement vanished from her face, and her voice became very low. "I had a beautiful dream. I felt we could be better than Europe. I dreamed of people in Egypt looking beautiful, healthy. We could rebuild our country together. But we got divided into political parties. How did this happen? That's not how we started this."

Naglaa thinks that the events at Mohamed Mahmood Street in front of the *dakhliyya* (Ministry of Interior)—often called the "second revolution" or the "Cabinet Clashes"—were the beginning of fragmentation. "This was a great battle. We all went to Tahrir on Friday the eighteenth of November 2011. Then on Saturday, I read online that they were dismantling the camps, so I went running down to the square. I was not aware of it, but my blood was boiling, and I started shouting at the officers, "How could you remove these people?" Ahmed Hassan, a reporting photographer, took a picture of me with my index finger raised in one of their faces. People still tease me about that. But I was only aware of the right of people for peaceful protest."

In the middle of all this violence, which erupted between the protesters and the army, people were falling in the square. The tear gas was blinding. She heard voices shouting that they were shooting protesters up the street. She covered her face with a mask someone gave her and started walking fast toward where they pointed. One young man pulled her back by her clothes. "No, no, stay back. I will go instead. You are an older woman. I will go!" She shook him off, but he insisted, shaking his head.

Another younger man, almost a teenager, came up to him and said, "Let her go! She won't find peace till she goes." So he did.

Naglaa slipped away and found herself in the middle of an inferno. She pulled a young boy to safety who had fallen on the ground and was about to be trampled underfoot. A man on a motorcycle came and took him to the midan's clinic. She turned around and saw from the corner of her eye a soldier raising the bottom of his shoe in the face of a group of protestors, and she just lost it. "I started chanting, *yasqut yasqut hukm al 3askar!* [Down with army rule.] This is when I got shot in my leg and my shoulder. I didn't care; I kept going. I ended up standing with the blood oozing out of my wounds, right in front of an army tank, and it stopped. After that, they arrested me; they seized my cell phone and ID. The officer warned me that if I did not stop this 'thuggery,' they would rape me. I was taken away from the midan with thirteen other women in an army truck towards the road leading to Upper Egypt. We were let go right there in the middle of nowhere, with no cell phones or any form of identification. [At the same time,] the minister of interior was saying on television, 'We delivered every lady we arrested right to her doorstep!'"

The next day, Naglaa and a few of the women who were arrested filed a complaint with the attorney general. The officer taking their testimony asked them why they were there in Tahrir and what they were doing there. "'Don't you know?' he asked me. 'People there do bad things?' 'Which people?' I asked him."

"You know and I know," he flashed back at Naglaa with a warning look in his eyes. Then the officer said to her, "If I put my finger in the eye of the person who put his finger in *my* eye, we will both be blind." And that was his wise advice to her. She looked at me while she recounted this meeting and then with a wry smile said, "This world is just off kilter (*il donya haysa*). If you ask for your rights, you get killed or maimed or ridiculed. We have to remain one people. Continue to surrender? No! We will get trampled if we do."

Naglaa's story is one of many that illustrate the encounters that women in Tahrir Square have had with state violence during the first eighteen days of revolution. Stories that not only produce a counter narrative to the dominant coverage of the local militaristic state and media but that reveal as well how the necropolitical practices of the state are played out over women's bodies during revolution. Offering these accounts that illustrate how gendered revolutionary bodies are imbricated in the politics of death, the lived experience of Egyptian revolutionary women like Naglaa encourages us to probe deeper into the ways violence and state bids for control are entangled with women's corporeality. While traditional gender roles were imposed on the daily accounts of the protestors by the state and the media alike, on the ground, the protestors themselves transcended not only class and religious boundaries but gender and state control as well.

A Tale of Two Revolutionaries

Pivotal events that marked the trajectory of the uprising in Egypt also shaped the fate of Hend Nafea and Shaimaa al Sabbagh—two young women revolutionaries whose stories epitomize the rearticulation of state power over its population through violence:

Saturday, December 17, 2011

Twenty-five-year-old Hend left her apartment early that morning, heading toward downtown Cairo. Her mind was full of the things she needed to do that day. Flyers to distribute, people to connect with, and calls to be made. It seemed that there was no time for respite from her job as a human rights researcher at the Hisham Mubarak Law Center in Cairo, one of the leading organizations that played an important role in monitoring the uprisings. Human rights activists founded the center in 1999 and named it after Hisham Mubarak, a leftist lawyer who championed human rights causes in Egypt. This Mubarak defended victims of government abuse and injustice, and in 1998 died suddenly at the age of thirty-five. In February 2011, Egyptian authorities arrested a number of the center's officers, journalists, and human rights activists, and then subsequently released them.

Foremost on her mind was a main concern with the safety of the protestors in Tahrir Square. Tensions between the military forces and the peaceful sit-in had been brewing, with protestors vowing to remain in Tahrir Square till their demands were met. Hend, like many others, was worried about violence escalating again after the previous day's clashes that left several dead and many others injured. Among those severely injured was Aboudi Ibrahim. Rumors had been spreading about the kidnapping of protestors from the square in large army trucks, so Aboudi, a young activist who was camped in Tahrir, decided to investigate a truck that was parked close to the square. According to a friend who witnessed what took place, an altercation developed between the driver of the truck and Aboudi, who was inquiring about the driver's papers. Within minutes, Aboudi and the group of activists who accompanied him were surrounded by two army units. Several of the young men managed to escape, but not Aboudi, who was struck on the side of the head by a gun and then taken away.

An hour later, a bloodied and mangled body was tossed out onto the street from the gates of the People's Assembly. It was Aboudi. He was immediately transported to Qasr al Eini Hospital, where he was treated for his wounds, but rumors of his death spread like wildfire, angering the protestors. A few of them allegedly resorted to throwing rocks and cocktail bombs at the military. This unleashed a torrent of military violence against the protestors. Soldiers had gained access to surrounding buildings, and in addition to the attacks on protestors that were taking place on the streets, there were other attacks underway from the rooftops. Tear gas, gunshots, and even large furniture and debris rained down on the throngs below, causing grave injuries and escalating the violence. The event marked the first day of what later became known as the "Cabinet Clashes," because they occurred next to the building where the Cabinet of Ministers is located.

Despite reports of the intensity of the violence in Tahrir from the day before, Hend stepped off the curb into the square and walked unafraid into the throngs of people. She believed in the revolution, and no threat of violence was going to keep her away from Tahrir. Driven by her strong conviction that people must protest injustice, she had no doubt that the people had the human right to do so. No progress could be achieved in any country without the hope of transformation. Hend was like many others who were in Tahrir Square that day, fueled by dreams of a better Egypt and motivated to remain in the square, no matter what may come. But the day that started with the hopes and dreams of a better Egypt turned quickly into mayhem right before her eyes. Tahrir Square near Qasr Al Eini Street erupted into a site of another bloody confrontation between the protestors and the military, whereupon military forces charged onto the square and began a brutal dispersal of the camps. The sound of bullets was heard as tear gas went off and tents were burned to the ground, including the first aid emergency center, the midan hospital, and the storage shed where all the medical supplies were kept. Women who were in the square were particularly targeted, pursued, and brutally clobbered by army truncheons.

According to Hend Nafea, the army specifically targeted women as a strategy to break the revolutionaries. Azza Hilal Suleiman was one of those who was brutalized by the army that day. She recounts in an interview how she stopped to help a young woman who had fallen on the ground, who was later called "the girl in the blue bra" by the media. She noticed the limp, naked body as it repeatedly got kicked by army boots and reached out to pull her from underneath their onslaught. She risked stopping and not fleeing, she later mused, because a part of her did not anticipate the extent of the ferocity of military violence on a woman—after all, her father and her uncles were all military men. Azza suffered a broken skull. She too was dragged under the batons of six soldiers—all clobbering her at the same time.

Others experienced that level of brutality. Twenty-four-year-old Aya Emad suffered a broken nose; twenty-eight-year-old April 6th movement activist Ghada Kamal was beaten and threatened with rape. Mona Seif, a twenty-five-year-old well-known activist from an activist family, was also subjected to violent treatment. Farida Al Hessy, a doctor and blogger who was delivering medical supplies to the midan hospital that day saw army soldiers closing in on her, so she ran as fast as she could. Ayman Nour, a young man who was in the square, tried as many other male protestors also did, to help a young woman escape army brutality, but this only infuriated the soldiers more. After both Ayman and Farida fell under the soldiers' blows, they were pulled by their hair into the building of the Cabinet Ministry, where they were subjected to more beatings, insults, and threats. The events of the Cabinet Clashes marked the most virulent and brutal treatment of women protestors by the military recorded to date, as the army made no secret of how they viewed the women of the midan. As has been discussed, the military carried out a public defamation campaign, alleging that the women who were in Tahrir were impure and impious.

Hend Nafea, who headed to Tahrir Square earlier that day to fight oppression and human injustice, joined the long list of those who were severely brutalized by the military's violent attack on Tahrir. Thus far, about fourteen people were killed, while 440 others were wounded. Hend never even had a chance to set foot in Tahrir Square itself; she was approaching the square from Qasr El Eini Street when she saw the throngs of people charging at her from all directions. Blinking, she tried to make sense of the situation, but she did not react quickly enough. As she turned to leave, two soldiers held her captive and tore her hijab off her head, kicked her, and screamed at her while they tore at her clothes. They dragged her by her hair, as they did to countless others, and as she fell, they pulled her to the curb. From then on, all Hend could see were the batons as they rapidly descended on her head. Blow after blow after blow, her head seemed about to explode. About twenty soldiers had swarmed around her, she later recalled, and were beating her viciously, everywhere. Some groped her private parts, while others shouted sexual expletives at her. They arrested Hend that day—all the while she recalls being kicked, spat on, slapped, shoved, and insulted by the worst possible verbiage as tears ran down her face.

While she was held captive for five days, the authorities continued to beat and torture her. When they finally released her to her family, pending charges of inciting violence and attempting to overthrow the government, Hend realized that the worst was not over yet. Her family showed up at the hospital to take her home as she lay bandaged in her bed. She was shipped off to her village, where she ended up a prisoner in her family home. She was to be disciplined for what they saw as wild and irresponsible behavior.

"I was transported to another battle," she said on the big screen, "the battle with my family."

In a theater in California, in September 2015, Hend sat next to me in the dark as we watched a documentary film about her activism in Tahrir, *The Trials of the Spring*. Hend filled me in on the details that the documentary did not cover. She laughed under her breath as she recalled the impossible situation she found herself in. "I was going to jump from the window," she whispered in my ear. Her family, a military one, could not conceive of any reason why Hend would do such a thing as to participate in a protest. Her younger brother, who was in the army at the time and with whom she had grown up orphaned in her uncle's home, no longer spoke to her. "He refused to speak to me," she told me. "It was as if I had committed a shameful crime." They were raised as orphans and she had protected him all her life and tried hard to replace their mother's absence as he was growing up, she was very hurt by his disapproval. It was a long time before he would talk to her again.

When the lights came on in the theater after an emotionally charged film that moved us all, Hend explained to the audience how she ended up in the United States. (I was invited there by Human Rights Watch to comment on the film, as well as help translate for Hend during the public discussion, but she did not need much help from me.) "I was sentenced to life in prison by a military court for participating in the protests the day of the Cabinet Clashes," she said. The audience gasped. She later told me that she managed to escape from Egypt and ended up in Lebanon; then she flew to the United States, where she sought political asylum. Two hundred other protestors were accused of similar charges, including Ahmed Douma, who was serving a life sentence in prison.

The year I met Hend Nafea in California had started with yet more devastating news. Violence continued to be committed against the protestors as activists attempted to commemorate the first uprising. The erasure of revolutionary memory came as a devastating blow to the millions of people who remained hopeful that the spirit of change could be kept alive. One of them was another woman from Alexandria.

Saturday, January 24, 2015

Alexandria is Egypt's "Bride of the Mediterranean Sea," a city named after Alexander the Great, the Macedonian conqueror who dreamed of Hellenizing the world. Instead, he left behind a legacy that stirred the imagination of generations and ignited unforgettable images of hegemonic military masculinity and ideals of heroism. His skills in the battlefield were enshrined in legend as he defeated one army after another. Alexander's ageless muscular body sits atop his horse, Bucephalus, looking over a busy square in Alexandria. Perhaps Shaimaa had passed the statue on her way to the train station that day. Perhaps she gazed at the epitome of military might and masculine heroism fictionalized in historical myth. There are many possible thoughts that could have crossed her mind as she left her city by the north coast and headed south to Cairo to commemorate not those misglorified military figures but the memory of the hundreds of young revolutionaries who had fallen to them. One thing is perhaps certain: thirty-one-year-old Shaimaa could not have anticipated that she too, by midafternoon of that day, would join the long list of victims of armed violence in Tahrir Square, that a senseless, unprovoked act by security forces blindly following orders would rob her of her young life.

Shaimaa Sabbagh was traveling with a group of friends and fellow activists to lay a wreath in memory of the martyrs of Tahrir Square during the Egyptian uprising of January 25, 2011. Her husband tells the story of a young woman who was not only driven by love for others but who was also a doting mother to their five-year-old son, Bilal. Sabbagh was an active member of the leftist Socialist People's Alliance Party (SPAP), and on that day, she was to attend their meeting in Cairo and then participate in the peaceful march in Tahrir. As her husband and friends told reporters, Shaimaa was devoted to social issues and worked to support laborers, street children, and all those who are dispossessed. Her main area of expertise, however, was the arts, with a Master of Arts degree from the Academy of Arts in Cairo. She was a folklorist who researched the dying traditions and cultural celebrations of villages along the Nile. The results of her work were to be the subject of a documentary about Egypt's villages. She wrote poetry and was part of a circle of friends who were artists and poets—often meeting in Alexandrian cafes, recalls a friend to the *New York Times*. Short, witty pieces that ascribe consciousness to even inanimate objects such as a woman's purse point to a sharp sense of humor and a curious empathy and voice:

> I am not sure
> Truthfully, she was nothing more than just a purse
> But when lost, there was a problem
> How to face the world without her
> Especially
> Because the streets remember us together
> The shops know her more than me
> Because she is the one who pays
> She knows the smell of my sweat and she loves it She knows the different buses

And has her own relationship with their drivers She memorizes the
ticket price
And always has the exact change
Once I bought a perfume she didn't like
She spilled all of it and refused to let me use it
By the way
She also loves my family
And she always carried a picture
Of each one she loves

What might she be feeling right now
Maybe scared?
Or disgusted from the sweat of someone she doesn't know Annoyed by
the new streets?
If she stopped by one of the stores we visited together Would she like
the same items?
Anyway, she has the house keys
And I am waiting for her

(Translated from the Arabic language by Maged Zaher, 2014)

Shaimaa Al Sabbagh, the mother, poet, and leftist activist, was shot dead
that day by security forces while peacefully protesting for only two minutes near
Cairo's Tahrir Square.

Human rights lawyer and founder of the Center for Egyptian Legal Aid
(CEWLA) Azza Soliman was having lunch with family and friends in downtown Cairo when around 3:30 p.m. she heard a commotion outside, so she got
up to see what was going on. In a statement she posted on Facebook the next
day, on January 25, 2015, Azza describes what she saw. Below is my translation from the original Arabic, "My testimony on the murder of Shaimaa Al
Sabbagh":

- Yesterday I was having lunch in [Café] Riche with my family and my friends
around half past three [in the afternoon]. I heard the sounds of a march. I went
to watch and found Mr. Helmy Shaarawi, Talaat Fahmy, Elham El Marghany,
and others from the Socialist Alliance. I greeted some of them, and we laughed,
and they were about twenty-five to thirty people, and they were carrying flowers. They moved to the opposite sidewalk near Talaat Harb [Square]. I started
taking pictures.
- The police put on their sirens and got closer to them, and some of them
were wearing masks and had long, black shotguns. My son Nadim came to
me and told me, "Please come with me; they will shoot. I have seen this many
times before." I said to him, "For sure, no. I am used to tear gas." I did not
complete the sentence when the shooting started and the gas. Everyone ran,
followed by the police on the opposite pavement from [Café] Riche. I saw

someone fall; I didn't know if they were a young man or a woman. Not till I moved to the passage next to [Café] Riche did I find out it was a girl, and I saw some blood. I did not see her face, and the person with her was shouting, "Ambulance!" A masked officer was closing on them.

- Talaat was moving toward us, but an officer took him to Talaat Harb Square. The friends of the girl took her to the ambulance—I didn't know the details. Of course, the police were [spreading] like locusts in Talaat Harb Street, and I saw them arrest two young people I didn't recognize.

- I began writing what had happened. A number of friends called me to make sure I was safe, so I asked them to let me know any news about the girl who was shot if they found out. On my way home, I called one of my girlfriends to ask after Talaat Fahmy. She called me back and told me that the girl had died and that Talaat had been arrested in Qasr el Nil Jail.

- I left home again, not believing that the girl had died. She died within minutes. I went to the morgue, and the scene was terrible there. Most of her friends were young men and women activists. The screaming and wailing grew loud, and I found out that the martyr had a son who was four or five years old.

Azza decided then to go with a group of lawyers to Abdeen District to give her testimony about what had happened. In a matter of hours, Azza—an eyewitness who was also a human rights lawyer—was put under arrest and charged with "unauthorized protesting" and the "breach of public security and public order" (FDH 2015). The legal ordeal that followed continued for months before Azza was acquitted and released.

There was no recourse, however, for Shaimaa Al Sabbagh, who never went home to Alexandria again.

Photographs of Sabbagh's dying moments went viral, as one of her colleagues clung to her body, keeping her upright so as not to fall on the pavement behind her. She was bleeding from the impact of the pellet gunshots that wracked her body. The shots—most likely because they were fired at such close range—tore through her lungs and heart. Shaimaa was pronounced dead upon arrival at the hospital.

Not Just Any Bodies

The day before Shaimaa Al Sabbagh's death, a seventeen-year-old girl whose name was Sondos Rida Abu Bakr was shot and killed during an Islamist protest in Alexandria (Al Jazeera 2015). Her death, like Sabbagh's, came amid a new surge in violence in Egypt after the ouster of former president Mohamed Morsi. Former chief of the army Abdel Fatah Al Sisi deposed Morsi following a massive show of popular support in Tahrir when thousands took to the square and the nearby streets, calling for him to take action. After the head of the Muslim Brotherhood's Freedom and Justice Party was removed from office and taken prisoner in an undisclosed location, General Abdel Fatah Al Sisi was promptly elected president by an overwhelming majority of Egyptian voters. Given these drastic changes in government, which followed closely on the heels of yet a bigger historical transformation that saw the toppling of Hosni Mubarak's thirty-year-long regime, violent protests spread once more across the country. The deadly dispersal of protestors in Rab'a Al Adawiya Square resulted in the killing of more than 817 of Muslim Brotherhood supporters, according to Human Rights Watch (2014).

Government anti protest violence in Egypt escalated after the first eighteen days of the January 25 uprising, but more dramatically in the year following the unseating of Mohamed Morsi from the presidency. According to Human Rights Watch, 846 people died during the first phase of the uprising and almost three thousand were injured, with the numbers of dead soaring between 2013 and 2014 to 3,143 deaths, according to a Carnegie Institute report by Michelle Dunne and Scott Williamson (2014), "Egypt's Unprecedented Instability by Numbers."

The new antiprotest law made actionable in 2013 gave security police legal authority to arrest protestors, but the use of violence during these arrests, unprovoked shootings, and the targeting of female protestors were markers of a process that was not simply about enforcing the law. What the state was implementing was a continuation of the process of intimidation and coercion witnessed during the events of the Cabinet Clashes. This was also an integral part of the Mubarak regime's practice of repressing protests, where women were specifically targeted and sexually harassed by thugs and security forces.

Gendering Violence

The events of the January 25 uprising witnessed a wide range of violence and brutal repression, yet the use of certain technologies of violence were reserved for women, whose bodies were viewed as transgressive as well as unruly. While nonmasculine bodies are often framed in such terms by patriarchal regimes and party politics in many areas around the world, in Egypt, the use of purity and piety complicated the repressive measures employed by the state. As discussed in the case of twenty-five-year-old Samira Ibrahim and at least seventeen other female protestors, the military subjected them to a special brand of violence—one that military personnel labeled as *kshufat al 'uzriyya* or "virginity tests." This form of assault that was reserved for "girls who . . . were not like your daughter or mine," as Major Emara, a member of SCAF (Supreme Council of Armed Forces) put it (Fleishman 2012). It left protestors like Samira Ibrahim wishing death upon themselves rather than being subjected to this form of violent assault and humiliation. Describing how their bodies become instruments of inflicting shame on themselves (Human Rights Watch 2011), these young women recounted the dehumanizing treatment by which bodies are separated from selves, signaling extreme alienation and estrangement from one's own familiar material being.

The case of Samira Ibrahim evokes a common trope in the discourses of male domination that rationalizes gendered ideologies of public space. Feminist scholarship has contributed extensively to this subject, for example Sherry Ortner (1974), Louise Lamphere (1997), and others. Although there are some limitations to viewing the public and private as binaries and perceiving women's political participation simplistically as strictly public, such theories do contribute to our understanding of larger dynamics that to some extent and in some cases do govern modern urban societies. (See Ann Fausto Sterling, 2000, for a rigorous critique of the role biology plays in sexing the nonmasculine body).

In these narratives, women's bodies are reduced to biological terms that link them to reproduction and domesticity, thus relegating them to the home and marginalizing them from the sphere of politics. Feminine bodies that challenge these normative ideals are therefore identified in negative terms and framed in discourses that validate punitive action against them. The violating procedure of virginity testing is one of the methods designed to marginalize the female body.

Sheer violence and brutality such as that unleashed on the bodies of women who dared trespass into the public or political realm is meant to link political protest to experiences of fear and terror. This was manifested in the horrific beating of female protestors in Tahrir Square during the military raids that took place to disperse the sit-in in the square. Female bodies were stomped on by the soldiers' heavy boots; brutal beatings were administered with sticks and batons, as well as acts of dragging by the hair and humiliating actions like slapping, spitting, and sexual threats. When the image of the woman in the blue bra went viral, state-owned media quickly judged her female body as transgressive of public space. Acting as judge of the military's human rights abuses, they instead chose to blame the young woman and criminalize her intentions. The image of the exposed naked body of the girl in the blue bra, however, continued to symbolize an autocratic state's attempt at thwarting local resistance, not simply through physical violence but also through the deliberate manipulation of patriarchal gender metaphors of sexuality and honor.

The images that circled social and public media of Shaimaa al Sabbagh's body as it teetered on the pavement, riddled with bullets, blood staining her clothes and streaking her face, pointed to the necropolitics of a state that knows no boundaries to the use of force. A small protest commemorating the deaths of the many who lost their lives in Tahrir met with a brutal response from state security forces. That Tahrir Square had been repossessed by the authorities and was being transgressed by protestors was not the only reason behind the brutal response, nor the fact that the protest might have posed a security threat. That moment when a young woman's body was the target of a rain of bullets was a moment about sovereignty and the disposability of vulnerable lives. She lay dying—an example of a vulnerable body that succumbed to the power of the state, not only for transgressing state boundaries but for simply being. A body rendered lifeless simply because the state willed it so. A feminine body that is already objectified by patriarchy and class becomes more easily deployed as a weapon against itself. Just as Samira Ibrahim, Hend Nafea, and others were made to experience their disempowerment over their bodies again and again in their brutal treatment and during their arrests and later by the media and accusing reports and allegations, here was Shaimaa being denied not only her body but her own life. That was the message written in symbolic bold letters over that young woman's corpse: "DENIED LIFE."

There were indeed words of sympathy and televised presidential statements, but the killing of yet another female, a young woman, who had participated in an Islamist march in Alexandria never made it to television and thus never received public sympathy. Sondos Rida Abu Bakr was a high school student shot dead by security forces during the dispersal of a protest on Friday, January 23, only two days before the anniversary of the uprising. A funerary procession headed to the local mosque, where her body was taken for prayers prior to its burial, turned into a protest. Holding signs with Sondos's name, hundreds of protestors marched to her working-class neighborhood, calling repeatedly "To heaven, to heaven," and "Down with military rule." Yet, the public outrage at her death never made it to Egyptian television, which remained silent about this tragedy and focused on Shaimaa's death instead. Shaimaa, a leftist activist who did not have ties to the now-banned Muslim Brotherhood organization, was deemed more acceptable as a victim than seventeen-year-old Sondos, whose affiliations rendered her not only suspect but also perhaps disqualified her as a victim in the public eye. Whatever the reason may be, the clear difference in the ways the media dealt with these cases of state violence mirrored the intersectionality of victimhood. Human Rights Watch (2016) also reports eighteen other deaths, a few with ties to Islamism and others anti-Islamist in various locations in Egypt.

Sondos's death and her affiliations to the Muslim Brotherhood group, which only one and a half years before had governed Egypt, brings into a focus how it is the purview of the hegemonic state to define the pure and the pious. For as military generals justified sexual assault on female protestors in the form of virginity tests, they based their claims on a social expectation of female chastity and honor. Piety and purity therefore are implied as prerequisites for women to access the public sphere. What happens when the female body embodies these qualities yet still participates politically? How does the state frame bodies that challenge its power from within the very corporeal rubrics it claims as requirements for public presence? This conundrum was exemplified in the case of the young *hara'ir* or young women cadets of the Muslim Brotherhood organization discussed previously. Their participation in protests early one morning in Alexandria in October 2013 put gendered state discourse to the test.

At 7:00 a.m., these twenty-one women, fourteen of whom ranged in age between fifteen and seventeen, headed out to protest against the unseating of the MB president Mohamed Morsi and his imprisonment by the military after a popular-backed army coup deposed the former president. The young women were arrested and immediately tried in an Alexandria court for inciting violence, as discussed previously.

To impugn the protesting female body, state and military discourse defined transgressive bodies participating in political action during the uprising as impure and impious, but these young female hara'ir defied the very tenets of state discourse because they represented the binary opposite of Emara's "not like your daughters or mine" rhetoric.

Khadiga, Naglaa, Hend, Sondos, and Shaimaa face the brutality of the encounter with state violence that intersects with their own sociocultural, religious, and political backgrounds. What about those bodies deemed sexually deviant by the state? What special brand of violence is reserved for them? In the aftermath of revolutionary Egypt, homosexuality is criminalized and singled out as an indicator of rampant sexuality that threatens the integrity of Egyptian heterosexual values.

"Morality Campaign"

Although subverting the revolutionary body is central to the rising discourse of authoritarianism, other bodies as well are drawn into the circle of disposability. Following the first uprising of 2011, the LGBT community in Egypt felt energized to build some institutional support for their members and to raise awareness in society. Because the Internet acted as an outlet for many to express their sexual orientation anonymously and to connect with others in the Middle East and around the world with similar views, thoughts turned to creating an online magazine to provide a forum for initial activism (El-Shenawi 2012). *Ehna*—meaning "us"—became an online magazine dedicated to the LGBT community. Next to the rainbow banner at the top of the page, a sentence read: *migalit sot al mithleen fi misr* (magazine for the voice of "mithleen" literally meaning "those of the same" is often translated inaccurately for expediency as homosexual, gay, or LGBT). Their first issue provided essential information about sexually transmitted diseases, included firsthand legal advice about homosexuality in Egypt as well as information about a national day against homophobia (ibid.). Yet, shortly following their first issues, the magazine was shut down, and their website apologized for the inconvenience. Since the magazine was anonymously run and its location was undisclosed, no further information seemed forthcoming. Many in the LGBT community were reportedly disappointed. Some attributed this shutdown to the Muslim Brotherhood government and fear of being targeted by religious extremists (ibid.).

In fact, *Ehna*'s fears were not unfounded, as Egyptian morality police began carrying out raids to clamp down on any alleged homosexual activity taking place in the country. While homosexuality is not prohibited by law, it is increasingly being framed as a legal matter in public and police discourse. To the beat of media and television drums, between 2013 and 2015, 111 criminal cases investigated individuals belonging to LGBT groups (HRW 2017). The added publicity connected to these investigations was central to framing nonconforming bodies as deviant and distortive of the heterosexual norm that constituted the state's image of Egypt's cultural and religious identity. The crackdown on LGBT groups intensified since the Muslim Brotherhood was removed from office in 2013. The police conducted these "morality campaigns," to demonstrate that the new government was committed to Muslim values despite the clampdown on the Muslim Brotherhood.

Illustrating this trend and how notions of deviance are employed to inculcate normative mainstream identities, I turn below to a set of events that created their own momentum around framing nonheterosexual orientations as sexual deviance.

In a sensationalist television program that opens with scenes of a back door leading into a dark corridor, the camera invites audiences to visit the underbelly of society. They watch as one frame after another appears in a mysterious ambience enhanced by dim lighting, intrigue, and suspicion. A splash of dark-red bloodstains appear on the darkened walls, and the program titles emerge as the cameras lead the spectator deeper into the darkness-filled passage. The titles read: drugs, prostitution, and forgery, hospital refuse. These are followed by the scene of a morgue and references to torture. The program is called *The Hidden*, (*Al mistakhabi*), the implication being that the show will unlock hidden societal secrets. Mona Iraqi is the program host and preparer. Her attitude is confrontational, and she makes her claims with a great sense of authority.

In a special series on the topic of homosexuality, Iraqi supports the idea that homosexuality is the problem and not the oppressive regime. The show focused on the trope of morality as a common strategy usually deployed during nationalist crises to rally populations around core values. Iraqi dedicated a series of episodes to exposing a gay sex-trafficking ring that operated through a public steam bath in a popular working-class area in the Ramsis neighborhood, on Bab al Bahr Street. "Gays" (she uses the English term), she claims, travel from all over Egypt's governorates to this "safe haven," to practice homosexuality. Mona Iraqi asserts with conviction that "Truth is never going to be lost," that is, as long as she has her TV show, which will ensure that this "truth"—however she defines it—will be exposed. Camera in tow, Mona is filmed as she conducts a surprise visit to the bath. The camera darts from one corner of the bath to the other, searching for debauchery. Just when none is captured, Mona leaps in front of the camera and puts one of the bath attendants on the spot, belligerently asking him about the sexual activity taking place there. The attendant is transfixed on the camera as he denies any knowledge of wrongdoing. Just then, behind Mona, coming out of the bath in shackles is a file of twenty-six half-naked men being led by the police, who had raided the establishment at the exact same time. The camera focuses on them, sparing no detail and making no attempt to preserve the men's privacy as they walk out of the bath naked save for towels wrapped around their middles. This was sensationalist television at its most cruel and vulgar. Twenty-six naked men filing out of the public bath were subjected not only to the violent gaze of the camera lens that consumed every aspect of their comportment but to the humiliating stares of onlookers gawking and pointing fingers at the sight of the men and shaking their heads at the "homosexuals." Watching their television screens, families and neighbors who must have recognized some of the faces, knowingly nodded as they heard Mona Iraqi claim, "There are many gays and many straights, but they are all there for the sex." All of the men were taken to jail and charged with debauchery. A number of them were accused of organizing a homosexual sex ring.

In the final episode of the season, dedicated solely to the topic of gay sex, Iraqi gives a history of why she invested her time and effort discussing masculine same-sex relations. Here she makes the grave announcement, "It was the spread of AIDS in Egypt!" She maintains that prior to making this announcement about AIDS, she had contacted Internal Security and several NGOs to obtain their support. Internal Security asked her not to air the show. She claims that they were afraid of bloodshed. Unblinking as she stared back through her cameras to the millions of Egyptian viewers who heard her outrageous manipulations of the truth, the show's host refers to a link on Google that mentions the steam bath by name and location as a gay haunt. But what is more interesting is the date when all this activity in the gay bath took place. She claims that it was 2011, the year of the uprising! The blatant attempt to link the revolution with what the program has described as deviant and perverse behavior pointed to the real agenda behind the show. The revolution of 2011 brought debauchery and deviance into the midst of Egyptian society according to Iraqi. Making that claim, Iraqi's motives behind revealing her alleged homosexual sex-trafficking ring became clear. Like various other television shows, *The Hidden* echoed public rationalizations for the status quo that the revolution is to blame for everything.

The show caused an uproar among human rights organizations and NGOs, who publicly voiced their criticism of Mona Iraqi for reporting the bath to the police without evidence to support her allegations. The reporting of the incident was provocative, linking the alleged sex circle to AIDS and historically relating it to Egypt's uprising. All the men under arrest were tried by the court and found innocent of the accused crimes. The attention shifted to Iraqi, scrutinizing her allegations and her methods. As public opinion and international LGBT activists turned their attention to her, Iraqi was arrested for defamation and sentenced to prison for six months.

Still unapologetic, even when one of the men who was dragged out of the bath attempted to self-immolate to end his public shame at being accused of homosexuality, Mona Iraqi decided to head out to the bath once again. This time she was determined to prove her innocence by asserting her original claims about the gay activities at the bath. The exchange she had with the men in the neighborhood was not only interesting in itself but spotlights the links between gender and regulation discussed thus far.

"This whole area is masculine," one man affirms to the camera. Another tells her, "It is good that you did this because all the women, men, and families in this area can be made aware of this story." While yet another says, "Thank you for broadcasting this show, so the foreigners out there know that we do not tolerate such things."

"The gays who came here from outside the neighborhood have no relation to us. This bath was started by a guy who meant to do something good for the area. All of us here just go about our business. We do not know if a man is homosexual or is a man," says another who ascribes an altogether different gender to nonheterosexual males.

After the acquittal of the accused men on January 12, 2015, Mona and her program were publicly criticized for broadcasting misinformation. She decided to continue absolving herself of irresponsible reporting by going scientific. This time, she hosted a slew of "scientists" who affirmed her claims that AIDS is endangering Egypt and that all effort needs to be expended in order to save the country from its ills. Although UNICEF puts the number of people infected with the HIV virus at 7,439 in 2013, it is hardly an epidemic.

More interviews with young men who recount their tales of male prostitution as they describe the impossibility of their lives under the conditions they have to endure enhance the sense of drama brought about by Iraqi's predictions of an AIDS epidemic. The more the attacks on her program, the further she went to affirm the seriousness of the conditions of immorality and sexual depravity that threatened Egypt after uprising and the more she validated political oppression and detracted from the real issues at hand.

Conclusion

Gender is crucial for understanding political change and for illuminating the dynamics of inclusionary/exclusionary boundaries. Violence as a dimension of the relationship between governmentality and gendered revolutionary bodies exposes the ugly underbelly of the necropolitics of the state. The very physical confrontation between women (the matriarchal figure, classed bodies, etc.) and security forces during uprising established new forms of politics of gender and corporeality that will define the history of women's resistance against state repression in the country for years to come. In these confrontations with state power, women activists' engagement with state security police transforms their role both socially and politically. It is paradoxical, since violence against women undermines the patriarchal idioms on which state patriarchy rests. Consequently, the revolutionary body must be gendered in ways that exonerate state violence and rationalize it as necessary for saving social values from deviance.

During these pivotal times, gender is deployed as a marker of difference and of deviance, as in the "Morality Campaigns" conducted by special police across the country to restore a sense of order and stability over perceived chaos. I discussed a particular controversy surrounding a television program that breaks a story about gay public baths in Cairo. The circumstances surrounding the program and the uproar it caused reveals how sexual practices and discourses illuminate the multilayered processes that imbricate gender into public politics to normalize the regulatory power of the state onto the body politic. As discussed in previous chapters, state power systematically implements its micropractices of control to shape the day-to-day operations of individuals reconfiguring individual subjectivity by instilling a sense of randomness, unpredictability, and helplessness.

The case of Khadiga El Hennawy illustrates how the meanings attached to gender roles can be manipulated and reversed, sometimes in dichotomous ways. Gender roles in the midan operated more fluidly. Gendered behaviors and expectations were challenged. Common masculine metaphors were applied to women. Those who are especially "brave" or "fearless" are compared to a "million men" (*million ragil*); others are called "a lion" (*asad*) or a "leopard" (*sab'*) which are masculine nouns. The "Lion of the Midan" is a woman whose direct engagement with state violence is explored in this chapter. Her fellow revolutionaries see her as the Lion of the Midan because to them she embodies masculine attributes of bravery and fortitude in the face of violent repression. Framing the bodies that protest in the midan as deviant, impious, depraved—even grotesque—enables authoritarian systems that gain validity from constructing and stigmatizing difference. While each of these bodies of Khadiga, Hend, the young MB cadets, Shaimaa, Sondos and the men taking a leisurely steam bath in Bab Al Bahr, have different motivations and experiences, they are all made to reinforce normative mainstream Egyptian values through their constructed deviance. State violence against these bodies is thus rational and logical—in fact, implementing their "death," determines the sovereignty of the regime.

7 Taking Resistance Virtually
Corporeality and Sexual Taboos

To whoever thinks our generation has just died
That our "voice" was just meaningless chatter
And that our revolution was only a story in a book
And that our role in history was to be absent
And that the judges in the courts were just
And whoever put us in prison had witnessed how much we sold (Egypt) for
All these statements are false
And the book and history will change
Before we die, before we die, before we die
History will not overlook us
Our voices, the midan, have no equal
(Hay ala al Falah, hay ala ili gaiy)
Rush to success, rush to what will come!

    k.h.
    # the revolution continues

CAIRO TRAFFIC GOES about its business as usual in Tahrir today—that is, it snakes noisily around the redesigned square with its newly erected twenty-meter flagpole carrying the Egyptian flag. It is difficult to imagine that only seven years ago in 2011, this very location was the epicenter of a grassroots revolution that toppled Hosni Mubarak's presidency. Since the popular-backed coup that seized power in the summer of 2013, Tahrir Square was reconceptualized from a space of revolution into one of national unity by the military, signaling a systematic project of erasure that was to take place in Egypt. Under the guise of security, progress, and rebuilding, a powerful propaganda machine spearheaded a campaign to reconstitute public memory. A new narrative propagated by state media outlets calls for a national project of "rebuilding now," reconceives the events of January 2011 in conspiratorial terms, criminalizing revolutionaries, a large percentage of whom have either left the country or languish in prison. Protests, except for those permitted by the state, are outlawed, while protestors are subjected to large fines and as long as fifteen-year prison sentences. Human Rights Watch reports that in recent years, as many as forty-one thousand individuals have been arrested or face criminal charges, while Al Nadim Center reports that hundreds have died in detention and prison (2016). Views perceived as disparaging religion, like atheism, are punishable by law, as a young blogger named Karim Ashraf al Banna recently found out (Greendlade 2015).

Social engineering projects that target morals and values rather than logistical issues such as the economy or development now dominate public discourse. "Our Morals Campaign," led by a prominent Muslim cleric, Ali Gomaa and psychiatrist Ahmed Okasha as well as actors and politicians, promotes ten Egyptian values that are to lay the groundwork for rebuilding society (Rabie 2016). This, as well as the arrests of perceived sexual deviants in frequent "morality raids," as discussed previously (Nader 2015) underscore the homogenizing objectives of the military regime. These technologies of rebuilding after the revolution of January 25 aim to unite the national community around its new leader. Through the manipulation of a cult of forgetting, differences are papered over to reinforce social cohesion through shared values and common identity. The latter are first and foremost constructed against "an other" already at the fringes of this community. As scholars since Michel Foucault have argued, the construction of "deviance" facilitates governance because it enables the conformity of the mainstream.

The current environment in Egypt has led analysts and commentators to conclude that the revolution is "dead." Egyptian prisons incarcerated almost 106,000 prisoners according to a report issued in September 2016 by the Arab Network for Human Rights Information. Almost sixty thousand of this number are political detainees (ANHRI 2016). Incarceration continues to be a response to civil disobedience, including simply participating in protest—now illegal according to constitutional law. Members of the Muslim Brotherhood live under scrutiny as their leadership remains in prison and their organization outlawed. Religious minorities such as Coptic Christians live in fear of terrorism and discrimination. This is while women still face the threat of violence and sexual harassment that affects their public mobility and political participation. After the introduction of a law in 2014 that bans sexual harassment, legal stipulations that expand the definition of rape, abuse, and assault for the protection of women are yet to be legislated (Egypt 2015). According to Human Rights Watch, between 2013 and 2016, 274 LGBT individuals were the focus of criminal investigations (2017). These conditions mirror a general regulatory authoritarian governmentality, but they also make visible a darker and systematic character of regime injustice, where particular constituents of the population are earmarked for selective lifelessness. The routinization of these systems is where their power is made viable.

It is not difficult to see how effective the campaign of rewriting the last years has been. Indeed, a number of revolutionaries believe the country has gone back to square one after the revolution (Bohn 2016). Countless others express the state of despondency and hopelessness they suffer from in the aftermath of the revolution. Nabila is a medical doctor in her fifties who spent years in the midan and elsewhere in Cairo, tending to the injured, organizing medical supplies, and marching in protests. Her children are now grown and have their own families to take care of. She works and takes care of her mother but cannot shake the feelings of despair. In fact, despair itself makes her feel ashamed. She describes how she and many others feel after the revolution:

> I beg of you to please give me some advice. What do I say to a nineteen-year-old who is handicapped in a wheelchair because a bullet lodged itself in his spine—deprived of playing soccer at night during the feast? What do I say to a young man who lost his eyesight—deprived of ever seeing his child's smile, the child for whom he had sacrificed to ensure his future? What do I say to the mother who lost her child who tells me every time she sees me, "As long as Mohamed's blood is warm, the revolution will not get cold. As long as his murderer is still free, the revolution will never be crushed"? What do I say to Nisma in her jail cell, who was a sweet butterfly all her life, flapping her wings as she took care of people, supporting them? I remember the days of Mohamed Mahmood, *maglis al wozara*, and *il itihadiyya*. It is true there was blood, and there was violence, and some of us lost their lives, got injured, and were arrested. But we were alive, we had a soul. Now, there are some of us who lose their lives, get injured, and are arrested, but we are dead. Our faces that watch them being taken away are ashen, our eyes lost their sparkle; they glance down at the ground. We cannot raise them in the faces of the victims. We are ashamed of our despair; it has chained our legs and our heads.
>
> No one is safe, no matter where they go. Our children are kidnapped and disappeared. Why hide in the folds of despair then?
>
> Death is coming . . .
>
> So die while you are standing, better than to live kneeling. Greatness to all who sacrificed and were martyred or were injured or arrested.
>
> Victory to the revolution.

Revolutionaries often express similar sentiments as the world around them keeps changing, obliterating any traces of their revolutionary history. The visible signs of state control are everywhere: the wide dissemination of morality campaigns, whitewashing revolutionary graffiti, the demolition of the incinerated National Democratic Party's headquarters, and the airbrushing of Tahrir Square's landscape. The process that Paul Connerton (1989) calls "organized forgetting" and the erasure of the social memory of the revolution is already underway.

Under these conditions, "rememory" as a practice of remembering is of particular importance. Rememory is a process of reconstruction as well as of remembering. It involves the resurrection of memories that are painful and traumatic to bring to the surface, but as it disinters the corporeal archive, it also reexperiences the power of resistance, the strength of the community, and reimagines the possibilities. By referring to the link between the corporeal and the archives of memory, this book has argued for a consideration of the body as a repository of knowledge. The corporeal has acted as the axis around which the complex and multilayered processes that have characterized the period known in Egypt as "the revolution" have revolved. Whether mirroring the tensions between neo-liberal structural adjustments and the modes of survival of local communities or acting as the platform of resistance against social and political hegemonic patriarchal systems, as a canvas for nationalism, marking deviance, the target of violence, or deployed as a strategy for embodying innocence and piety, and most important, as the mass force of rebellion, the centrality of the corporeal cannot be overemphasized.

Thus, the corporeal acts as the archive of these often-conflicting discourses that have the potential to disrupt normative knowledge. Tapping into these archives, the rememories of the women revolutionaries narrated here describe how gendered bodies become the signifying agents of collective action and of transformation. Their accounts inspire a reimagining of the corporeal at the center of civil disobedience, processes of citizenship-making and political trans-formation. The rememories of these revolutionaries thus—under the conditions of collective amnesia postuprising—reanimate social memory if not the revolu-tionary body itself.

The wide campaigns of arrests and disappearances of young activists also underscore the importance of the corporeal in bids for power and control, as systems of governance establish their status quo as normative. After a period of revolution and national awakening, the sheer magnitude of corporeal dissent putting millions in the streets of Egypt must be a disconcerting thought to an autocratic regime charged with the impossible task of subduing the largest popu-lation in the Arab world (ninety-two million in 2017). This last chapter of the book is not intended to pay homage to a bygone revolution—though the despair and loss of hope among many of my interlocutors could suggest such a direction may be merited. Instead, I wish to suggest that corporeal dissent can assume alternative forms to protest and revolution. With the containment of political work and the regulation of bodies in the public sphere, a new but familiar space has emerged as a medium of communication and social change for dissidents and social visionaries—a virtual one.

A Virtual Corporeality

There is one revolutionary space today that eludes the Egyptian state's recon-structive campaign, and that is the virtual world. The space where it all began is Facebook (FB). Paralleling the state's landscaping campaigns over the debris left behind by revolution, social activist groups in Egypt have spearheaded their own forms of social mobilization in recent years—in virtual scapes. Though multipronged, these efforts expand Facebook's potential as a virtual space for groups of people to come together. Through the creation of "confession pages" that enable FB subscribers to "confess" their most intimate problems in a safe and private virtual environment, they address issues particularly relevant to the younger generation of Egyptians who constitute roughly a quarter of the population. Facebook groups such as Cairo Confessions and Confessions of a Married Woman directly challenge the state's monopoly over defining morals and values by challenging hegemonic notions of "deviance" and bringing to their membership a more tolerant, open space that unabashedly addresses issues deemed as taboo by society.

In these private virtual spaces, a more candid and unrepressed corporeality is at the center of the discussions. Mental, emotional, or sexual problems—issues of an intimate nature not often the topic of public conversation and especially not in today's Egypt—are the focal point of these confession groups, where membership is protected and postings are afforded anonymity. Despite social stigma and state emphasis on conservative values and morals in Egypt today, tens of thousands of individuals post confessions while receiving advice in the form of comments. Young people in particular gravitate in large numbers to these virtual groups, creating in the process collective spaces of social support that unshackle public narrative from the grasp of the state and reclaim it for their own.

Virtual Revolutionary Space

In a widely quoted interview with CNN, Wael Ghoneim proclaimed, "This revolution started online. This revolution started on Facebook. . . . I've always said that if you want to liberate a society, just give them the Internet." Some 33 percent of Egypt's population has Internet privileges, amounting to 30,835,256 people (Internet Users 2016). While not the majority of the population, this remains a staggering number of people. Taking into consideration that active engagement with the Internet requires a certain measure of literacy (only 75 percent of Egyptians are literate), these numbers of individuals among the literate who have access to the Internet seem even more impressive. Moreover, 68 percent of all Internet users in Egypt are between fifteen and twenty-five years of age, according to a 2015 study by Nielsen Egypt pointing to a vast segment of the population. Nevertheless, this brings up the issue of class and socioeconomic privilege as important factors affecting people's access to Internet technology. It is to be noted that almost 80 percent of women's responses in the page Confessions of a Married Woman are in the Arabic language. Posts are filtered and summarized and often translated from Arabic into English by the site administrators, yet the majority of the responses are made in Arabic, suggesting that English may not be the language of choice of most of the respondents.

While bilingual fluency is not to be taken as an indicator of class privilege, it could be more likely that preference for Arabic indicates that access to this forum is more inclusive of various class levels. Discussions on the Cairo Confessions page are conducted entirely in Arabic, with few members and administrators sporadically interjecting words in English, also suggesting that the group may be more class inclusive. The question regarding access and resources cannot be addressed fully without mention of the wide prevalence of smartphones and Internet cafes in Egypt that also afford greater access to the Internet and social media without requiring the additional expenses of a computer.

As a space that provides access to alternative sources of information to state-controlled media, the potential for social media and particularly Facebook to provoke dissent and insurrection is not lost on the Egyptian government. There is no shortage of lawsuits seeking to regulate the use of Facebook in Egypt (Mikhail 2016). While not initiated by state actors, these lawsuits reflect the desires of a key group in society who may ostensibly benefit from restricting the flow of information. Parliamentarian Gamal Abdel Nasser, who is working to develop legislation to limit Facebook, inadvertently alludes to the accountability that comes with freedom of information by stating, "The West sold us Facebook only to blackmail us with it" (ibid.). Though Abdel Nasser is not alone in this view, there are countless others on the opposite side of this issue who have publicly opposed the feasibility and legality of these proposals and who have questioned the democratic credibility of an elected parliament that seeks to limit public freedoms (ibid.).

The backlash against social media in the country has not deterred its users in Egypt, who are estimated to be the largest Facebook users in the Arab world (ARE 2012). Thirty-one percent of the population is believed to be members of the "face," the majority of whom at 75 percent are below the age of thirty (Daily News 2016). Looking at the periods when sudden increases in Facebook memberships have been reported, it becomes apparent that political transformations are a major catalyst. The numbers of FB users increased by approximately five million in 2011, the year of the revolution, followed by a three million increase in 2012 and then again by five million in the summer of 2013, when General Al Sisi deposed Mohamed Morsi (ibid.). The appeal of Facebook to a youthful Egyptian public lies in its ability to create a virtual space that enables users to stay connected while also controlling and shaping their own social media worlds.

Collective Virtual Spaces

"A community that is filled with the bright, open minds of the Egyptian people, where you can anonymously get your problems heard and responded (to)," states the short description of the Facebook page Cairo Confessions. Founded by twenty-one-year-old student Mohamed Ashmawy in 2013, Cairo Confessions has become the first and only media outlet to deal with mental health in the Middle

East and the North African region. Ashmawy, who was then majoring in computer science at the University of Minnesota, recounts that he and his then vice president Ali Khalifa challenged one another to take on the project, though they never imagined the extent to which they would eventually become known. Their team is now twenty individuals strong and is joined by a growing number of psychiatrists and counselors working to provide instant care to a public in need of airing its problems to community members, experts, and mental health providers. Because the posts are anonymous, the group does not rely on memberships but rather on "likes."

In the beginning, the people who were posting were mostly Ashmawy's friends, but gradually within a very short period of time, there was a surge in postings. People with whom he was not acquainted started their own postings on the page, and soon there were thousands of posts. Mohamed Allam, who co-runs CC (short for Cairo Confessions) with Ashmawy recounts how "The whole idea was that we wanted to create a safe space for people to open up about taboo issues. When I joined CC, I said let's gather people, create a community. Let's create a judgment-free zone. To those ends, we focus quite a bit on the moderation of the comments to the postings to ensure that there is no judgmental feedback or comments that injure people. This was our vision to create a social network. I can imagine that the name 'Confessions' came from a silly Facebook group called College Confessions that Ashmawy probably picked up from when he attended college in Minnesota. I don't know that for sure, but I am just surmising."

The majority of the topics of the postings were focused on relationships. To Allam, this is the number one issue plaguing young people in Egypt today, followed by family issues. The third category that prevails among the postings is sexuality. Issues like masturbation, virginity, and homosexuality are top comments. "But most importantly," says Allam, "the relationship between a boy and a girl is considered taboo in our conservative Arab society, which causes guys to be very repressed. This starts from the teens and continues through college and university. It increases social anxiety and complicates young people's lives because they do not know how to tell the opposite sex, 'I like you.'" He went on to say that Cairo Confessions allows people to vent, to find release in unloading. "People (mostly young people) today cannot take it anymore. Many feel they cannot speak out loud, like homosexuals, for instance, they feel persecuted by society. Problems from family relations are also quite prominent in the postings. Family problems can be the result of financial problems or of aggressive parents treating their children badly—this is a very common concern for young people."

From the anonymity they afforded their membership on their Facebook page, they ventured into a new, uncharted territory, "meet-ups." Because of the strong indicators that showed them how much young people suffered from social anxiety issues, they decided to provide these members with opportunities to meet others with similar interests and needs. So, they asked those who were interested to fill out applications, and from their responses they created groups that brought people with similar interests together. CC then organized events in "real life" for people which they called, "meet ups." These new meet ups provided the physical spaces that bridged the virtual with the material. They had ice-breaking exercises for strangers to loosen up and get to know one another, and most recently they put on a treasure hunt in Zamalek. While Facebook is their main platform, the team uses Twitter and has weekly podcasts to supplement access to their followers. Still, their activities transcend the virtual by providing opportunities for real-time interactions, organized gatherings for participants, monthly storytelling events, and field trips.

The founders and organizers of Cairo Confessions view themselves on a mission to challenge the stigma of "confession" and what they call "the power of the social secret," by bringing taboo issues out into the open. Ultimately, this will "change society from within," states Ashmawy. CC is not directly related to the revolution, in Allam's opinion, however. "The link [to the revolution] is indirect," says Allam thoughtfully. "The repression people suffered from before the revolution was quite high. People were preoccupied with other things, but after what happened [the revolution] people's [minds] began to open up. During the revolution, however, people's level of awareness about [social and political] issues became quite high. Our generation is more aware than any other generation. This created a momentum. An irreversible change took place in society. After this period of revolution, things can never be the same again."

The Cairo Confessions group enjoys a great deal of popularity, with over sixty thousand likes and a staggering number of individuals seeking help. What is at the core of the endeavor, however, is to ultimately create a more tolerant society that is open about its problems. "We are very passionate about improving mental health and promoting self-expression; our idea is a model for an open, more accepting community. Changing society from within takes a lot of effort and a lot of time, so patience is needed—and a bit of good luck wouldn't hurt!" says Ashmawy in an interview with Cairohub (Mahmoud 2014).

Mental health issues in Egypt are generally neither socially acknowledged nor openly discussed, unless they are viewed as widespread phenomena. Cable television channels occasionally host prominent psychiatrists and secretary general of "Our Morals campaign" Ahmed Okasha, professor of psychiatry. Discussions center around general issues such as how to be happy (CBC 2 2014), overcome depression (Al Mehwar 2015), or provide input on social phenomena such as sexual harassment (ONTV 2014) and even terrorism (ONTV 2014). These are indeed relevant issues after the revolution, when a recent United Nations report has relayed that Egypt's population ranks 130th out of 156 countries in happiness (UN 2013, 2014). Though conceptual understanding of happiness cannot be universally applied, let alone to measure these sentiments among vast populations, it is not difficult to imagine that a population that has faced sudden changes in rates of violence, political instability, and increased poverty would also experience a decline in its general disposition. Though the trauma of the last few years after the revolution has hit some more than others, deeply ingrained sociopsychological issues that are rooted in traditions and practices considered taboo are the subject of many of the posts on the Cairo Confessions Facebook page.

Another "confessions" page that operates on a much wider scale and enjoys a unique place of its own in Egyptian women's lives is a page that has acquired almost notorious fame in Cairo, Confessions of a Married Woman. Twenty-eight-year-old Zeinab Al Ashry began the Facebook page when she was on maternity leave. She still manages the site as she ponders her next career move. An accomplished young woman who holds an MBA degree and had a career as an accounts manager at media giant Yahoo for more than two years, she will have no problem making a career leap. Three years ago, Zeinab started Confessions of a Married Woman, a secret FB page that allows its members-only group to discuss the most intimate details of their married lives openly and without any of the social stigma that often comes with the topic:

> I had recently gotten married and was hanging out with a group of my girl-friends when the topic turned to divorce. One of our close friends was going through the difficult process for reasons that seemed all too familiar. As my friends hinted towards similar issues in their marriages I too realized that I was going through the same challenges but that I daren't elaborate because we are taught to keep our marital life to ourselves. In our conservative Eastern society, women are taught that they should not air their house secrets out in the open. The tradition to keep home life private is not a bad one in itself and it is worth preserving. After all, I wouldn't want to do that when these are friends with whom one frequently socializes and it would be embarrassing to my husband if others were to know about our intimate life details. But that does not mean that staying silent is a healthy tradition, it isolates women and actually leads to divorce in some cases because women think it is only them who suffer and that there is nothing to be done about it.

Zeinab realized she could *do* something about this herself. So, she started an anonymous group on Facebook, and in the first year, she had two to three thousand members. Now the membership has risen to fifty thousand. "Can you imagine what fifty thousand women in one place could look like?" She laughs at the empowering thought.

> In the last three years, many cases have come across my screen. The most common issues are sexually related. These are often performance issues. You might think that the majority of the cases have to do with women who lack sexual

drive. In Egyptian society, when a couple is divorced and people say that the wife had been glum and morose, this is code for "not into sex." But in reality, and in my experience from the forum, almost 50 percent of the sexual problems that women reported had to do with their husband's lack of sexual drive and not their own! Yes, of course there are many cases where women could not keep up with their husband's sexual drive, but the numbers are much less. I would put these at 15 to 20 percent, but these are my rough estimates. In my view, these marital problems are often the effect of wider social issues. Men enter into marriage in Egypt thinking that they will reenact their father's role. But times have changed, and women now have careers and contribute to the finances of the couple. In some cases, they earn more than their husbands. Some men cannot reconcile their internalized notions of masculinity as the main breadwinner who is the head of the household in these new scenarios. Life can also be stressful, and work is very demanding in some cases. I think this produces a lack of confidence in men. Wives, on the other hand, do not understand these pressures and cannot fathom why their husbands have no desire for sex. When they finally confront each other, husbands often try to convince their wives that this is normal and happens in all families. They say they are busy or that work is stressful.

Like the Cairo Confessions team, Zeinab viewed the 2011 revolution as sparking a sense of agency in a population that had long felt disempowered.

After the revolution, people realized that they can make change happen. They assumed a new look on life. Our generation is more self-aware and more globally aware. Young people look at what other people around the world are doing, and they think, *why not us too? We too can change things and do something.* Egyptians were able to see that collective action brings about results because of the revolution and that community and having our own place to air our differences and our problems is the first step toward healing. I saw this happen firsthand on the Facebook page I started. In the beginning, women were afraid to discuss their issues; they held back, but eventually they realized that anonymity provides safety. People lived in their own virtual worlds, their own bubbles, but now, new groups are emerging online that are making use of this engagement with social media to further causes in society or to do business. There are now groups for mothers, for car sales, a variety of What's Up groups ranging from university alumni to neighborhoods, and entrepreneurial groups have appeared as well.

The surge in new Facebook pages that engage people in actual social and economic projects points to the fluidity in virtual engagement. Like Cairo Confessions' "meet up" events, Zeinab is also organizing workshops that focus on empowering women. This was not only in response to hundreds of posts by housewives and stay-at-home mothers asking for suggestions for home-based business project ideas, but also to provide married women in unhappy unions with alternatives, as most have no choice but to remain married due to financial need. An upcoming workshop will address how to have a start-up business for women. "I am building a bridge between women and the professional world. I am also trying to spread knowledge and tolerance for psychiatric help. I am calling for the removal of stigma from sexual matters in society and for empowering women," says Zeinab.

Change and Its Proponents

Hundreds of thousands of Egyptians have turned to Facebook pages and online forums since the 2011 revolution as a source of self-help and support for their problems in daily life. Although many popular virtual spaces avoid formal politics, the discussions do political work by building communities and demystifying subjects that the state deems taboo, such as homosexuality, sexuality, atheism, divorce, and the difficulties of dealing with domineering parents. These vibrant virtual spaces redefine exclusionary boundaries by challenging the state's efforts to monopolize moral codes. When young people openly discuss career plans, parents, difficult breakups, and sexual frustration—even if they do so anonymously—they push back against traditional taboos and begin to define a new normal. To be sure, such transgressions of conventional norms are not as dramatic as the assembly of protesters in Tahrir Square in January 2011. But the online camaraderie of these online groups echoes the bonds forged among Tahrir protesters. And while the Internet on its own cannot a revolution make, the participants in these online forums have begun to cross the line from the virtual to the real, through workshops and meet-ups that put them face to face.

Conclusion

What does it mean to gender a revolution? And why does a revolution need to be gendered? Revolution means a status quo has been disrupted, a disruption that is marked by a rejection of sociopolitical norms that shackle generations of populations. The Egyptian uprising elevated women's participation in the public sphere to another level. Women marched on Tahrir in the thousands—their numbers reaching 50 percent of the protestors on some days, as many eyewitness accounts have recalled. Yet, regardless of their efforts, women are often overlooked in historical and social science analysis of the Arab revolutions, despite the fact that such events as revolutions also intervene in the gender domain because of the centrality of gender to the social, economic, and political structuring processes. A social and political force, women's presence in the revolution in Egypt was central to the collective effort, not only because they increased the surge in mass bodies, which was radical, but also their very presence in the midan in large numbers was transformative of the most socially grounded gender norms. Men alone could not disrupt the status quo by themselves; they had to partner with women, and every social, religious, and political constituency needed to be represented to create a unified collectivity. Women's participation in the revolution in Tahrir Square was also necessary for various political purposes. Their presence even challenged the military's masculine and paternalistic ethic. Women's participation in civil disobedience was not unprecedented, however, as this book has shown. Egyptian women have engaged in dissent for many decades. Their presence signaled revolution itself. It was instantly disruptive because it changed established frames of dominance and pronounced a powerful statement about the future.

It is therefore this disruptive power that women wielded which directly challenged the terms of state power and governing systems in the country. They continued to demonstrate despite harassment and reported human rights violations committed against them. In a number of cases that have occupied both local and global attention, the pivotal importance of female corporeality in public debate during and after the "Arab Uprisings" becomes clear. These cases demonstrate the struggle over defining women's bodies as demarcators of public space and as conduits of state power and religious control. Ultimately, gender becomes the principal instrument that defines the kind of urban space envisioned by the state versus the space envisioned by the revolutionaries.

The research study presented in this book is based on accounts culled from interviews with nearly one hundred Egyptian women who lived the realities of the revolutionary period that began with January 25, 2011 and continues through the elections that brought Muslim Brotherhood candidate Mohamed Morsi to government, to the events that surrounded the beginning of the current military regime of President El Sisi. Over a five-year period, the data was collected from open-ended discussions, conversations, social media postings, and virtual online chats with women from various backgrounds, classes, and religious backgrounds. The main objective of this work was to produce a counter-hegemonic account of Egyptian revolutionaries who were either ignored or whose objectives were misrepresented by a gaze that shapes women, their actions, and their sociopolitical participation to serve male dominated politics, whether these are local or global. Tracing a corporeal history of dissent that made possible women's intervention in the revolution made it clear how important it is to begin thinking theoretically about the body in the context of the Middle East and outside of the usual topics of FGM, veiling and virginity.

The accounts of revolutionary and activist women presented here address these goals as they capture the mutually productive, fluid processes that characterize the body and the forces that act upon it to understand how gendered human subjectivity is shaped in a revolutionary context. These accounts also trouble the public discourses that frame women's bodies as either pious or promiscuous, (along the lines of the virgin/whore dichotomy) take gendered bodies as surfaces for reproducing and rationalizing dominant ideologies. While women's bodies bear the mark of repression and dominance, women simultaneously rework these markers to reinvent new forms of participation and resistance that often challenge and/or negotiate social values. We witness how they transcend the boundaries of gendered discourse and rework the terms of gender injustice through their activism.

Women's lived experiences during Egypt's revolution also help clarify how the necropolitical practices of the state are enacted over women's, children's and sexually nonconforming bodies. Gendered revolutionary bodies are imbricated in the politics of death. Violence—no matter how brutal in these cases—was once more justified by framing the nonmasculine body in denigrating terms that question its purity and piety and hence value or disposability in society. The multiple violences, both discursive as well as physical, inflicted on the bodies of revolutionaries contributed to the inculcation of subjectivities of worthlessness and marginality that oftentimes validated the systems of repression and regulation during and after the events of revolution. Equally important is how rememory as a process of recollection enabled a reactivation of revolutionary experiences among my women interlocutors. The details of the recounted lived experiences, the sounds, smells, and emotions of revolution were often retold with graphic realism as the retelling enabled the women to reimagine their corporeality within the original context of Tahrir Square as well as in other locations in Egypt.

This book highlights the narratives of gendered corporeality as a counter-hegemonic force that rearticulates the historiography of the revolution through a gendered perspective. The accounts of women revolutionaries can be read against the dominant discourses of state media, the military junta, and Islamism throughout the chapters, to point to the ways that gender is regulated in Egyptian society. The nonmasculine bodies that this book reimagines intervene in public spaces where as they are constructed as transgressive, unruly, and grotesque, they push the boundaries of public space, troubling systems of male privilege, normative politics and state control. Understanding how diverse these bodies are and appreciating the variety in embodied experience is integral to analysis of the revolutionary public space, because it reveals the complexity and multiple processes—often contradictory, other times in tandem—that compete over political supremacy. The violence that was unleashed on the protestors by various perpetrators, and in particular the sexual violence against women (whether by the military, secret police, violent masculinity, or pro-Mubarak thugs) cannot be understood without examining these nuances in experience, the shifts in history, and the sociopolitical events unraveling in the midan explored in this book.

Feminist theory and particularly the work of Judith Butler (1998) afford a view on the body that radically departs from naturalistic and/or biological frameworks. The fluidity and temporality of the body frees it from rigid material and discursive restraints, while allowing us to see the corporeal form as constantly mutating and transformative. Problematizing the social construction of the gendered body not as a prediscursive material being but as an affect of discourse and performance has opened a path breaking approach to studying the corporeal and appreciating its creative potential. Collective corporeal action has the potential, therefore, of restructuring public space and creating news ways of viewing and experiencing the body. According to similar analysis by Susan Bordo (2003), this can begin to make a fissure in what is otherwise an impermeable system of power that undergirds society.

These fissures in public performance are referred to as "bodily insurgency" by Daphne Brooks (2006). Though speaking in the context of black performers' bodies in the nineteenth century, Brooks notes how as black actors, singers, and activists in the United States reconstituted their bodies, they pushed against normative understandings of the black body thereby "defamiliarizing" them. The performing African body in the transatlantic context thus reconstitutes powerful racial and gendering discourses through movements, gestures, and visual/audio variations. These disruptions ultimately reinform the public space creating the possibility of change within entrenched discriminatory systems that manifest the body.

Years after the first uprising took place in Tahrir Square in 2011, when even memories of the revolution are now derided by authority figures and thousands of protestors have been thrown into Egypt's overcrowded jails, the discourse about those who engaged fully and completely in the revolution is organized around alienation and marginality. Yet, public performance in particular holds much potential for transformation for disruptive and unruly bodies.

*   *   *

I end with a short exchange with Amal, the government official entrusted with thousands every day at her job, yet who has to clean houses in her free time so she can save enough for a one-bedroom apartment in one of the new cities. This is what she said when we talked right before Al Sisi's sweeping success at his first election. It is a good reminder after Egypt completed yet another presidential election with similar results.

"Hopefully, things will get better under Sisi." (Referring to the former chief of the armed forces under deposed president Morsi.) She said it with what seemed like more bravado than conviction, as if to convince herself more than me. "Yes, Al Sisi will come through for us. He will put this right."

Wondering what Amal's views of the political challenges in Egypt today looked like in the months prior to the presidential elections, I asked her, "How do you know this?"

"He is the right person for the job," she replied. "But they are already turning him into a president. He is not a president yet, *rabina yustur* [may God protect us]."

"But what if Al Sisi became like everyone else?"

"We will *not* stand for it," came the swift reply. "We will go to the streets again and demand his resignation," Amal said firmly.

Works Cited

Abd Allah, AbdelHalim H. 2014. "Al-Dostour Elects Egypt's First Female Party Leader. Hala Shukrallah Will Succeed Mohamed ElBaradei." *Daily News Egypt* Feb. 22. http://www.dailynewsegypt.com/2014/02/22/al-dostour-elects-egypts-first-female-party-leader/.

Abdel Kader, Soha. 2001."Impact of Labor Mobility and Labor Migration on Gender Relations and Division of Labor." UNDP Report. The Situation of Rural Women Within the Context of Globalization, United Nations Division for the Advancement of Women (DAW) and the United Nations Development Fund for Women (UNIFEM). Mongolia.

Abou Bakr, Thouraia. 2013. "The Multi-Talented Pakinam El Sharkawy," Apr. 23. http://www.dailynewsegypt.com/2013/04/23/the-multi-talented-pakinam-el-sharkawy/.

Abouelnaga, Shereen, 2016. *Women in Revolutionary Egypt: Gender and the New Geographics of Identity.* Cairo: The American University in Cairo Press.

Abu-Lughod, Lila. 1993. *Writing Women's Worlds: Bedouin Stories.* Berkeley: University of California Press.

Abu-Lughod, Lila. 2013. *Do Muslim Women Need Saving?* Cambridge: Harvard University Press.

Ahmed, Gamal. 2014. *"Al do'ah al gudud wel thawra.da'wa lil tanaqid."* ("The New Preachers and the Revolution. An Invitation for Contradiction.") *masr al arabia.com,* 18:28.

Ahmed, Leila. 1992. *Women and Gender in Islam: Historical Roots of a Modern Debate.* New Haven: Yale University Press.

Ahram English. 2012. "Military Prosecution Interrogating Over 170 after Abbasiya Clashes: Military Source." May 4. http://english.ahram.org.eg/NewsContent/1/64/40867/Egypt/Politics-/Military-prosecution-interrogating-over--after-Abb.aspx.

Aikau, Hokulani, Karla A. Erickson, and Jennifer Pierce, eds. 2007. *Feminist Waves, Feminist Generations: Life Stories from the Academy.* Minneapolis: University of Minnesota Press.

Ajbaili, Mustapha. 2012. "Egypt Activist Who Protested Nude Says She Wants to Make Change, Differently." Al Arabiya News. Dec. 2012. Accessed November 30, 2013.

Al Ahram Online. 2013. "PROFILE: Mona Mina, New Sec-Gen of the Doctors Syndicate: The First Non-Brotherhood Syndicate Head in Decades Is a Campaigner for Doctors' Rights and Improved Healthcare." Ahram Online. December 20, 2013.

Al-Ali, Nadje. 2007. *Iraqi Women: Untold Stories from 1948 to the Present.* London: Zed Books.

Al-Ali, Nadje. 2012. "Gendering the Arab Spring." *Middle East Journal of Culture and Communication.* 5, 26–31.

Al-Ali, Nadje and Nicola Pratt. 2009. *What Kind of Liberation? Women and the Occupation of Iraq.* Berkeley: University of California Press.

Al-Ali, Zaid. 2013. "Another Egyptian Constitutional Declaration." *Foreign Policy.* July 9. Accessed March 20, 2017. http://foreignpolicy.com/2013/07/09/another-egyptian-constitutional-declaration/.

Al Jazeera. 2011. "Egypt Bans Virginity Tests by Military." December 27. Accessed March 31, 2016. http://www.aljazeera.com/news/africa/2011/12/2011122713262460116.html.

Al Jazeera. 2012. "Wedad el Demerdash: *wahida min ashga' nisaa al 'alam.*" ("Wedad el Demerdash: One of the World's Bravest Women.") https://www.youtube.com /watch?v=3ZlBDU7M0BE&t=22s.

Al Jazeera. 2015. "Egyptian Student Killed Ahead of Uprising Anniversary. Anti-Government Protests Erupt across the Country to Mark Anniversary of 2011 Uprising That Toppled Hosni Mubarak." http://www.aljazeera.com/news/2015/01/egyptian-student-killed -uprising-anniversary-150124070647710.html.

Al Mahdi, Aliaa. 2011. Aliaa Al Mahdi Blog. Accessed December 19, 2013. http://www.blogger .com/profile/16313561420852855838.

Al Nadim Center. "The Harvest of Oppression 2015." January 2016. http://www.alnadeem .org/content/-2015حصاد-القهر-في-عام.

Ambrose, Stephen E. and Douglas G. Brinkley. 2011. *Rise to Globalism: American Foreign Policy Since 1938.* 9th revised ed. New York: Penguin Books.

Anderson, Elizabeth. 2004. "Feminist Epistemology and Philosophy of Science." In Edward Zalta, ed., *The Stanford Encyclopedia of Philosophy.* https://stanford.library.sydney.edu .au/archives/sum2004/entries/feminism-epistemology/.

Arab Republic of Egypt Ministry of Communication and Information Technology. "Egypt, the Biggest User Population in the Region." November 2012. http://www.mcit.gov.eg /Media_Center/Latest_News/News/2491.

Bach, Kirsten Haugaard. 1998. "The Vision of a Better Life: New Patterns of Consumption and Changed Social Relations." In *Directions of Change in Rural Egypt,* edited by Nicholas Hopkins and Kirsten Westergaard, 184–200. Cairo: American University in Cairo Press.

Badr, Intisar, principal investigator. 2007. *Nisa' fi suq al-'amal: al-'amilat wa-siyyasat al-khaskhasa.* Cairo: New Woman Foundation.

Badran, Margot. 1996. *Feminists, Islam, and Nation: Gender and the Making of Modern Egypt.* Cairo: AUC Press, 1996.

Baker, Mona, ed. 2015. *Translating Dissent: Voices from and with the Egyptian Revolution.* New York: Routledge.

Bakhtin, M. M. 1941, 1965. *Rabelais and His World.* Trans. Hélène Iswolsky. Bloomington: Indiana University Press, 1993.

Barlas, Asma. 2009. "Islam and Body Politics: Inscribing (Im)morality," Conference on Religion and Politics of the Body, Nordic Society for Philosophy of Religion, University of Iceland, Reykjavik, June 26–28, 2009.

Baron, Beth. 2005. *Egypt as a Woman: Nationalism, Gender, and Politics.* Berkeley: University of California Press.

Barraclough, Ruth and Elyssa Faison, eds. 2009. *Gender and Labor in Korea and Japan: Sexing Class.* London: Routledge.

Barsoum, Ghada. 2015. "Youth and Unemployment in Egypt." *Ahramonline.* June 11. http:// english.ahram.org.eg/NewsContentP/4/132530/Opinion/Youth-and-unemployment-in -Egypt.aspx.

Bartky, Sandra Lee. 2003. "Foucault, Femininity, and the Modernization of Patriarchal Power." In *The Politics of Women's Bodies: Sexuality, Appearance, and Behavior,* 3rd edition, edited by Rose Weitz, 25–45. New York: Oxford University Press.

Bayat, Asef. 2017. *Revolution Without Revolutionaries: Making Sense of the Arab Spring.* Stanford: Stanford University Press.

Beinin, Joel. 2001. *Workers and Peasants in the Modern Middle East* (The Contemporary Middle East). Cambridge: Cambridge University Press.

Beinin, Joel. 2011. *Social Movements, Mobilization, and Contestation in the Middle East and North Africa.* Redwood City, CA: Stanford University Press.

Beinin, Joel with Hossam el-Hamalawy. 2007. "Egyptian Textile Workers Confront the New Economic Order." *Middle East Report Online.* March 25, 2007.

Beinin, Joel with Hossam el-Hamalawy. 2010. "Egyptian Textile Workers: From Craft Artisans Facing European Competition to Proletarians Contending with the State." In *Covering the World: A Global History of Textile Workers,* edited by Lex Heerma van Voss, et al., 1650–2000. Farnham, UK: Ashgate Press.

Beinin, Joel and Zachary Lockman. 1989. *Workers on the Nile: Nationalism, Communism, Islam, and the Egyptian Working Class, 1882–1954.* Princeton: Princeton University Press.

Berger, Iris. 1992. *Threads of Solidarity: Women in South African Industry, 1900–1980.* Bloomington: Indiana University Press.

Berliner, David. 2005. "Social Thought & Commentary: The Abuses of Memory: Reflections on the Memory Boom in Anthropology." *Anthropological Quarterly* 78 (1 Winter): 197–211.

Bhattacharya, Tithi. 2013. "Explaining Gender Violence in the Neoliberal Era." *International Socialist Review* 21 (Winter 2013–2014).

Bohn, Lauren. "A Revolution Devours Its Children." *The Atlantic.* January 2016. http://www.theatlantic.com/international/archive/2016/01/egypt-revolution-arab-spring/426609/.

Bordo, Susan. 2003. *Unbearable Weight: Feminism, Western Culture, and the Body,* 2nd edition. Berkeley: University of California Press.

Boyarin, Jonathan. 1991. *Polish Jews in Paris: The Ethnography of Memory.* Bloomington: Indiana University Press.

Brickner, R. K. 2006. "Mexican Union Women and the Social Construction of Women's Labor Rights." *Latin American Perspectives* 33 (6): 55–74.

Brickner, R. K. 2009. "The Evolution of Union Women's Activism in Mexico City after Structural Adjustment." *Canadian Woman Studies/les cahiers de la femme* 27 (1): 82–86.

Brook, Barbara. 1999. *Feminist Perspectives on the Body.* London: Longman.

Brooks, Daphne A. 2006. *Bodies in Dissent: Spectacular Performances of Race and Freedom, 1850–1910.* Durham, NC: Duke University Press.

BSR. 2010. "Female Factory Workers' Health Needs Assessment: Egypt." https://herproject.org/doc_repository/Female_Factory_Workers_HNA_Egypt_FINAL.pdf.

Butler, Judith. 1998. "Subjects of Sex/Gender/Desire." In *Feminism and Politics,* edited by Ann Philips, 273–294. London: Oxford University Press.

CAPMAS. Central Agency for Public Mobilization and Statistics. 2016. "Report. Egypt." http://www.capmas.gov.eg/Pages/IndicatorsPage.aspx?page_id=6154&ind_id=1124.

Chakrabarty, Dipesh. 1992. "Postcoloniality and the Artifice of History: Who Speaks for 'Indian' Pasts?" *Representations* 37 (Winter): 1–26.

Childress, Sarah. 2013. "Timeline: What's Happened Since Egypt's Revolution?" Frontline. September 17. http://www.pbs.org/wgbh/frontline/article/timeline-whats-happened-since-egypts-revolution/.

Clifford, James and George E. Marcus. 1986. *Writing Culture: The Poetics and Politics of Ethnography*. Berkeley: University of California Press.

Climo, Jacob and Maria Cattell. 2002. *Social Memory and History: Anthropological Perspectives*. Walnut Creek, CA: Altamira Press.

CNN. 2011. "CNN Official Interview: Egyptian Activist Wael Ghonim— 'Welcome to Egypt Revolution 2.0.' http://edition.cnn.com/videos/#video/bestoftv/2011/02/11/exp.ghonim.facebook.thanks.cnn?iref=allsearch.

Cole, Juan. 2008. *Napoleon's Egypt: Invading the Middle East*. New York: St. Martin's Griffin.

Connell, R. W. 1985. "Theorizing Gender." Sociology 19(2): 260–272. 1995. Masculinities. Berkeley: University of California Press.

Connerton, Paul. 1989. *How Societies Remember*. Cambridge: Cambridge University Press.

Conteh-Morgan, Earl. 2006. "Globalization, State Failure, and Collective Violence: The Case of Sierra Leone." *International Journal of Peace Studies* 11 (2): 87–103.

Dahi, Omar S. 2011. "Understanding the Political Economy of the Arab Revolts." *Middle East Report, North Africa: The Political Economy of Revolt* (Summer), 41: 2–6.

Daily News Egypt. 2016. "Report Details Internet and Social Media Use among Egyptians." January 2016. http://www.dailynewsegypt.com/2016/01/04/report-details-internet-and-social-media-use-among-egyptians/.

Daily News Egypt. 2017. "25 January Revolution Was Turning Point in Egypt's History: Al-Sisi." http://www.dailynewsegypt.com/2017/01/25/25-january-revolution-turning-point-egypts-history al-sisi/.

Deif, Farida. 2004. "Divorce from Justice: Women's Unequal Access to Divorce in Egypt. *Human Rights Watch* 16 (8 E): 1–68.

Di Leonardo, Micaela. 1987. "The Oral History as Ethnographic Encounter." *The Oral History Review* 15 (1): 1–20.

Dorman, W. J. and E. Stein. 2013. "Informality Versus the State Islamists, Informal Cairo and Political Integration by Other Means." *Alternatives: Turkish Journal of International Relations* 12 (4): 5–19.

Douglas, Mary. 2000. *Purity and Danger: An Analysis of Concepts of Pollution and Taboo*. London: Routledge.

DuPlessis, Rachel and Ann Snitow. 2007. *The Feminist Memoir Project: Voices from Women's Liberation*. New Brunswick, NJ: Rutgers University Press.

Egypt Independent. 2013. "US Cancels Award for Samira Ibrahim after Incendiary Tweets." March 9, 2017. http://www.egyptindependent.com//news/us-cancels-award-samira-ibrahim-after-incendiary-tweets salience.

Egypt Independent. 2016. "Aswat Masriya." July 27, 2016. http://www.egyptindependent.com//news/278-percent-egyptian-population-lives-below-poverty-line-capmas.

Egyptian Center for Women's Rights. 2015. "12 Successful Female Candidates on Individual Seats Out of 18." ecwronline.org. December 6, 2015. http://ecwronline.org/?p=6693.

Egyptian Initiatve for Personal Rights. 2013. "Non-peaceful Assembly Does Not Justify Collective Punishment—Rights Groups Condemn Lethal Violence against Those in Sit-in and Terrorist Acts of the Muslim Brotherhood," news release, August 15, 2013. http://eipr.org/en/pressrelease/2013/08/15/1782.

"An Egyptian Lady Worth a Million Men Attacks an Officer after He Assaulted a Protestor: (سيدة مصرية بمليون راجل تهاجم ظابط بعد تعديه علي شاب في التحرير)." https://www.youtube.com/watch?v=Z4i59_EAmjM.

Elders, The. 2012. http://www.theelders.org/liveblogs/middle-east-visit-2012.

Eletribi, Amor and March LeVine. 2012. "The Labor Movement and the Future of Democracy in Egypt." Al Jazeera. http://www.aljazeera.com/indepth/opinion/2012/04/20124117523568936.html.

El-Hennawy, Noha. 2011. "Despite Footage of Violence, Military General Denies Use of Excessive Force." *Egypt Independent*. December 19, 2011. http://www.egyptindependent.com//news/despite-footage-violence-military-general-denies-use-excessive-force.

Elias, Norbert. 1982. *The Civilizing Process: State Formation and Civilization*. Oxford: Basil Blackwell.

El-Mahdi, Rabab. 2011. "Orientalizing the Egyptian Uprising." *Jadaliyya*. April 11, 2011. http://www.jadaliyya.com/Details/23882/Orientalising-the-Egyptian-Uprising.

El Saadawi, Nawal. 1972. *al mar'a wal jins*. (*Women and Sex*). Cairo: al nashirun al Arab.

El Saadawi, Nawal. 1999. *A Daughter of Isis: An Autobiography of. Nawal El Saadawi*. London: Zed Books Ltd.

El Saadawi, Nawal. 2013. "From the (Female) Martyrs of the Revolution of January 25th." *Al Masry Al Youm* 21 (29).

El Said, Maha. 2015. "She Resists: Body Politics Between Radical and Subaltern." In *Rethinking Gender in Revolutions and Resistance: Lessons from the Arab World*, edited by Maha El Said, Lena Meari, and Nicola Pratt, 109–134. Chicago: Zed Books.

El Said, Maha, Lena Meari, and Nicola Pratt, eds. 2015. *Rethinking Gender in Revolutions and Resistance: Lessons from the Arab World*. Chicago: Zed Books.

El Shakry, Omnia. 2007. *The Great Social Laboratory: Subjects of Knowledge in Colonial and Postcolonial Egypt*. Stanford, CA: Stanford University Press.

El-Shinawy, Eman. 2012. "The Curious Case of Egypt's First Gay Magazine." *Al Arabiya News*. August 24, 2012. https://english.alarabiya.net/articles/2012/08/24/233994.html. Accessed March 26, 2017.

Elsadda, Hoda. "Article 11: Feminists Negotiating Power in Egypt." January 5, 2015. https://www.opendemocracy.net/5050/hoda-elsadda/article-11-feminists-negotiating-power-in-egypt

Elsheshtawy, Yasser. 2017. "Urban Rupture: A Fire, Two Hotels and the Transformation of Cairo." In *Urban Violence in the Modern Middle: From the Imperial Age to the Arab Spring*, edited by Nelida Fuccaro, 211–230. Stanford: Stanford University Press.

Enloe, Cynthia. 2000. *Maneuvers: The International Politics of Militarizing Women's Lives*. Berkeley: University of California Press.

Fabian, Johannes. 1999. "Remembering the Other: Knowledge and Recognition in the Exploration of Central Africa." *Critical Enquiry* 26: 49–69.

Fahmy, Khaled. 1989. "Women, Medicine and Power in Nineteenth-Century Egypt." In *Remaking Women: Feminism and Modernity in the Middle East*, edited by Lila Abu-Lughod, 35–72. Princeton: Princeton University Press.

Fahmy, Mohamed Fadel and Mohammed Jamjoom. 2011. "Women March in Cairo to Protest Violence; Military Promises to Listen." CNN. December 21, 2011. http://www.cnn.com/2011/12/20/world/africa/egypt-unrest/.

Farah, Nadia Ramsis. 2012. "The Political Economy of Egypt's Revolution." In *Egypt's Tahrir Revolution*, edited by Dan Tschirgi, Walid Kazzih, and Sean F. McMahon, 47–65. Boulder, CO: Lynne Rienner Publishers.

Fathi, Yasmine. 2012. "Egypt's Battle of the Camel: The Day the Tide Turned." *Al Ahramonline*. February 2, 2012. http://english.ahram.org.eg/News/33470.aspx.

Fausto-Sterling, Anne. 2000. *Sexing the Body: Gender Politics and the Construction of Sexuality*. New York: Basic Books.

FIDH, Nazra for Feminist Studies, New Women Foundation and Uprising of Women in the Arab World. "Egypt: Keeping Women Out: Sexual Violence Against Women in the Public Sphere." n.d. Accessed August 16, 2018. https://www.fidh.org/IMG/pdf/egypt _sexual_violence_uk-webfinal.pdf.

FIDH. 2015. "Egypt: Acquittal of Ms. Azza Soliman, Human Rights Lawyer and Founder of the Centre for Egyptian Women Legal Aid (CEWLA)." https://www.fidh.org/en /issues/human-rights-defenders/egypt-acquittal-of-ms-azza-soliman-human-rights -lawyer-and-founder-of.

Fleishman, Jeffrey. "Egyptian Army Doctor Acquitted of Giving Virginity Tests to Arrestees." March 11, 2012. http://latimesblogs.latimes.com/world_now/2012/03/reporting-from -cairo-an-egyptianmilitary-tribunal-sunday-acquitted-an-army-doctor-of-giving -women-activistsvirginity. Accessed June 21, 2013.

Foucault, Michel. 1977. *Discipline and Punish: The Birth of the Prison*. Trans. Alan Sheridan. New York: Random House.

Foucault, Michel. 1980. *Power/Knowledge: Selected Interviews and Other Writings, 1972–77*. Ed. Colin Gordon. London: Harvester.

Foucault, Michel. 1990. *The History of Sexuality, Vol. 1, An Introduction*. Trans. Robert Hurley. Pantheon Books: New York.

Franke-Ruta, Garance. 2011. "Egypt: Why the Kiss Picture Is So Radical." *The Atlantic.* January 31, 2011. http://www.theatlantic.com/international/archive/2011/01/egypt -why-the-kiss-picture-is-so-radical/70518/.

Fricker, Miranda. 2009. *Epistemic Injustice: Power and the Ethics of Knowing*. New York: Oxford University Press.

Ganguly, Debjani and John Docker. 2008. *Rethinking Gandhi and Non-Violent Relationality: Global Perspectives*. London: Routledge.

Garcia-Navarro, Lulu. 2012. "In Egypt's New Parliament, Women Will Be Scarce." NPR. January 19, 2012. http://www.npr.org/2012/01/19/145468365/in-egypts-new -parliament-women-will-be-scarce.

Geer, Benjamin. 2013. "Autonomy and Symbolic Capital in an Academic Social Movement: The March 9 Group in Egypt." *European Journal of Turkish Studies* 17. https://ejts .revues.org/4780.

Ghoneim, Wael. 2012. *Revolution 2.0. The Power of the People Is Greater than the People in Power*. Boston: Houghton Mifflin Harcourt.

Goldschmidt, Arthur. 2000. *Biographical Dictionary of Modern Egypt*. Cairo: American University in Cairo Press.

Greenslade, Roy. "Egyptian Student Jailed for Proclaiming That He Is an Atheist." *The Guardian*. January 13, 2015. https://www.theguardian.com/media/greenslade/2015 /jan/13/egyptian-student-jailed-for-proclaiming-that-he-is-an-atheist.

Guenena, Nemat. 1986. *The Jihad: An Islamic Alternative in Egypt* (Cairo Papers in Social Science). Cairo: American University in Cairo Press.

Guenena, Nemat. 2013. "Women in Democratic Transition: Political Participation Watchdog UNIT." http://www.un.org/democracyfund/sites/www.un.org.democracyfund/files /UDF-EGY-08-241_Final%20UNDEF%20evaluation%20report.pdf.

Hafez, Sherine. 2012. "No Longer a Bargain," *American Ethnologist*, 39:1, Feb.

Hale, Sondra. 2013. "The Memory Work of Anthropologists: Notes Towards a Gendered Politics of Memory in Conflict Zones—Sudan and Eritrea." In *Anthropology of the Middle East and North Africa: Into the New Millennium*, edited by Sherine Hafez and Susan Slyomovics, 125–144. Bloomington: Indiana University Press.

Haraway, Donna. 1988. "Situated Knowledges: The Science Question in Feminism and the Privilege of Partial Perspective." *Feminist Studies* 14 (3): 575–599.

Harding, S. 1996. "Borderlands Epistemologies." In *Science Wars*, edited by A. Ross, 331–340. Durham, NC: Duke University Press.

Hardt, Michael and Antonio Negri. 2000. *Empire*. Cambridge: Harvard University Press.

Hasso, Frances S. and Zakia Salime, eds. 2016. *Freedom without Permission: Bodies and Space in the Arab Revolutions*. Durham, NC: Duke University Press.

Hatem, Mervat F. 1992. "Economic and Political Liberation in Egypt and the Demise of State Feminism." *International Journal of Middle East Studies* 24 (No. 2): 231–251.

Hatem, Mervat F. 1994. "Egyptian Discourses on Gender and Political Liberalization: Do Secularist and Islamist Views Really Differ?" *Middle East Journal* 48 (4): 661–676.

Hatem, Mervat F. 1997. "The Professionalization of Health and the Control of Women's Bodies as Modern Governmentalities in Nineteenth-Century Egypt." In *Women in the Ottoman Empire: Middle Eastern Women in the Early Modern Era*, edited by Madeline C. Zilfi, 66–80. Leiden: Brill.

Hatem, Mervat F. 2012. "Gender and Revolution in Egypt." *Middle East Report*, 261 41(4): 36–41.

Haug, F. 1987. *Memory Work. Female Sexualization: A Collective Work of Memory*. London: Verso.

Hawas, Sarah. 2012. "Global Translations and Translating the Global: Discursive Regimes of Revolt." In *Translating Egypt's Revolution: The Language of Tahrir*, edited by Samia Mehrez, 277–305. Cairo: American University in Cairo Press.

Henderson, Margaret. 2006. *Marking Feminist Times: Remembering the Longest Revolution in Australia*. Bern: Peter Lang European University Studies.

Hirsch, M., and V. Smith. 2002. "Feminism and Cultural Memory: An Introduction." *Signs: Journal of Women in Culture and Society* 28 (1): 1–19.

Hoodfar, Homa. 2001. "The Veil in Their Minds and on Our Heads: Veiling Practices and Muslim Women in the Politics and Culture in the Shadow of the Capital." In *Women, Gender, and Religion*, edited by Elizabeth Anne Castelli and Rosamond C. Rodman, 440–446. New York: Palgrave Press.

Hooks, Bell. 1994. "Theory as a Liberatory Practice." In *Teaching to Transgress: Education as the Practice of Freedom*, 59–76. New York: Routledge.

Hubbard, Ruth. 1987. "Constructing Sex Difference." *New Literary History* 19: 129–134.

Human Rights Watch. 2011. "Egypt: Military 'Virginity Test' Investigation a Sham. Impunity Highlights the Lack of Independence of Justice System." http://www.hrw.org/news/2011 /11/09/egypt-military-virginity-test-investigation-sham. Accessed December 19, 2013.

Human Rights Watch. 2011. "Impunity Highlights Lack of Independence of Justice System," November 9, 2011. https://www.hrw.org/news/2011/11/09/egypt-military-virginity-test -investigation-sham. Accessed December 19, 2013.

Human Rights Watch. 2013. "Egypt: Dangerous Message for Protesters: Harsh Sentences for Pro-Morsy Women, Girls Violate Rights." https://www.hrw.org/news/2013/12/07 /egypt-dangerous-message-protesters.

Human Rights Watch. 2014. "Egypt: Take Concrete Action to Stop Sexual Harassment, Assault Committee Assessment Should Lead to Reforms." June 13, 2014. https://www.hrw.org/news/2014/06/13/egypt-take-concrete-action-stop-sexual-harassment-assault.

Human Rights Watch. 2014. "All According to Plan: The Raba'a Massacre and the Mass Killing of Protestors in Egypt." https://www.hrw.org/report/2014/08/12/all-according-plan/raba-massacre-and-mass-killings-protesters-egypt.

Human Rights Watch. 2017. "World Report: Egypt." https://www.hrw.org/world-report/2017/country-chapters/egypt.

IFAD. 1999. "The Mobility Barrier to Women's Poverty Reduction in the Near East and North Africa." http://www.ifad.org/gender/learning/challenges/women/65.htm.

Ikhwan Web. 2011. "MB Announces Establishment of Political Party: Freedom and Justice Egypt's Largest Political Opposition, the Muslim Brotherhood, Has Confirmed That It Is Preparing to Establish a Political Party, Calling It the Freedom and Justice Party, or Horeya and Adala." February 21, 2011. http://www.ikhwanweb.com/article.php?id=28077.

Index Mundi. "Egypt Female-Headed Households." http://www.indexmundi.com/facts/egypt/female-headed-households.

Internet Users by Country. 2016. http://www.internetlivestats.com/internet-users/egypt/.

Joseph, Suad, ed. 2000. *Gender and Citizenship in the Middle East*. Syracuse: Syracuse University Press.

Kahanah, Ephraim and Sagit Stivi-Kerbis. 2014. "The Assassination of Anwar al Sadat: An Intelligence Failure." *International Journal of Intelligence and Counter Intelligence* 27: 178–192.

Kanaaneh, Rhoda Ann. 2002. *Birthing the Nation: Strategies of Palestinian Women in Israel*. Berkeley: University of California Press.

Kandiyoti, Deniz, ed. 1991. *Women, Islam and the State*. Basingstoke, UK: Macmillan.

Khalil, Andrea, ed. 2014. *Gender, Women and the Arab Spring*. New York: Routledge.

Khodair, Amany A. and Bassant Hassib. 2015. "Women's Political Participation in Egypt: The Role of the National Council for Women." *International Journal of Political Science and Development* 3 (7): 326–337.

King, Laura. 2011. "Protests Raise Hope for Women's Rights in Egypt." *Los Angeles Times*, February 2, 2011. http://articles.latimes.com/2011/feb/02/world/la-fg-egypt-women-20110203.

Kirkpatrick, David. 2014. "Egyptian Leader Apologizes to Victim of Sexual Assault in Tahrir Square." *New York Times*. June 11, 2014. http://www.nytimes.com/2014/06/12/world/middleeast/president-sisi-of-egypt-apologizes-to-victim-of-mass-sexual-assaults.html?_r=0.

Kirkpatrick, David. 2015. "Killing of Shaimaa el-Sabbagh in Cairo Angers Egyptians." *New York Times*. February 3, 2015. http://www.nytimes.com/2015/02/04/world/middleeast/shaimaa-el-sabbagh-tahrir-square-killing-angers-egyptians.html?_r=0.

Kolhatkar, Sonali. 2002. "The Impact of U.S. Intervention on Afghan Women's Rights." *Berkeley Journal of Gender, Law and Justice* 17 (1): 12–30.

Korany, Bahgat and Rabab El-Mahdy. 2014. *Arab Spring in Egypt: Revolution and Beyond*. Cairo: The American University in Cairo Press.

Kortam, Hend. 2014. "NGOs Condemn Minister's Intention to Exclude Women from Governor Reshuffle: Head of the Media Division in the Ministry Says Minister's Statements 'Were Taken out of Context.'" *Daily News Egypt*. August 25, 2014.

http://www.dailynewsegypt.com/2014/08/25/ngos-condemn-ministers-intention
-exclude-women-governor-reshuffle/.

Lamphere, Louise. 1997. "The Domestic Sphere of Women
and the Public World of Men: The Strengths and Limitations of an Anthropological
Dichotomy." In *Woman, Culture and Society,* edited by M. Rosaldo and Louise
Lamphere, 90–98. Stanford: Stanford University Press.

Lazreg, Marnia. 1994. *The Eloquence of Silence. Algerian Women in Question.* New York:
Routledge.

Lorber, Judith. 2009. "Believing Is Seeing: Biology as Ideology." In *The Politics of Women's
Bodies: Sexuality, Appearance, and Behavior,* 3rd ed., edited by Rose Weitz, 12–24. New
York: Oxford University Press.

Lynch, Marc. 2013. *The Arab Uprising: The Unfinished Revolutions of the New Middle East.*
New York Public Affairs.

MacLeod, Arlene E. 1994. *Accommodating Protest: Working Women, the New Veiling and
Change in Cairo.* Chicago: Columbia University Press.

Mada Masr. 2014. "Students Could Be Expelled for Criticizing President Sisi." August
29, 2014. http://www.madamasr.com/en/2014/08/29/news/u/students-could-be
-expelled-for-criticizing-president-sisi/.

Mahmoud, Cherry. "Q & A: Mohamed Ashmawy, Founder & CEO of Cairo Confessions."
Cairohub. October 9, 2014. http://www.cairohub.com/qa-mohamed-ashmawy
-founder-ceo-of-cairo-confessions/.

Marshall, Lucinda. 2005. "The Connection between Militarism and Violence against
Women." In *Beyond Borders: Thinking Critically about Global Issues,* edited by Paula S.
Rothenberg, 307–310. New York: Worth.

Martin, Emily. 1991. "The Egg and the Sperm: How Science Has Constructed a Romance
Based on Stereotypical Male-Female Roles." *Signs* 16 (3): 485.

Mayhall, Laura E. Nym. 2000. "Reclaiming the Political: Women and the Social History of
Suffrage in Great Britain, France, and the United States." *Journal of Women's History* 12
(1): 172–181.

Mbembe, Achille. "Necropolitics." Public Culture 15 (1): 11–40,

McLarney, Ellen. 2016. "Women's Rights and Equality: Egyptian Constitutional Law." In
Women's Movements in Post-"Arab Spring" North Africa, edited by Fatima Sadiqi,
109–126. New York: Palgrave Macmillan.

MEE Staff. 2014. "Egypt: Timeline of Key Human Rights Violations since the 2011
Revolution." November 4, 2014. http://www.middleeasteye.net/news/egypt-timeline
-key-human-rights-violations-2011-revolution-872433931.

Meer, Shamim. 1991. *Black Women Workers: A Study in Patriarchy, Race and Women
Production Workers in South Africa.* Durban: Madiba Publications, Institute for Black
Research.

Mehrez, Samia, ed. 2012. *Translating Egypt's Revolution: The Language of Tahrir.* Cairo: The
American University in Cairo Press.

Meky, Shounaz. 2014. "Egypt Criminalizes Sexual Harassment." Al Arabiya English.
June 6, 2014. http://english.alarabiya.net/en/News/middle-east/2014/06/06/Egypt
-criminalizes-sexual-harassment.html.

Mernissi, Fatima. 1987. *Beyond the Veil: Male-Female Dynamics in Modern Muslim Society.*
Bloomington: Indiana University Press.

Michael, Marc. 2011. "Is Liberalism Killing Copts?" Al Jazeera. November 19.http://www
.aljazeera.com/indepth/opinion/2011/11/2011111616317813239.html.

Mihaila, Liliana. 2012. "Cabinet Clashes Remembered, Egypt Ended 2011 with Street
Fighting That Left Many Dead." *Daily News Egypt*. December 15, 2012. http://www
.dailynewsegypt.com/2012/12/15/cabinet-clashes/.

Mikhail, George. "Will Egypt's Parliament Pass Facebook Law?" Al Monitor. May 10, 2016.
http://www.al-monitor.com/pulse/originals/2016/05/egypt-law-regulate-facebook
-parliament-opposition.html.

Moghadam, V. M. 1999. "Gender and Globalization: Female Labor and Women's
Mobilization." *Journal of World-Systems Research* 5 (2): 301–314.

Mohanty, Chandra Talpade. 2003. "Under Western Eyes." In *Feminism Without Borders:
Decolonizing Theory, Practicing Solidarity*, 17–42. Durham, NC: Duke University Press.

Moraga, Cherríe and Gloria Anzaldúa. 1983. *Theory in the Flesh. In This Bridge Called My
Back: Writings by Radical Women of Color*. New York: Kitchen Table, Women of Color
Press.

Morrison, Toni. 1987. *Beloved*. New York: Knopf Doubleday Publishing Group.

Morsi, Eman S. 2008. "Strikes in Egypt: Female Workers," BANewscenter. http://bianet.org
/english/world/107336-strikes-in-egypt-female-workers.

Mukurasi, Laetisha. 1991. *Post Abolished: One Woman's Struggle for Employment Rights in
Tanzania*. New York: IRL Press.

Murphy, William. 2014. *Political Imprisonment and the Irish, 1912–1921*. Oxford: Oxford
University Press.

Nader, Emir. "11 Homosexuals Arrested in Pre-Eid Morality Raids." *Daily News Egypt*.
September 2015. https://www.dailynewsegypt.com/2015/09/21/11-homosexuals
-arrested-in-pre-eid-morality-raids/.

National Center for Social and Criminological Research (NSCR). 2011. "Street Children in
Egypt."

Nelson, Cynthia. 1996. *Doria Shafik: Egyptian Feminist: A Woman Apart*. Gainesville:
University Press of Florida.

Nora, P. 1989. "Between Memory and History: Les Lieux de Mémoire." *Representations* 26: 7–25.

Nov 20 A 1000 chant with the downfall of Tantawi 20, Nov.
(الألف في التحرير يهتفوا بإسقاط طنطاوي 20 نوفمب) https://www.youtube.com/watch?v=
SdSLmh6P61s.

Odekon, Mehmet. 2006. *Encyclopedia of World Poverty, Vol. 1*. Thousand Oaks, CA: Sage
Publications.

Olimat, Muhamad, ed. 2013. *Arab Spring and Arab Women: Challenges and Opportunities*.
New York: Routledge International Handbooks.

Ong, Aihwa. 2010. *Spirits of Resistance and Capitalist Discipline: Factory Women in Malaysia*.
Albany: State University of New York Press.

Ortner, Sherry. 1974. "Is Female to Male as Nature Is to Culture?" In *Woman, Culture, and
Society*, edited by M. Z. Rosaldo and Louise Lamphere, 67–87. Stanford, CA: Stanford
University Press.

Osman, Tarek. 2010. *Egypt on the Brink: From the Rise of Nasser to the Fall of Mubarak*. New
Haven, CT: Yale University Press.

Pateman, Carol. 1988. *The Sexual Contract*. Stanford, CA: Stanford University Press.

Peach, Lucinda J. 1993. *Women at War: The Ethics of Women in Combat*. Bloomington:
Indiana Center on Global Change and World Peace.

Pfeifer, Karen. 1999. "How Tunisia, Morocco, and even Egypt became IMF 'Success Stories' in the 1990s." *Middle East Report* 210 (Spring): 23–27.

Pfeifer, Karen, Marsha Pripstein-Posusney, and Djavad Salehi-Isfahani. 1999. "Reform or Reaction? Dilemmas of Economic Development in the Middle East." *Middle East Report* 210 (Spring): 9–47.

POMEPS Arab Uprising Bibliography. 2015. http://pomeps.org/category/academic-works /arabuprisings/. Updated October 26, 2015.

Power, Carla. 2011. "Silent No More: The Women of the Arab Revolutions." *Time*. March 24, 2011. http://content.time.com/time/world/article/0,8599,2059435,00.html.

Rabie, Dalia. 2016. "Adjusting Egypt's Moral Compass." Mada Misr. March 2016. http://www.madamasr.com/sections/politics/adjusting-egypts-moral-compass.

Radwan, Noha. 2011. "How Egyptian Women Took Back the Street between Two 'Black Wednesdays': A First-Person Account." *Jadaliyya*. February 20, 2011. http://www .jadaliyya.com/pages/index/694/how-egyptian-women-took -back-the-street -between-tw.

Rahman, Anika and Nahid Toubia. 2000. *Female Genital Mutilation: A Practical Guide to Worldwide Laws & Policies. Center for Reproductive Law & Policy*. London: Zed Books.

Russell, Mona L. 2004. *Creating the New Egyptian Woman: Consumerism, Education and. National Identity 1863–1922*. New York: Palgrave, Macmillan.

Saad, Oud. 2012. "Exclusive Interview with Mama Khadiga, Tahrir's Godmother." What Women Want. January 24, 2012. https://www.youtube.com/watch?v=Cmeqnjtfvc8. Accessed March 20, 2017.

Sadiqi, Fatima, ed. 2016. *Women's Movements in Post-"Arab Spring" North Africa*. New York: Palgrave Macmillan.

Said, Edward. 1981. *Covering Islam*. New York: Vintage Books.

Salem, Sarah. 2012. "Femen's Neocolonial Feminism: When Nudity Becomes a Uniform." *English al akhbar*. http://english.al-akhbar.com/node/14494. Accessed November 30, 2013.

Salzinger, Leslie. 2003. *Genders in Production*. Berkeley: University of California Press.

Scott, James. 1985. *Weapons of the Weak: Everyday Forms of Resistance*. New Haven, CT: Yale University Press.

Shaarawi, Huda. 1987. *Harem Years: The Memoirs of an Egyptian Feminist (1879–1924)*. New York: Feminist Press.

Shahine, Selim. 2011. "Youth and Revolution in Egypt." *Anthropology Today*. 27 (2): 1–3.

Shalhoub-Kevorkian, Nadera. 2009. *Militarization and Violence against Women in Conflict Zones in the Middle East: A Palestinian Case Study*. Cambridge: Cambridge University Press.

Shihata, Samer. 2004. "Egypt after 9/11: Perceptions of the United States." Contemporary Conflicts. SSRC. March 26, 2004. http://conconflicts.ssrc.org/archives/mideast /shehata/. Accessed February 4, 2017.

Shukralla, Salma. 2011. "10,000 Egyptian Women March Against Military Violence and Rule." Jadaliyya. December 20, 2011. http://www.jadaliyya.com/pages/index/3671 /10000-egyptian-women-march-against-military-violen.

Silvey, Rachel. 2003. "Spaces of Protest: Gendered Migration, Social Networks, and Labor Activism in West Java, Indonesia." *Political Geography* 22: 129–155.

Singerman, Diane. 2013. "Youth, Gender and Dignity in the Egyptian Uprising." *Journal of Middle East Women's Studies* 9 (3): 1–27.

Singerman, Diane and Homa Hoodfar, eds. 1996. *Development, Change, and Gender in Cairo: A View from the Household*. Bloomington: Indiana University Press.

Sivakumaran, Sandesh. 2007. "Sexual Violence Against Men in Armed Conflict." *The European Journal of International Law* 18 (2), 253–276.

Skalli, Loubna Hanna. 2014. "Young Women and Social Media against Sexual Harassment in North Africa." In *Gender, Women and the Arab Spring*, edited by Andrea Khalil, 114–128. New York: Routledge.

Slyomovich, Susan. 1998. *The Object of Memory: Arab and Jew Narrate the Palestinian Village*. Philadelphia: University of Pennsylvania Press.

Smith, Andrea. 2006. *Colonial Memory and Postcolonial Europe: Maltese Settlers in Algeria and France*. Bloomington: Indiana University Press.

Solidarity Center. 2010. "Justice for All: The Struggle for Workers' Rights in Egypt." http://hrlibrary.umn.edu/research/Egypt/The%20Struggle%20for%20Workers%20rights.

Sowers, Jeannie and Chris Toensing, eds. 2012. *The Journey to Tahrir*. London: Verso.

Stichter, Sharon and Jane L. Parpart. 1990. *Women, Employment, and the Family in the International Division of Labor*. London: Macmillan.

Stork, Joe. 2015. "Egypt's Political Prisoners." Human Rights Watch. March 2015. https://www.hrw.org/news/2015/03/06/egypts-political-prisoners.

Sutter, John. 2011. "The Faces of Egypt's Revolution 2.0." CNN. http://www.cnn.com/2011/TECH/innovation/02/21/egypt.internet.revolution/.

Tadros, Mariz. 2013. *Copts at the Crossroads: The Challenges of Building Inclusive Politics in Egypt*. Oxford: Oxford University Press.

Tahrir Diaries. 2011. *Samira w3l gish, qisit f3ta misriyya*. ("Samira and the Army: The Story of an Egyptian Girl.") http://www.youtube.com/watch?v=c29CAXR141s. Accessed December 2013.

Talal, Omneya. 2015. "Egypt: Women's Achievements in 2015—Presiding Judges and Elected Parliamentarians." All Africa. December 28, 2015. http://allafrica.com/stories/201512282073.html.

Trétiack, Philippe. 2013. *"Aliaa Magda Mahdy: la rage au corps." Elle*. January 28, 2013. http://www.elle.fr/Societe/Les-enquetes/Aliaa-Magda-Elmahdy-la-rage-au-corps-2305974.

UNESCO. 2002. "UNDP, Arab Human Development Report 2002. Creating Opportunities for Future Generations." http://www.arab-hdr.org.

UNICEF. 2013. "UNICEF Egypt." https://www.unicef.org/egypt/hiv_aids.html.

United Nations. 2013. *World Happiness Report*. http://unsdsn.org/wp-content/uploads/2014/02/WorldHappinessReport2013_online.pdf.

Visweswaran, Kamala. 1994. *Fictions of Feminist Ethnography*. Minneapolis: University of Minnesota Press.

Ward, Kathryn, ed. 1990. *Women Workers and Global Restructuring*. Ithaca, NY: ILR Press.

Wickham, Carrie. 2002. *Mobilizing Islam: Religion, Activism and Political Change in Egypt*. New York: Columbia University Press.

Winegar, Jessica. 2012. "Egypt: A Multigenerational Revolt." Jadaliyya. http://www.jadaliyya.com/pages/index/703/egypt_a-multi-generational-revolt.

Wolf, Naomi. 2011."The Middle East's Feminist Revolution." *The Globe and Mail*, March 2, 2011. http://www.theglobeandmail.com/globe-debate/the-middle-easts-feminist-revolution/article568783/.

World Bank. 2010. "Most Improved in Doing Business." http://www.doingbusiness.org/reforms/top-reformers-2010. Accessed August 9, 2016.

You Tube. 2012. "Gamal Abdel Nasser on the Muslim Brotherhood." https://www.youtube
.com/watch?v=TX4RK8bj2Wo. Accessed January 17, 2017.

Zaher, Maged. 2014. *The Tahrir of Poetry: Seven Contemporary Egyptian Poets.* Washington:
Alice Blue Books.

Zainab al-Ghazali, 1988. *"Ayam min Hayati"* ("Days from My Life.") Cairo: Dar al-Shuruq.
http://latimesblogs.latimes.com/world_now/2012/03/reporting-from-cairo-an
-egyptian-military-tribunal-sunday-acquitted-an-army-doctor-of-giving-women
-activists-virginity.html. Accessed June 21, 2013.

Zohry, Ayman. 2007. "Migration and Development in Egypt." Paper presented at Bosch
Foundation Institute for Migration and Cultural Studies, Berlin.

Index

SHERINE HAFEZ is Associate Professor in the Department of Gender and Sexuality at the University of California, Riverside. She is author of *An Islam of Her Own: Reconsidering Religion and Secularism in Women's Islamic Movements* and editor (with Susan Slyomovics) of *Anthropology of the Middle East and North Africa: Into the New Millennium.*

CPSIA information can be obtained
at www.ICGtesting.com
Printed in the USA
BVHW042059160223
658701BV00013B/197